World Facts

The Earth

AREA: 196,951,900 sq mi (510,066,000 sq km)

LAND: 57,313,000 sq mi (148,647,000 sq km)—29.1%

WATER: 139,638,900 sq mi (361,419,000 sq km)— 70.9%

POPULATION: 6,067,000,000 people

The Continents

	AREA (sq mi)	(sq km)	Percent of Earth's Land
Asia	17,213,300	44,579,000	30.0
Africa	11,609,000	30,065,000	20.2
North America	9,449,500	24,474,000	16.5
South America	6,880,500	17,819,000	12.0
Antarctica	5,100,400	13,209,000	8.9
Europe	3,837,400	9,938,000	6.7
Australia	2,968,200	7,687,000	5.2

Highest Point On Each Continent

	feet	meters
Everest, Asia	29,035	8,850
Aconcagua, South America	22,834	6,960
McKinley (Denali), N. America	20,320	6,194
Kilimanjaro, Africa	19,340	5,895
El'brus, Europe	18,510	5,642
Vinson Massif, Antarctica	16,067	4,897
Kosciuszko, Australia	7,310	2,228

Lowest Point On Each Continent

	feet	meters
Dead Sea, Asia	-1,349	-411
Lake Assal, Africa	-512	-156
Death Valley, N. America	-282	-86
Valdés Peninsula, S. America	-131	-40
Caspian Sea, Europe	-92	-28
Lake Eyre, Australia	-52	-16
Antarctica (ice covered)	-8,366	-2,550

Ten Longest Rivers

	LENGTH miles	kilometers
Nile, Africa	4,241	6,825
Amazon, South America	4,000	6,437
Yangtze (Chang), Asia	3,964	6,380
Mississippi-Missouri, N. America	3,710	5,971
Yenisey-Angara, Asia	3,440	5,536
Yellow (Huang), Asia	3,395	5,464
Ob-Irtysh, Asia	3,361	5,410
Amur, Asia	2,744	4,416
Lena, Asia	2,734	4,400
Congo, Africa	2,715	4,370

Ten Largest Lakes

	AREA (sq mi)	(sq km)	Greatest Depth (feet)	(meters)
Caspian Sea, Europe-Asia	143,254	371,000	3,363	1,025
Superior, N. America	31,701	82,100	1,332	406
Victoria, Africa	26,836	69,500	269	82
Huron, N. America	23,013	59,600	751	229
Michigan, N. America	22,318	57,800	922	281
Tanganyika, Africa	12,587	32,600	4,823	1,470
Baikal, Asia	12,163	31,500	5,371	1,637
Great Bear, N. America	12,086	31,300	1,463	446
Aral Sea, Asia	11,854	30,700	167	51
Malawi, Africa	11,159	28,900	2,280	695

Ten Largest Islands

	AREA (sq mi)	(sq km)
Greenland	840,065	2,175,600
New Guinea	306,008	792,500
Borneo	280,137	725,500
Madagascar	226,658	587,000
Baffin	195,961	507,500
Sumatra	164,993	427,300
Honshu	87,806	227,400
Great Britain	84,215	218,100
Victoria	83,906	217,300
Ellesmere	75,759	196,200

The Oceans

	AREA (sq mi)	(sq km)	Percent of Earth's Water Area
Pacific	64,190,671	166,241,000	46.0
Atlantic	33,422,271	86,557,000	23.9
Indian	28,352,382	73,427,000	20.3
Arctic	3,662,445	9,485,000	2.6

Deepest Point In Each Ocean

	feet	meters
Challenger Deep, Mariana Trench, Pacific	35,827	10,920
Puerto Rico Trench, Atlantic	28,232	8,605
Java Trench, Indian	23,376	7,125
Molloy Deep, Arctic	18,399	5,608

Ten Largest Seas

	AREA (sq mi)	(sq km)	Average Depth (feet)	(meters)
South China	1,148,583	2,974,600	4,803	1,464
Caribbean	971,465	2,515,900	8,448	2,575
Mediterranean	969,187	2,510,000	4,924	1,501
Bering	873,079	2,261,100	4,892	1,491
Gulf of Mexico	582,130	1,507,600	5,298	1,615
Sea of Okhotsk	537,532	1,392,100	3,192	973
Sea of Japan	391,111	1,012,900	5,469	1,667
Hudson Bay	281,912	730,100	305	93
East China	256,622	664,600	620	189
Andaman	218,125	564,900	3,668	1,118

Earth's Extremes

HOTTEST PLACE: Dalol, Denakil Depression, Ethiopia; annual average temperature— 93°F (34°C)

COLDEST PLACE: Plateau Station, Antarctica; annual average temperature— -134°F (-56.7°C)

WETTEST PLACE: Mawsynram, Assam, India; annual average rainfall— 467 in (1,187.3 cm)

DRIEST PLACE: Atacama Desert, Chile; rainfall barely measurable

HIGHEST WATERFALL: Angel, Venezuela— 3,212ft (979 m)

LARGEST DESERT: Sahara, Africa— 3,475,000 sq mi (9,000,000 sq km)

LARGEST CANYON: Grand Canyon, Colorado River, Arizona; 277 mi (446 km) long along river; 1,801 ft (549 m) to 18 mi (29 km) wide, about 1 mi (1.6 km) deep

LONGEST REEF: Great Barrier Reef, Australia— 1,250 mi (2,012 km)

GREATEST TIDES: Bay of Fundy, Nova Scotia— 52 ft (16 m)

ABBREVIATIONS

COUNTRY NAMES

ARM.	Armenia
AZERB.	Azerbaijan
B. & H.;	Bosnia and
BOSN. & HERZ.	Herzegovina
BELG.	Belgium
CRO.	Croatia
EST.	Estonia
HUNG.	Hungary
LATV.	Latvia
LIECH.	Liechtenstein
LITH.	Lithuania
LUX.	Luxembourg
MACED.	Macedonia
MOLD.	Moldova
N.Z.	New Zealand
NETH.	Netherlands
SLOV.	Slovenia
SWITZ.	Switzerland
U.A.E.	United Arab Emirates
U.K.	United Kingdom
U.S.	United States
YUG.	Yugoslavia

PHYSICAL FEATURES

I.-s.	Islands
L.	Lake
Mt.-s.	Mont, Mountains
R.	River

OTHER

Eq.	Equatorial
Pop.	Population
Rep.	Republic
St.	Saint
&	and

NATIONAL GEOGRAPHIC
Student Atlas
of the
World

NATIONAL GEOGRAPHIC SOCIETY
WASHINGTON, D.C.

About the Earth

Learning About Maps

Physical Systems

Human Systems

The Continents

40 North America

56 South America

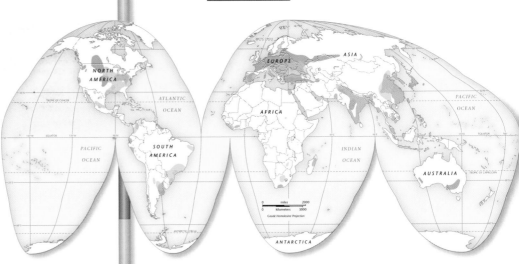

MERCURY

VENUS

EARTH

MARS

SUN

JUPITER

SATURN

URANUS

NEPTUNE

• PLUTO

▲ *Nine planets* orbit the sun, held in place by its gravitational field. Mercury's orbit (below) is the shortest: 88 Earth days; Pluto's is the longest: 248 Earth years.

PLUTO

MERCURY

The Earth in Space

At the center of our solar system is the sun, a huge mass of hot gas that is the source of both light and warmth for Earth. Third in a group of nine planets that revolve around the sun, Earth is a terrestrial, or mostly rocky, planet. So are Mercury, Venus, and Mars. Earth is about 93 million miles (150 million kilometers) from the sun, and its journey, or revolution, around the sun takes 365¼ days. Farther away from the sun, five more planets—Jupiter, Saturn, Uranus, and Neptune (all made up primarily of gases) plus tiny, mostly icy Pluto—complete the major heavenly bodies that make up our solar system. The solar system, in turn, is part of the Milky Way galaxy.

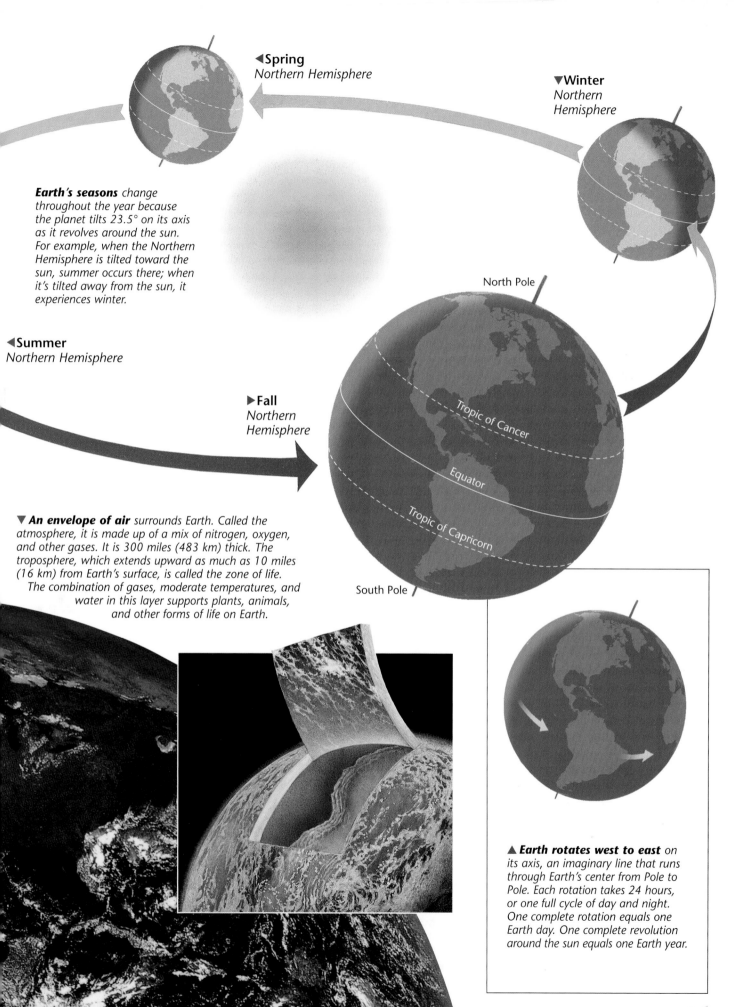

◄Spring
Northern Hemisphere

▼Winter
Northern Hemisphere

Earth's seasons change throughout the year because the planet tilts 23.5° on its axis as it revolves around the sun. For example, when the Northern Hemisphere is tilted toward the sun, summer occurs there; when it's tilted away from the sun, it experiences winter.

◄Summer
Northern Hemisphere

►Fall
Northern Hemisphere

North Pole

Tropic of Cancer

Equator

Tropic of Capricorn

South Pole

▼ *An envelope of air* *surrounds Earth. Called the atmosphere, it is made up of a mix of nitrogen, oxygen, and other gases. It is 300 miles (483 km) thick. The troposphere, which extends upward as much as 10 miles (16 km) from Earth's surface, is called the zone of life. The combination of gases, moderate temperatures, and water in this layer supports plants, animals, and other forms of life on Earth.*

▲ *Earth rotates west to east* *on its axis, an imaginary line that runs through Earth's center from Pole to Pole. Each rotation takes 24 hours, or one full cycle of day and night. One complete rotation equals one Earth day. One complete revolution around the sun equals one Earth year.*

Learning About Maps

MAP PROJECTIONS

Maps tell a story about physical and human systems, places and regions, patterns and relationships. This atlas is a collection of maps that tell a story about Earth.

Understanding that story requires a knowledge of how maps are made and a familiarity with the special language used by cartographers, the people who create maps.

Globes present a model of Earth as it is—a sphere—but they are bulky and can be difficult to use and store. Flat maps are much more convenient, but certain problems result from transferring Earth's curved surface to a flat piece of paper, a process called projection. There are many different types of projections, all of which involve some form of distortion: area, distance, direction, or shape. Web Link

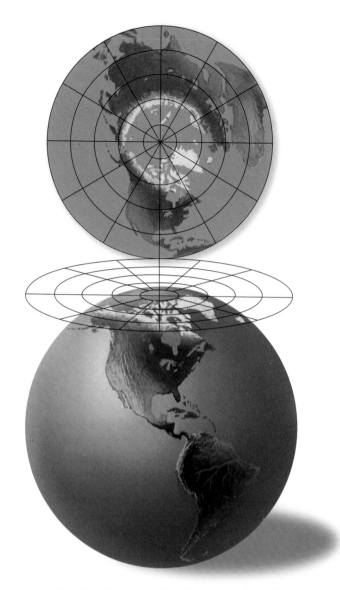

▲ **Azimuthal Projection Map.** *This kind of map is made by projecting a globe onto a flat surface that touches the globe at a single point, such as the North Pole. These maps accurately represent direction along any straight line extending from the point of contact. Away from the point of contact, shape is increasingly distorted.*

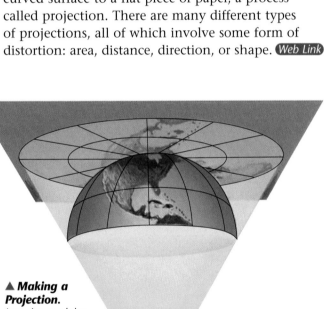

▲ **Making a Projection.** *Imagine a globe that has been cut in half as this one has. If a light is shined into it, the lines of latitude and longitude and the shapes of the continents will cast shadows that can be "projected" onto a piece of paper, as shown here. Depending on how the paper is positioned, the shadows will be distorted in different ways.*

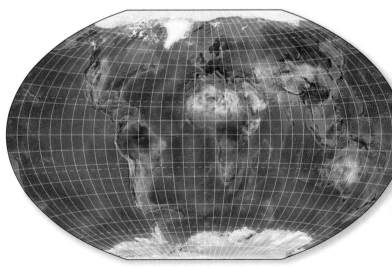

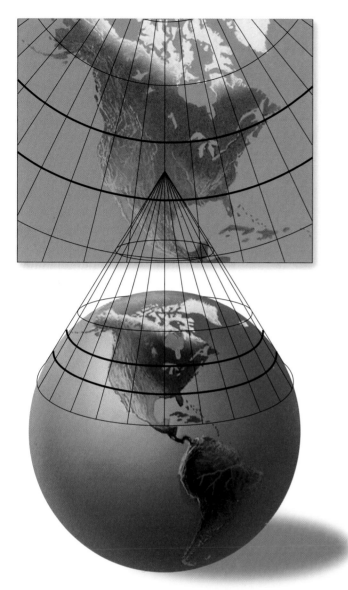

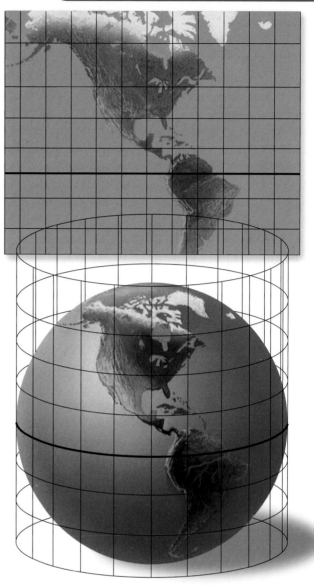

▲ **Conic Projection Map.** *This kind of map is made by projecting a globe onto a cone. The part of Earth being mapped touches the sides of the cone. Lines of longitude appear as straight lines; lines of latitude appear as parallel arcs. Conic projections are often used to map mid-latitude areas with great east-west extent, such as North America.*

▲ **Cylindrical Projection Map.** *A cylindrical projection map is made by projecting a globe onto a cylinder that touches Earth's surface along the Equator. Latitude and longitude lines on this kind of map show true compass directions, which makes it useful for navigation. But there is great distortion in the size of high-latitude landmasses.*

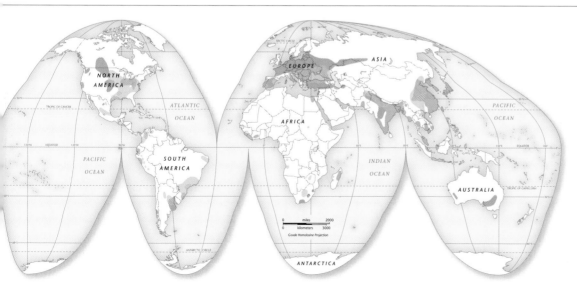

◄ **Other Projections.** *Sometimes cartographers create general purpose world projections, such as the Winkel Tripel (far left), in which distortion of both size and shape is minimized. This creates a reasonably accurate image of Earth. Another general purpose projection is the Goode's Interrupted Homolosine (left), which interrupts ocean areas to preserve the relative size and shape of land areas.*

READING MAPS

People can use maps to find locations, to determine direction or distance, and to understand information about places. Cartographers rely on a special graphic language to communicate through maps.

An imaginary system of lines, called the global grid, helps us locate particular points on Earth's surface. The global grid is made up of lines of latitude and longitude that are measured in degrees, minutes, and seconds. The point where these lines intersect identifies the absolute location of a place. No other place has the exact same address. Web Link

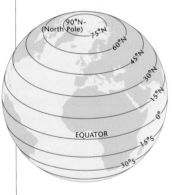

◀ **Latitude.** Lines of latitude—also called parallels because they are parallel to the Equator—run east to west around the globe and measure location north or south of the Equator. The Equator is 0° latitude.

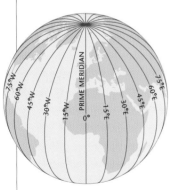

◀ **Longitude.** Lines of longitude, also called meridians, run from Pole to Pole and measure location east or west of the prime meridian. The prime meridian is 0° longitude, and it runs through Greenwich, near London, England.

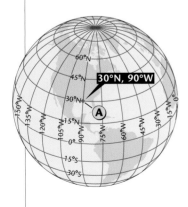

◀ **Latitude and Longitude.** When used together, latitude and longitude form a grid that provides a system for determining the exact, or absolute, location of every place on Earth. For example, the absolute location of point A is 30°N, 90°W.

▲ **Direction.** Cartographers put a north arrow or a compass rose, which shows the four cardinal directions—north, south, east, and west—on a map. On this map, point B is northwest (NW) of point A. Northwest is an example of an intermediate direction, which means it is between two cardinal directions. Grid lines can also be used to indicate north.

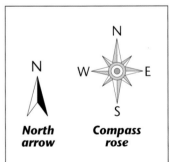

North arrow   **Compass rose**

▶ **Scale.** A map represents a part of Earth's surface, but that part is greatly reduced. Cartographers include a map scale to show what distance on Earth is represented by a given length on the map. Scale can be graphic (a bar), verbal, or a ratio.

To determine how many miles point A is from point B, place a piece of paper on the map above and mark the distance between A and B. Then compare the marks on the paper with the bar scale on the map.

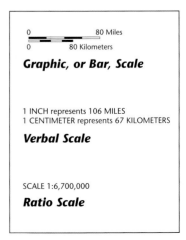

Graphic, or Bar, Scale

1 INCH represents 106 MILES
1 CENTIMETER represents 67 KILOMETERS

Verbal Scale

SCALE 1:6,700,000

Ratio Scale

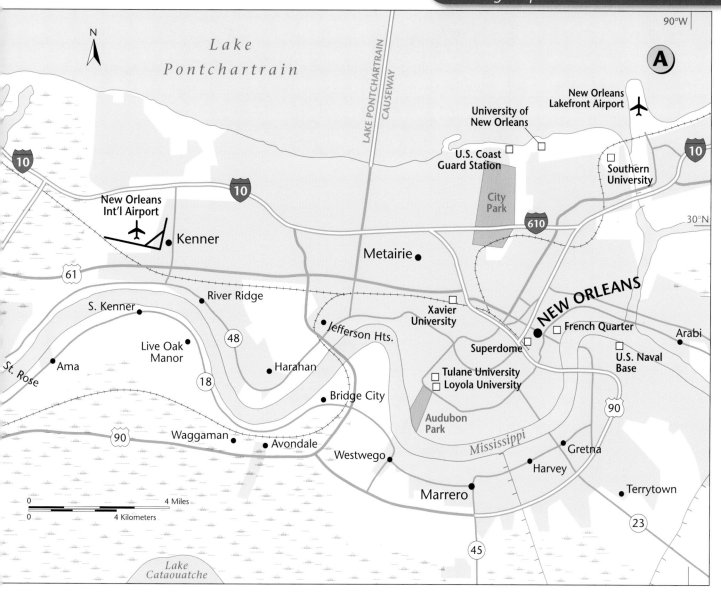

▼ Symbols. *Finally, cartographers use a variety of symbols, which are identified in a map key or legend, to tell us more about the places represented on the map. There are three general types of symbols:*

Point symbols *show exact location of places (such as cities) or quantity (a large dot can mean a more populous city).*

Line symbols *show boundaries or connections (such as roads, canals, and other trade links).*

Area symbols *show the form and extent of a feature (such as a lake, park, or swamp).*

Additional information may be coded in color, size, and shape.

▲ Putting It All Together. *We already know from the map on page 8 which states A and B are located in. But to find out more about city A, we need a larger scale map—one that shows a smaller area in more detail (see above).*

Metropolitan area		Road	
Lake or river		Railroad	
Park		Runway	
Swamp		Airport	
Canal		Point of interest	
Highway		Town	

TYPES OF MAPS

This atlas includes many different types of maps so that a wide variety of information about Earth can be presented. Three of the most commonly used types of maps are physical, political, and thematic.

A **physical map** identifies natural features, such as mountains, deserts, oceans, and lakes. Area symbols of various colors and shadings may indicate height above sea level or, as in the example here, ecosystems. Similar symbols could also show water depth.

A **political map** shows how people have divided the world into countries. Political maps can also show states, counties, or cities within a country. Line symbols indicate boundaries, and point symbols show the locations and sometimes sizes of cities.

Thematic maps use a variety of symbols to show distributions and patterns on Earth. For example, a choropleth map uses shades of color to represent different values. The example here shows the amount of energy consumed each year by various countries. Thematic maps can show many different things, such as patterns of vegetation, land use, and religions.

A **cartogram** is a special kind of thematic map in which the size of a country is based on some statistic other than land area. In the cartogram at far right, population size determines the size of each country. This is why Nigeria—the most populous country in Africa—appears much larger than Sudan, which has more than double the land area of Nigeria (see the political map). Cartograms allow for a quick visual comparison of countries in terms of a selected statistic.

Web Link

This globe *is useful for showing Africa's position and size relative to other landmasses, but very little detail is possible at this scale. By using different kinds of maps, mapmakers can show a variety of information in more detail.*

Physical Map

Madeira Islands
Canary Islands
Cape Verde Islands
Atlas Mountains
Mediterranean Sea
Dead -1,349 (-411
Nile
Libyan Desert
Red Sea
S A H A R A
S A H E L
AFRICA
White Nile
Blue Nile
Ethio High
Niger
Upper Guinea
Gulf of Guinea 0°
Congo
Lake Victoria
Congo Basin
Great Rift Valley
Lake Tanganyika
Lower Guinea
OCEAN
Zambezi
Namib Dese
Kalahari Desert

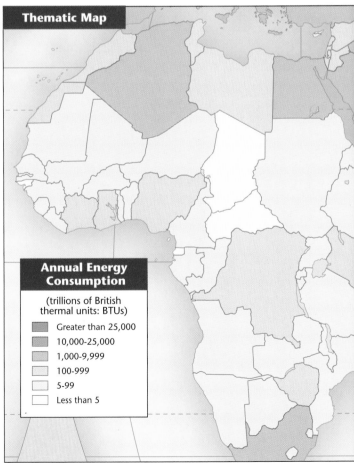

Thematic Map

Annual Energy Consumption

(trillions of British thermal units: BTUs)

- Greater than 25,000
- 10,000-25,000
- 1,000-9,999
- 100-999
- 5-99
- Less than 5

Political Map

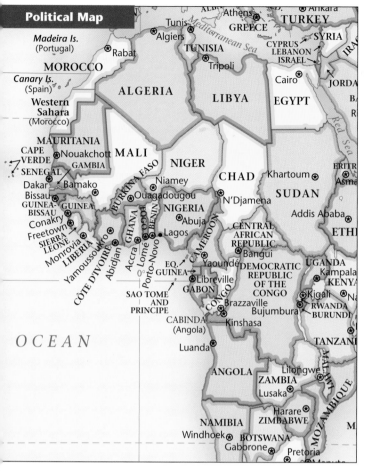

Madeira Is. (Portugal)
Canary Is. (Spain)
Western Sahara (Morocco)

TURKEY
GREECE
Athens
Ankara
Tunis
Algiers
Rabat
TUNISIA
Tripoli
CYPRUS
LEBANON
SYRIA
ISRAEL
IRAQ
Cairo
JORDAN
MOROCCO
ALGERIA
LIBYA
EGYPT
Red Sea
MAURITANIA
Nouakchott
MALI
NIGER
CHAD
Khartoum
ERITREA
Asmara
CAPE VERDE
GAMBIA
Niamey
SUDAN
N'Djamena
Addis Ababa
SENEGAL
Bamako
BURKINA FASO
NIGERIA
ETHI
Dakar
Bissau
Ouagadougou
Abuja
GUINEA-BISSAU
GUINEA
GHANA
BENIN
Lagos
CENTRAL AFRICAN REPUBLIC
Conakry
Freetown
SIERRA LEONE
LIBERIA
Monrovia
Yamoussoukro
CÔTE D'IVOIRE
Abidjan
Accra
Lomé
TOGO
Porto-Novo
0°
EQ. GUINEA
CAMEROON
Yaoundé
Bangui
DEMOCRATIC REPUBLIC OF THE CONGO
UGANDA
Kampala
KENYA
Libreville
GABON
CONGO
Brazzaville
Kinshasa
Kigali
RWANDA
BURUNDI
Bujumbura
SAO TOME AND PRINCIPE
CABINDA (Angola)
OCEAN
Luanda
TANZANIA
ANGOLA
ZAMBIA
Lusaka
Lilongwe
MALAWI
MOZAMBIQUE
Harare
ZIMBABWE
NAMIBIA
Windhoek
BOTSWANA
Gaborone
Pretoria

Cartogram

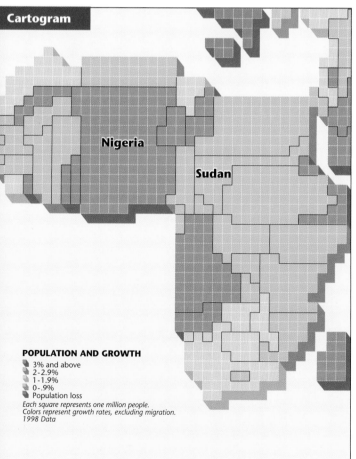

Nigeria

Sudan

POPULATION AND GROWTH
- 3% and above
- 2-2.9%
- 1-1.9%
- 0-.9%
- Population loss

Each square represents one million people.
Colors represent growth rates, excluding migration.
1998 Data

Satellite Image Maps

Satellites orbiting Earth transmit images of the surface to computers on the ground. These computers translate the information into special maps (below) that use colors to show various characteristics. Such maps are valuable tools for identifying patterns or comparing changes over time.

▼ **Cloud Coverage**

▼ **Topography/Bathymetry**

▼ **Sea Level Variability**

▼ **Sea Surface Temperature**

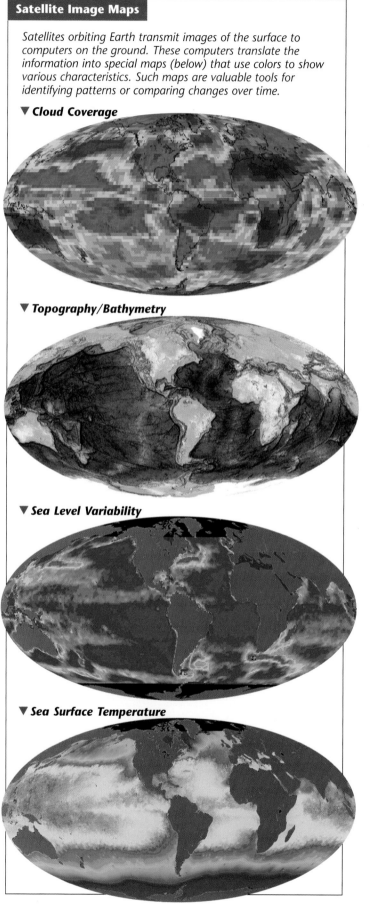

Physical Systems
THE PHYSICAL WORLD

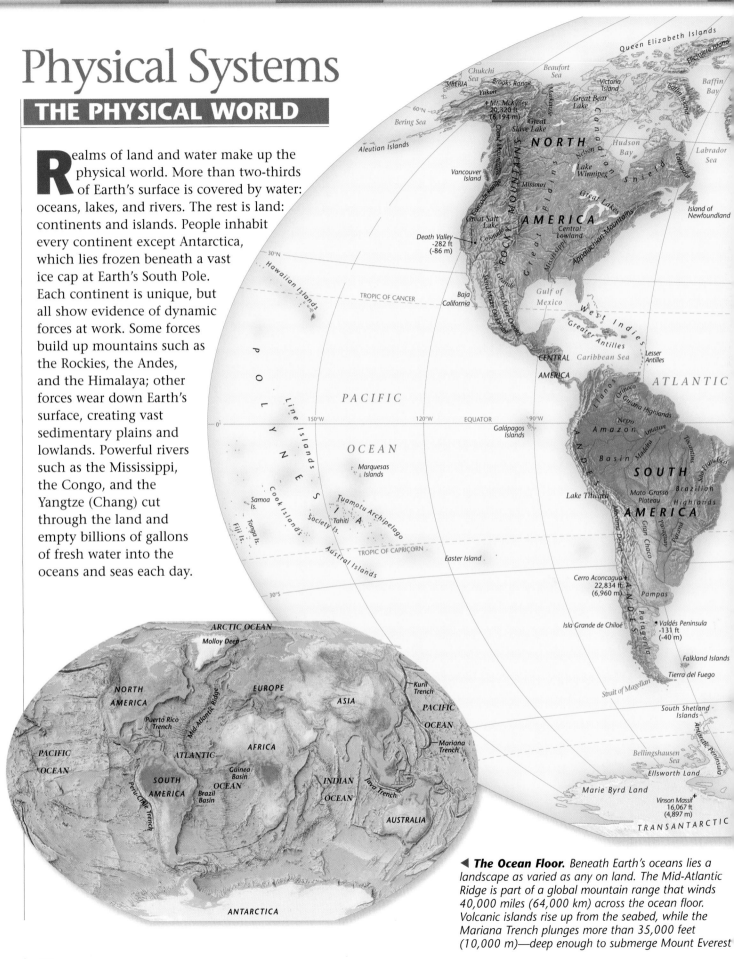

Realms of land and water make up the physical world. More than two-thirds of Earth's surface is covered by water: oceans, lakes, and rivers. The rest is land: continents and islands. People inhabit every continent except Antarctica, which lies frozen beneath a vast ice cap at Earth's South Pole. Each continent is unique, but all show evidence of dynamic forces at work. Some forces build up mountains such as the Rockies, the Andes, and the Himalaya; other forces wear down Earth's surface, creating vast sedimentary plains and lowlands. Powerful rivers such as the Mississippi, the Congo, and the Yangtze (Chang) cut through the land and empty billions of gallons of fresh water into the oceans and seas each day.

◀ **The Ocean Floor.** Beneath Earth's oceans lies a landscape as varied as any on land. The Mid-Atlantic Ridge is part of a global mountain range that winds 40,000 miles (64,000 km) across the ocean floor. Volcanic islands rise up from the seabed, while the Mariana Trench plunges more than 35,000 feet (10,000 m)—deep enough to submerge Mount Everest

ARCTIC OCEAN

GREENLAND

Greenland Sea

Svalbard

Novaya Zemlya

Kara Sea

Laptev Sea

East Siberian Sea

Barents Sea

ARCTIC CIRCLE

Iceland

Norwegian Sea

Scandinavia

Ural Mountains

West Siberian Plain

Central Siberian Plateau

Angara

Lena

Lena

60°N

Bering Sea

Kamchatka Peninsula

Aleutian Is.

British Isles

Ireland

North Sea

Great Britain

Baltic

Northern European Plain

Volga

Ob

Irtysh

Ob

SIBERIA

Amur

Lake Baikal

Sea of Okhotsk

Kuril Islands

Hokkaido

EUROPE

Alps

Danube

Black Sea

Elbrus 18,510 ft (5,642 m)

Caucasus Mts.

Aral Sea

Caspian Sea

The Steppes

Altay Mountains

Tian Shan

ASIA

GOBI

North China Plain

Yellow (Huang)

Sea of Japan

JAPAN

Honshu

Korea

Yellow Sea

Nampo Shoto

30°N

Azores

Madeira Islands

Mediterranean Sea

Atlas Mountains

Zagros Mountains

Persian Gulf

Taklimakan Desert

Kunlun Mountains

Plateau of Tibet

HIMALAYA

Brahmaputra

Yangtze (Chang)

East China Sea

Ryukyu Islands

Taiwan

PACIFIC

Canary Islands

SAHARA

LIBYAN Desert

Nile

Red Sea

ARABIAN PENINSULA

Dead Sea -1,349 ft (-411 m)

Indus

Ganges

Mt. Everest 29,035 ft (8,850 m)

INDIA

Salween

Mekong

Hainan

Luzon

Philippine Sea

Mariana Islands

OCEAN

Cape Verde Islands

S A H E L

AFRICA

Blue Nile

White Nile

Gulf of Aden

Somali Peninsula

Ethiopian Highlands

Arabian Sea

Deccan Plateau

Bay of Bengal

Andaman Islands

Indochina Peninsula

South China Sea

Philippine Islands

MICRONESIA

Marshall Islands

Upper Guinea

Gulf of Guinea

0°

Congo

Lower Guinea

Congo Basin

Lake Victoria

Great Rift Valley

Lake Tanganyika

Kilimanjaro 19,340 ft (5,895 m)

Seychelles

Sri Lanka

Nicobar Is.

Maldive Islands

Andaman Sea

Malay Peninsula

Sumatra

Borneo

INDONESIA

Greater Sunda Islands

Java

Celebes

Moluccas

New Guinea

Gilbert Islands

EQUATOR

MELANESIA

Bismarck Archipelago

Solomon Islands

OCEAN

Namib Desert

Zambezi

Madagascar

Mascarene Islands

INDIAN

OCEAN

Arafura Sea

New Caledonia

Vanuatu

Coral Sea

Fiji Islands

Kalahari Desert

Drakensberg

Great Sandy Desert

Central Lowlands

AUSTRALIA

Great Dividing Range

South Sandwich Islands

0   miles   2000

0   kilometers   3000

Winkel Tripel Projection

Kerguélen Islands

Lake Eyre -52 ft, (-16 m)

Great Victoria Desert

Murray

Darling

Mt. Kosciuszko 7,310 ft (2,228 m)

Tasman Sea

North Island

NEW ZEALAND

Tasmania

South Island

30°S

ANTARCTIC CIRCLE

60°S

Queen Maud Land

Auckland Islands

MOUNTAINS

ANTARCTICA

Transantarctic Mountains

Victoria Land

30°E   60°E   90°E   150°E

◄ **The Physical World.** *Great land-masses called continents break Earth's global ocean into four smaller ones. Each continent is unique in terms of the landforms and rivers that etch its surface and in the ecosystems that lend colors ranging from the deep greens of the tropical forests of northern South America and southeastern Asia to the browns and yellows of the arid lands of Africa and Australia. Most of Antarctica's features are hidden beneath its ice cap.*

EARTH'S GEOLOGIC HISTORY

Earth is truly a living planet. Its outer shell, or crust, is broken into huge pieces called plates. These plates ride on the slowly moving molten rock, or magma, that lies beneath the crust. Their movement constantly changes Earth's surface. For instance, along one convergent boundary—a place where two plates meet—the plate carrying India is colliding with the Eurasian Plate, heaving up the still growing mountains of the Himalaya. Along another convergent boundary, the Nazca Plate dives beneath the South American Plate in a process called subduction. Volcanoes may occur along subduction zones. Along transform zones, such as California's San Andreas Fault, plates grind past each other, triggering earthquakes. The Mid-Atlantic Ridge is a divergent boundary where plates are pulling apart and molten rock is rising to form new ocean floor. At places called hot spots magma breaks through the crust, forming new land, as in the Hawaiian Islands. Web Link

▼ **Our Changing Planet.** *The Latin phrase terra firma implies planet Earth is solid and unchanging. However, Earth's surface has been anything but unchanging. Geologic evidence suggests that moving plates have collided and moved apart more than once over the course of the planet's long history. As the main map shows, the forces of change show no signs of stopping.*

[Map labels: JUAN DE FUCA PLATE, NORTH AMERICAN PLATE, ROCKY MOUNTAINS, San Andreas Fault, Hawaiian Islands, PACIFIC PLATE, EQUATOR, PACIFIC OCEAN, CARIBBEAN PLATE, COCOS PLATE, ATLANTIC, NAZCA PLATE, SOUTH AMERICAN PLATE, MID-ATLANTIC RIDGE, EAST PACIFIC RISE, ANDES, ANTARCTIC PLATE, SCOTIA PLATE]

▶ **Pangaea.**
About 240 million years ago, all of Earth's continents had collided to form a vast land-mass (now called Pangaea) that stretched from Pole to Pole.

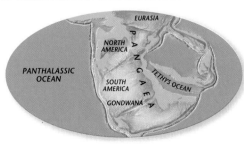

[Map labels: EURASIA, NORTH AMERICA, PANGAEA, PANTHALASSIC OCEAN, SOUTH AMERICA, TETHYS OCEAN, GONDWANA]

▶ **Drifting Apart.**
By 94 million years ago, Pangaea had been pulled apart into smaller landmasses. In the warm global climate, dinosaurs evolved into Earth's dominant animal group.

[Map labels: NORTH AMERICA, EURASIA, ATLANTIC OCEAN, PACIFIC OCEAN, TETHYS OCEAN, SOUTH AMERICA, AFRICA, AUSTRALIA]

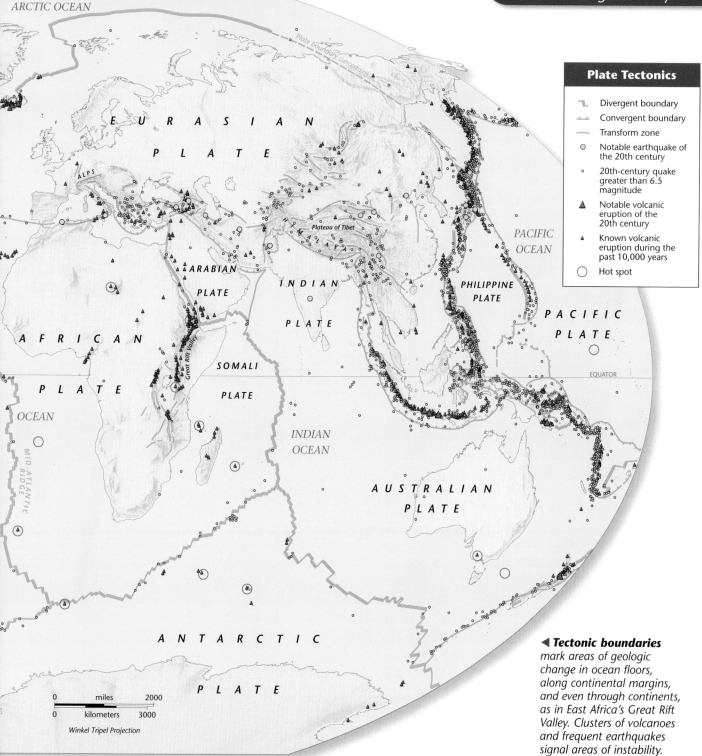

ARCTIC OCEAN

E U R A S I A N   P L A T E

ALPS

ARABIAN PLATE

HIMALAYA

Plateau of Tibet

PACIFIC OCEAN

PHILIPPINE PLATE

PACIFIC PLATE

INDIAN PLATE

PLATE

AFRICAN PLATE

Great Rift Valley

SOMALI PLATE

EQUATOR

OCEAN

MID-ATLANTIC RIDGE

INDIAN OCEAN

AUSTRALIAN PLATE

A N T A R C T I C   P L A T E

| 0 | miles | 2000 |
| 0 | kilometers | 3000 |

Winkel Tripel Projection

Plate boundary (uncertain)

Plate Tectonics

⌐	Divergent boundary
⌐	Convergent boundary
—	Transform zone
○	Notable earthquake of the 20th century
○	20th-century quake greater than 6.5 magnitude
▲	Notable volcanic eruption of the 20th century
▲	Known volcanic eruption during the past 10,000 years
○	Hot spot

◀ **Tectonic boundaries**
mark areas of geologic
change in ocean floors,
along continental margins,
and even through continents,
as in East Africa's Great Rift
Valley. Clusters of volcanoes
and frequent earthquakes
signal areas of instability.

▶ **Eve of Destruction.**
By 65 million years
ago, continents were
moving toward their
current positions.
The impact (✳) of an
asteroid in the Gulf
of Mexico probably
extinguished the
dinosaurs and many
other species.

NORTH AMERICA · EUROPE · ASIA · ATLANTIC OCEAN · PACIFIC OCEAN · PACIFIC OCEAN · AFRICA · SOUTH AMERICA · AUSTRALIA

▶ **Deep Freeze.**
By 18,000 years
ago, the continents
resembled their
current shapes.
A great ice age
had the far
northern and
southern regions
locked under huge
ice sheets.

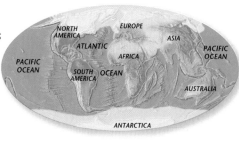

NORTH AMERICA · EUROPE · ASIA · ATLANTIC · AFRICA · PACIFIC OCEAN · PACIFIC OCEAN · SOUTH AMERICA · OCEAN · AUSTRALIA · ANTARCTICA

15

EARTH'S LAND & WATER FEATURES

The largest land and water features on Earth are the continents and the oceans, but many other features—large and small—make each place unique. Mountains, plateaus, and plains give texture to the land. The Rockies and the Andes rise high above the lowlands of North and South America. In Asia, the Himalaya and the Plateau of Tibet form the rugged core of Earth's largest continent. These features are the result of powerful forces within Earth pushing up the land. Others, such as canyons and valleys, are created when weathering and erosion wear down parts of Earth's surface.

Dramatic features are not limited to the land. Submarine mountains, appearing like pale blue threads against the deep blue on the satellite map, rise from the seafloor and trace zones of underwater geologic activity. Deep trenches form where plates collide, causing one to dive beneath the other.

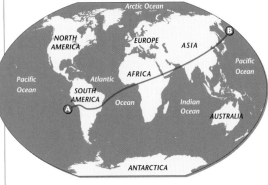

▼ **A Slice of Earth.**
This cross section of Earth's surface extends from Lake Titicaca near South America's Pacific coast to the Kuril Islands in the North Pacific Ocean. It shows towering mountains, eroded highlands, broad coastal plains, and deep ocean basins.

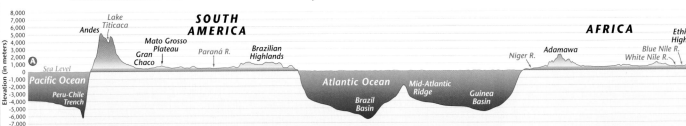

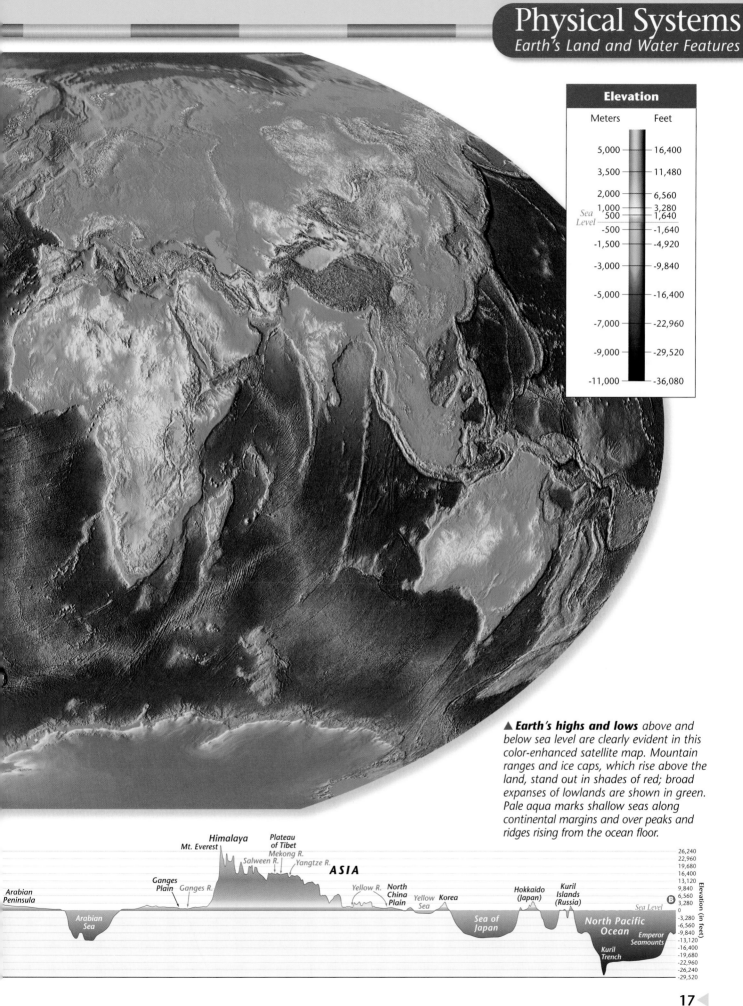

Elevation

Meters	Feet
5,000	16,400
3,500	11,480
2,000	6,560
1,000	3,280
500	1,640
-500	-1,640
-1,500	-4,920
-3,000	-9,840
-5,000	-16,400
-7,000	-22,960
-9,000	-29,520
-11,000	-36,080

Sea Level

▲ **Earth's highs and lows** above and below sea level are clearly evident in this color-enhanced satellite map. Mountain ranges and ice caps, which rise above the land, stand out in shades of red; broad expanses of lowlands are shown in green. Pale aqua marks shallow seas along continental margins and over peaks and ridges rising from the ocean floor.

Himalaya
Mt. Everest
Plateau of Tibet
Mekong R.
Salween R.
Yangtze R.
ASIA
Ganges Plain
Ganges R.
Yellow R.
North China Plain
Yellow Sea
Korea
Hokkaido (Japan)
Kuril Islands (Russia)
Arabian Peninsula
Arabian Sea
Sea of Japan
North Pacific Ocean
Emperor Seamounts
Kuril Trench
Sea Level
Ⓑ

Elevation (in feet)

| 26,240 |
| 22,960 |
| 19,680 |
| 16,400 |
| 13,120 |
| 9,840 |
| 6,560 |
| 3,280 |
| 0 |
| -3,280 |
| -6,560 |
| -9,840 |
| -13,120 |
| -16,400 |
| -19,680 |
| -22,960 |
| -26,240 |
| -29,520 |

EARTH'S CLIMATES

Climate is not the same as weather. Climate is the long-term average of conditions in the atmosphere at a particular location on Earth's surface. Weather refers to the momentary conditions of the atmosphere. Climate is important because it influences vegetation and soil development. It also influences people's choices about how and where to live.

There are many different systems for classifying climates. One commonly used system was developed by Russian-born climatologist Wladimir Köppen and later modified by American climatologist Glenn Trewartha. Köppen's system identifies five major climate zones based on average precipitation and temperature, and a sixth zone for highland, or high elevation, areas. Except for continental climate, all climate zones occur in mirror image north and south of the Equator. Web Link

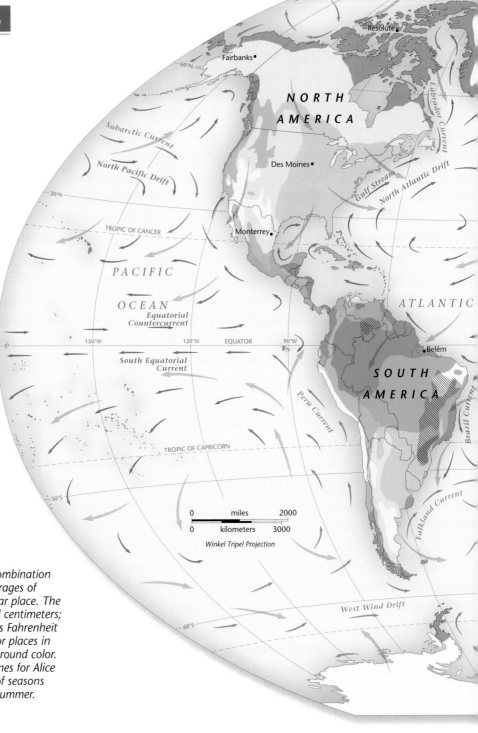

▼ **Climate Graphs.** *A climate graph is a combination bar and line graph that shows monthly averages of precipitation and temperature for a particular place. The bar graph shows precipitation in inches and centimeters; the line graph shows temperature in degrees Fahrenheit and Celsius. The graphs below are typical for places in the climate zone represented by their background color. The seeming inversion of the temperature lines for Alice Springs and McMurdo reflects the reversal of seasons south of the Equator, where January is midsummer.*

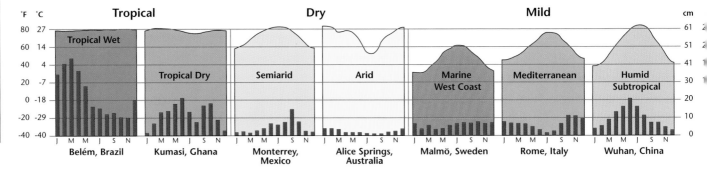

Tropical	Dry	Mild
Tropical Wet — Belém, Brazil	Semiarid — Monterrey, Mexico	Marine West Coast — Malmö, Sweden
Tropical Dry — Kumasi, Ghana	Arid — Alice Springs, Australia	Mediterranean — Rome, Italy
		Humid Subtropical — Wuhan, China

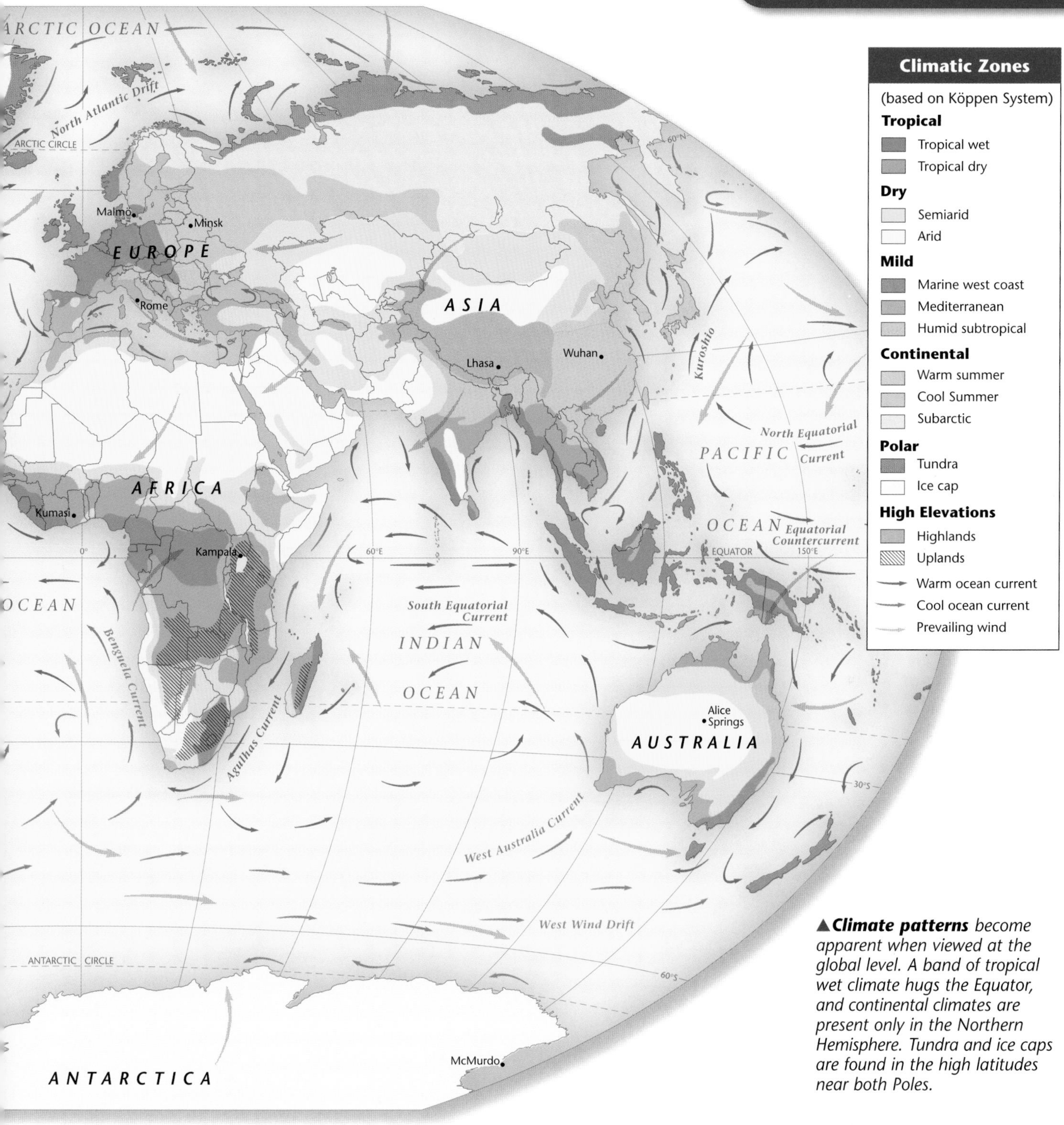

Climatic Zones
(based on Köppen System)

Tropical
- Tropical wet
- Tropical dry

Dry
- Semiarid
- Arid

Mild
- Marine west coast
- Mediterranean
- Humid subtropical

Continental
- Warm summer
- Cool Summer
- Subarctic

Polar
- Tundra
- Ice cap

High Elevations
- Highlands
- Uplands
- → Warm ocean current
- → Cool ocean current
- → Prevailing wind

ARCTIC OCEAN

North Atlantic Drift

ARCTIC CIRCLE

Malmö

Minsk

EUROPE

Rome

ASIA

Lhasa

Wuhan

Kuroshio

60°N

AFRICA

Kumasi

Kampala

0°

North Equatorial Current

PACIFIC

OCEAN Equatorial Countercurrent

150°E

EQUATOR

Benguela Current

Agulhas Current

South Equatorial Current

INDIAN

OCEAN

60°E

90°E

AUSTRALIA

Alice Springs

30°S

West Australia Current

West Wind Drift

West Wind Drift

60°S

ANTARCTIC CIRCLE

ANTARCTICA

McMurdo

▲ **Climate patterns** *become apparent when viewed at the global level. A band of tropical wet climate hugs the Equator, and continental climates are present only in the Northern Hemisphere. Tundra and ice caps are found in the high latitudes near both Poles.*

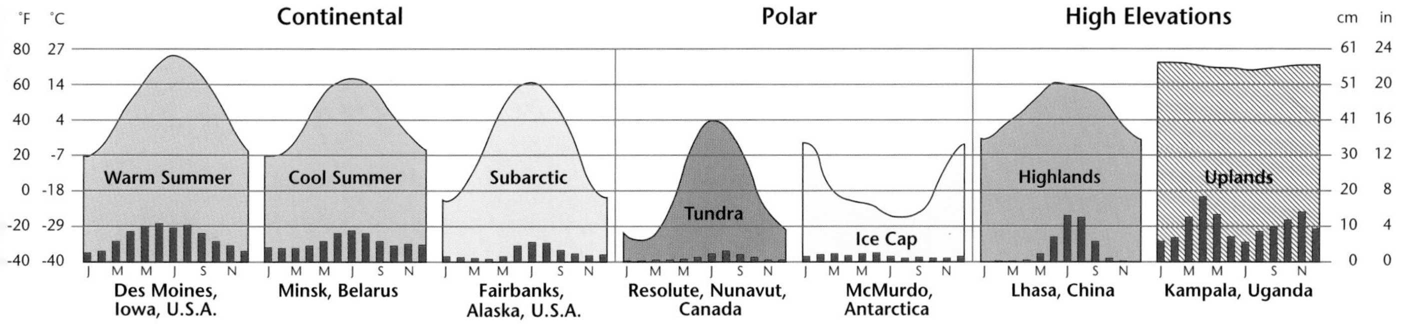

	Continental		Polar		High Elevations	

°F °C

80 27
60 14
40 4
20 -7
0 -18
-20 -29
-40 -40

cm in
61 24
51 20
41 16
30 12
20 8
10 4
0 0

Warm Summer
Cool Summer
Subarctic
Tundra
Ice Cap
Highlands
Uplands

J M M J S N (×7 for each chart)

Des Moines, Iowa, U.S.A.

Minsk, Belarus

Fairbanks, Alaska, U.S.A.

Resolute, Nunavut, Canada

McMurdo, Antarctica

Lhasa, China

Kampala, Uganda

CLIMATE CONTROLS

The patterns of climate vary widely. Some climates, such as those near the Equator and the Poles, are nearly constant year-round. Others experience great seasonal variations, such as the wet and dry patterns of the tropical dry zone and the monthly average temperature extremes of the subarctic.

Climate patterns are not random. They are the result of complex interactions of basic climate controls: **latitude**, **elevation**, **prevailing winds**, **ocean currents**, **landforms**, and **location**.

These controls combine in various ways to create the bands of climate that can be seen on the world climate map on pages 18–19 and on the climate maps in the individual continent sections of this atlas. At the local level, however, special conditions may create microclimates that differ from those that are more typical of the region.

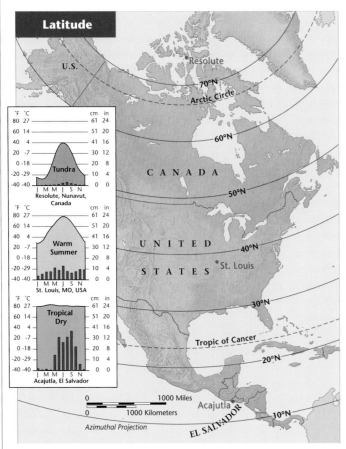

Latitude

▲ *Latitude. Energy from the sun strikes the Equator at a right angle. As latitude (distance north or south of the Equator) increases, the angle becomes increasingly oblique, or slanted. Less energy is received from the sun, and annual average temperatures fall. Therefore, the annual average temperature decreases as latitude increases from Acajutla, El Salvador, to St. Louis, Missouri, to Resolute, Canada.*

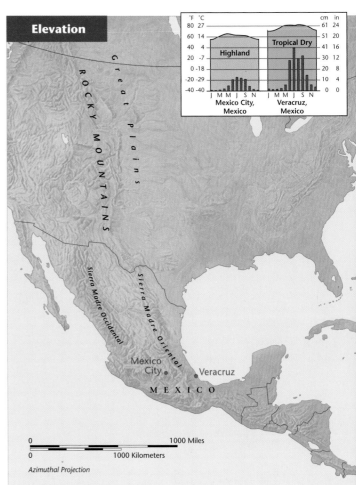

Elevation

Azimuthal Projection

▲ *Elevation. Not all locations at the same latitude experience similar climates. Air at higher elevations is cooler and holds less moisture than air at lower elevations. This explains why the climate at Veracruz, Mexico, which is near sea level, is warm and wet, and the climate at Mexico City, which is more than 7,000 feet (11,000 m) above sea level, is cooler and drier.*

▶ *Landforms. Air carried by prevailing winds blowing off the ocean is full of moisture. If that air encounters a mountain when it reaches land, it is forced to rise. It becomes cooler, causing precipitation on the windward side of the mountain (see Portland graph). When air descends on the side away from the wind—the leeward side— the air warms and absorbs available moisture. This creates a dry condition known as rain shadow (see Wallowa graph).*

Landforms

▶ Prevailing Winds and Ocean Currents. *Earth's rotation combined with heat energy from the sun creates patterns of movement in Earth's atmosphere called prevailing winds. In the oceans similar movements of water are called currents. Prevailing winds and ocean currents bring warm and cold temperatures to land areas. They also bring moisture or take it away. The Gulf Stream and the North Atlantic Drift, for example, are warm-water currents that influence average temperatures in eastern North America and northern Europe. Prevailing winds—trade winds, polar easterlies, and westerlies—also affect temperature and precipitation averages.*

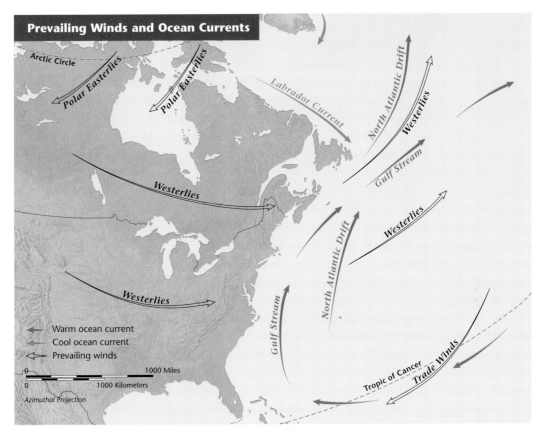

Prevailing Winds and Ocean Currents

▼ Location. *Marine locations—places near large bodies of water—have mild climates with little temperature variation because water gains and loses heat slowly (see San Francisco graph). Interior locations—places far from large water bodies—have much more extreme climates. There are great temperature variations because land gains and loses heat rapidly (see Wichita graph). Richmond, which is relatively near the Atlantic Ocean but which is also influenced by prevailing westerly winds blowing across the land, has moderate characteristics of both conditions.*

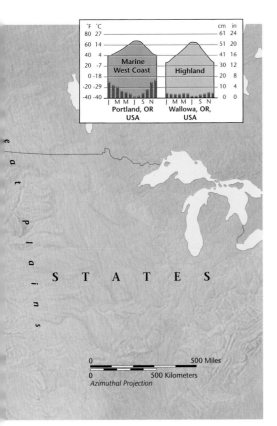

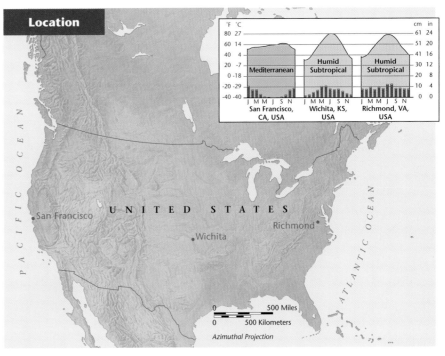

Location

EARTH'S NATURAL VEGETATION

Natural vegetation is the plant life that would be found in an area if it were undisturbed by human activity. Natural vegetation varies widely depending on climate and soil conditions. In the rain forest, trees tower as much as 200 feet (60 m) above the forest floor. In the tundra, dwarf species of shrubs and flowers are adaptations to harsh conditions at high latitudes and high elevations.

Vegetation is important to human life. It provides oxygen, food, fuel, products with economic value, even lifesaving medicines. Human activities, however, have greatly affected natural vegetation. Huge forests have been cut to provide fuel and lumber. Grasslands have yielded to the plow as people extend agricultural lands. As many as one in eight plants may become extinct as a result of human interference. *Web Link*

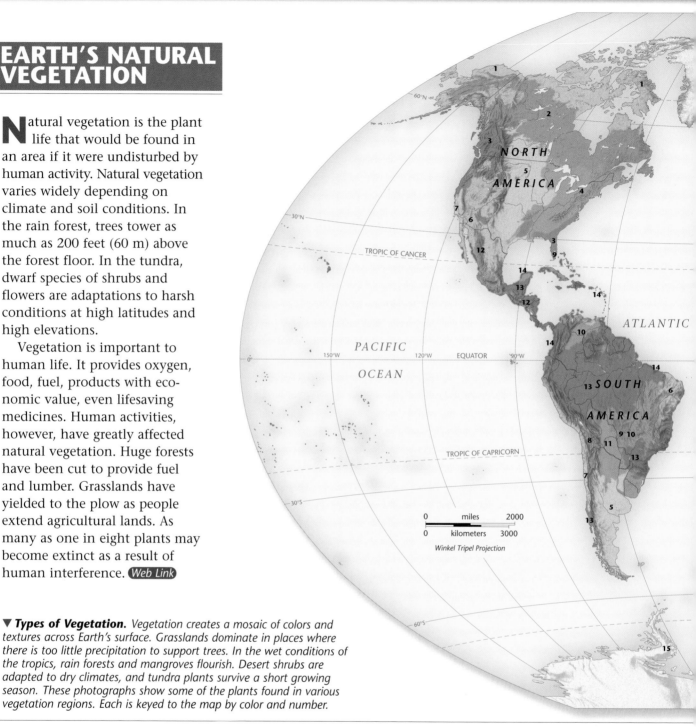

▼ **Types of Vegetation.** *Vegetation creates a mosaic of colors and textures across Earth's surface. Grasslands dominate in places where there is too little precipitation to support trees. In the wet conditions of the tropics, rain forests and mangroves flourish. Desert shrubs are adapted to dry climates, and tundra plants survive a short growing season. These photographs show some of the plants found in various vegetation regions. Each is keyed to the map by color and number.*

▲ **Tundra**

▲ **Northern coniferous forest**

▲ **Temperate broadleaf forest**

▲ **Desert shrub**

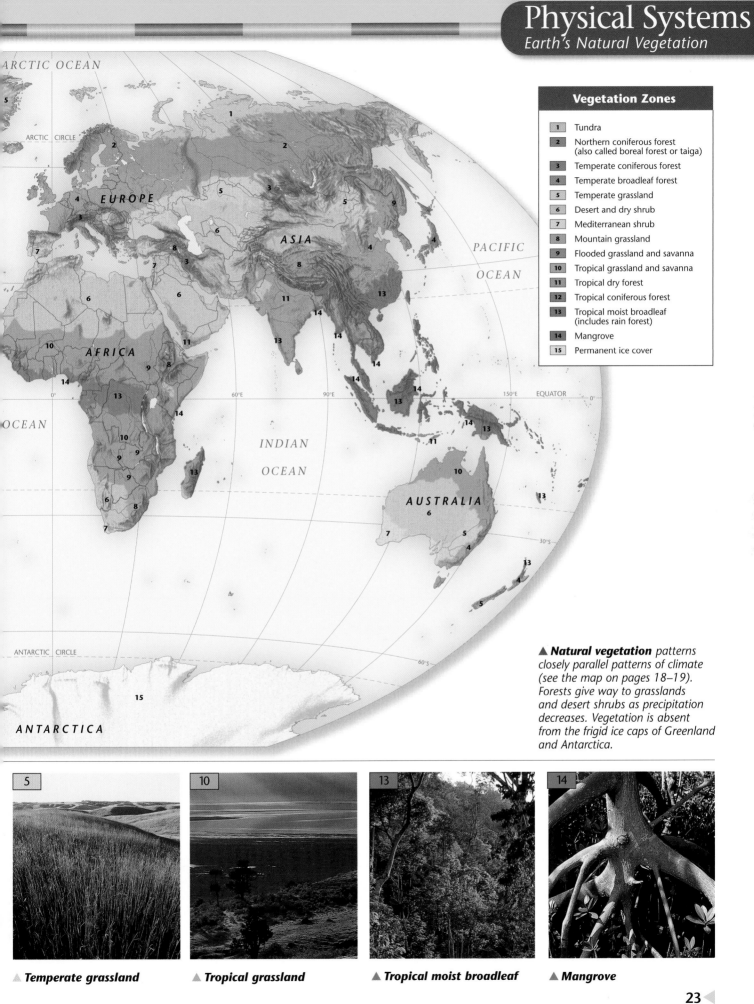

ARCTIC OCEAN

ARCTIC CIRCLE

EUROPE

ASIA

PACIFIC OCEAN

AFRICA

INDIAN OCEAN

AUSTRALIA

OCEAN

ANTARCTIC CIRCLE

ANTARCTICA

Vegetation Zones

1	Tundra
2	Northern coniferous forest (also called boreal forest or taiga)
3	Temperate coniferous forest
4	Temperate broadleaf forest
5	Temperate grassland
6	Desert and dry shrub
7	Mediterranean shrub
8	Mountain grassland
9	Flooded grassland and savanna
10	Tropical grassland and savanna
11	Tropical dry forest
12	Tropical coniferous forest
13	Tropical moist broadleaf (includes rain forest)
14	Mangrove
15	Permanent ice cover

▲ **Natural vegetation** patterns closely parallel patterns of climate (see the map on pages 18–19). Forests give way to grasslands and desert shrubs as precipitation decreases. Vegetation is absent from the frigid ice caps of Greenland and Antarctica.

▲ **Temperate grassland**   ▲ **Tropical grassland**   ▲ **Tropical moist broadleaf**   ▲ **Mangrove**

23

Human Systems

THE POLITICAL WORLD

A map with the names and boundaries of countries shows the political world. Boundaries—some arrived at peacefully, others after years of conflict and war—carve up the land into 191 independent units, or countries, at the close of the 20th century. Boundaries are dynamic, meaning they change over time as political power shifts. For example, in 1990, West and East Germany became one country, removing a boundary that had separated them since 1949. In 1993 a new boundary divided Czechoslovakia into two separate countries, the Czech Republic and Slovakia.

Countries vary in size. Russia, the largest, stretches across northern Asia into Europe. Other countries are small enough to fit inside another country. For instance, the country of Lesotho, lies entirely within the country of South Africa. Web Link

▶ **The scale of this map** makes it impossible to name all 191 independent countries and their capital cities. For a complete listing, refer to pages 112–119 or use the place-name index and the political maps in each continent section.

▶ **View From the North Pole.** Ocean, not land, surrounds the area of the North Pole, so there are no political boundaries there. The Arctic Ocean, icebound much of the year, is part of the coastal waters of Earth's northernmost countries.

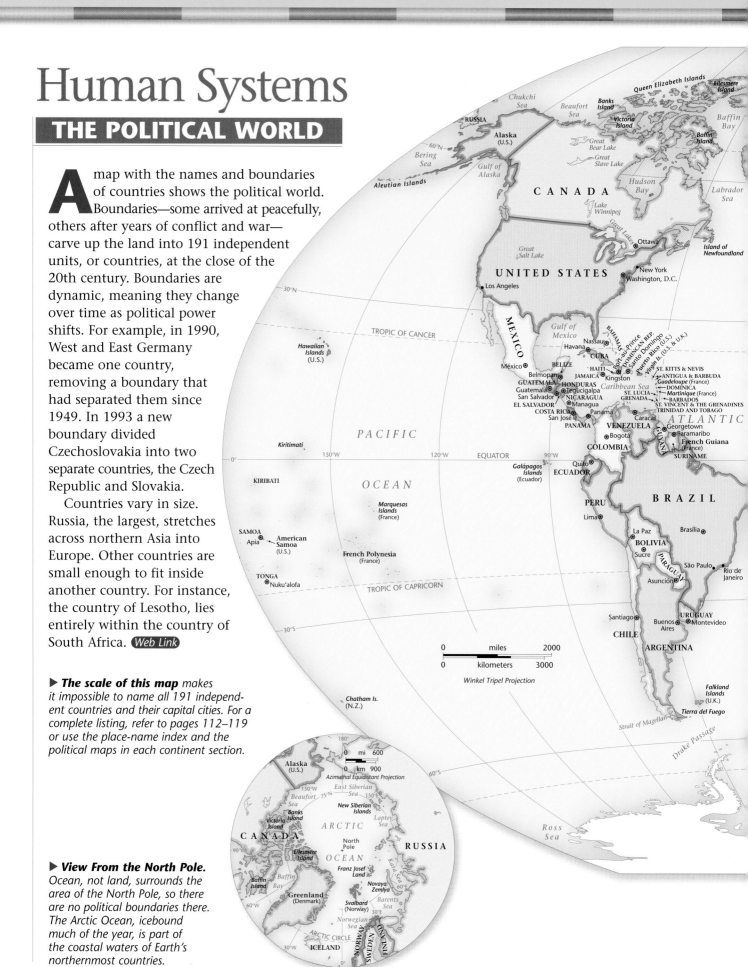

ARCTIC OCEAN

Greenland
(Denmark)

Greenland Sea

Franz Josef Land

Svalbard (Norway)

Barents Sea

Severnaya Zemlya

New Siberian Islands

East Siberian Sea

Laptev Sea

Kara Sea

Novaya Zemlya

ARCTIC CIRCLE

Norwegian Sea

ICELAND
Reykjavik

R U S S I A

Bering Sea

Kamchatka Peninsula

Sea of Okhotsk

Sakhalin

Oslo
Stockholm
Helsinki
Moscow

NORWAY
SWEDEN
FINLAND

UNITED
KINGDOM
DENMARK
Copenhagen
Dublin
IRELAND
London
Berlin
GERMANY
Warsaw
POLAND
Minsk
BELARUS
Kiev
UKRAINE

Paris
FRANCE
SWITZ.
ITALY
Rome

Madrid
SPAIN
PORTUGAL
Lisbon

Astana

KAZAKHSTAN
Aral Sea

Ulaanbaatar
MONGOLIA

Lake Baikal

Hokkaido

NORTH KOREA
Pyongyang
Seoul
SOUTH KOREA

Honshu
JAPAN
Tokyo
Osaka
Kyushu

Beijing

ROMANIA
BULGARIA
Black Sea
GEORGIA
ARM.
AZER.
Bishkek
KYRGYZSTAN
Dushanbe
TAJIKISTAN

The People's Republic of China claims Taiwan as its 23rd province.

ALBANIA
GREECE
Athens
Ankara
TURKEY
Tunis

UZBEKISTAN
Tashkent
TURKMENISTAN
Ashgabat

C H I N A

Shanghai

Taipei
TAIWAN

PACIFIC

Philippine Sea

CYPRUS
LEBANON
ISRAEL
SYRIA
IRAQ
Baghdad
Tehran
IRAN
Kabul
AFGHANISTAN

Islamabad

Luzon
Northern Mariana Islands (U.S.)

OCEAN

MARSHALL ISLANDS

Azores (Portugal)

MOROCCO
Rabat

Canary Is. (Spain)
Western Sahara (Morocco)

ALGERIA
TUNISIA
Tripoli

Algiers
Mediterranean Sea

LIBYA
EGYPT
Cairo

JORDAN
KUWAIT
BAHRAIN
QATAR
Riyadh
U.A.E.
SAUDI ARABIA
OMAN
Muscat

NEPAL
New Delhi
Kathmandu
BHUTAN
Thimphu
BANGLADESH
Dhaka
Calcutta

PAKISTAN
Karachi

Hanoi
VIETNAM
Hainan
South China Sea
Manila
PHILIPPINES

Mindanao
PALAU

FEDERATED STATES OF MICRONESIA

KIRIBATI

MAURITANIA
Nouakchott
MALI
CAPE VERDE
SENEGAL
GAMBIA
Dakar
Bamako
GUINEA-BISSAU
GUINEA
Conakry
SIERRA LEONE
Freetown
Monrovia
LIBERIA
Yamoussoukro

NIGER
Niamey
CHAD
N'Djamena
SUDAN
Khartoum

ERITREA
Asmara
YEMEN
Sanaa
DJIBOUTI

Arabian Sea
Socotra (Yemen)

Mumbai (Bombay)
I N D I A

Bay of Bengal

MYANMAR (BURMA)
Yangon
LAOS
Vientiane
THAILAND
Bangkok
CAMBODIA
Phnom Penh

BRUNEI
Bandar Seri Begawan
MALAYSIA
Kuala Lumpur
SINGAPORE

COTE D'IVOIRE
Abidjan
BURKINA FASO
Ouagadougou
GHANA
Accra
TOGO
BENIN
Porto-Novo
Lomé
NIGERIA
Lagos
Abuja

CENTRAL AFRICAN REPUBLIC
Bangui

ETHIOPIA
Addis Ababa
SOMALIA

SRI LANKA
Colombo
Sri Jayewardenepura Kotte
Male
MALDIVES

EQUATOR

NAURU

EQ. GUINEA
SAO TOME AND PRINCIPE
GABON
Libreville
CONGO
CAMEROON
Yaoundé
Brazzaville
DEMOCRATIC REPUBLIC OF THE CONGO
Kinshasa

UGANDA
Kampala
RWANDA
Kigali
BURUNDI
Bujumbura
KENYA
Nairobi

Mogadishu

I N D O N E S I A

Jakarta
Java
Sumatra
Borneo
Celebes

New Guinea
PAPUA NEW GUINEA
Port Moresby

SOLOMON ISLANDS
Honiara

TUVALU

OCEAN

CABINDA (Angola)

TANZANIA
Dar es Salaam
SEYCHELLES

COMOROS
Moroni

East Timor

ANGOLA
Luanda
ZAMBIA
Lusaka
MALAWI
Lilongwe

Coral Sea

VANUATU
Port-Vila

FIJI
Suva

INDIAN OCEAN

Antananarivo
MAURITIUS
Port Louis
Réunion (France)

New Caledonia (France)

NAMIBIA
Windhoek
BOTSWANA
Gaborone
ZIMBABWE
Harare
MOZAMBIQUE
MADAGASCAR

A U S T R A L I A

Pretoria
Bloemfontein
SWAZILAND
Maputo
LESOTHO
SOUTH AFRICA
Cape Town

Great Australian Bight

30°S

Tasman Sea
North Island

Canberra

NEW ZEALAND
Wellington

Tasmania

South Island

ANTARCTIC CIRCLE

Kerguélen Islands (France)

OCEAN

A N T A R C T I C A

Ross Sea

Cities

⊛ National capital

• Urban area with more than 10 million people

▶ View From the South Pole.
Covered by ice, the continent of Antarctica has been set aside by treaty for scientific research. It has no permanent population and no political boundaries, although 7 countries claim territory there and 23 operate year-round research stations (see map page 111).

ATLANTIC OCEAN
ANTARCTIC CIRCLE
Weddell Sea
Antarctic Peninsula
Ronne Ice Shelf
West Antarctica
South Pole
East Antarctica
A N T A R C T I C A
Ross Ice Shelf
Ross Sea
PACIFIC OCEAN
INDIAN OCEAN

0 mi 600
0 km 900
Azimuthal Equidistant Projection

WORLD POPULATION

Late in 1999 the United Nations announced that Earth's population had surpassed six billion. Although more than 80 million people are added each year, the rate, or annual percent, at which the population is growing is gradually decreasing. Earth's population has very uneven distribution, with huge clusters in Asia and in Europe. Population density, the number of people living in each square mile (or square kilometer) on average, is high in these regions. For example, there are more than 2,000 people per square mile (800 people per sq km)) in Bangladesh. Other areas, such as deserts and Arctic tundra, have less than 2 people per square mile (1 person per sq km). Web Link

▼ **Crowded streets,** like this one in Shanghai, may become commonplace as Earth's population continues to increase and as more people move to urban areas.

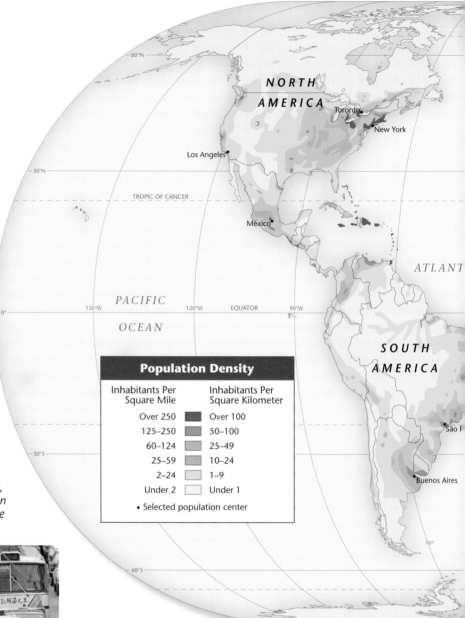

Population Density

Inhabitants Per Square Mile	Inhabitants Per Square Kilometer
Over 250	Over 100
125–250	50–100
60–124	25–49
25–59	10–24
2–24	1–9
Under 2	Under 1

• Selected population center

Population Growth Over Time

The population's rate of increase—the percent by which it changes each year—was slow until industrial and scientific discoveries in the 1800s brought improved health, a more reliable food supply, and other changes that improved the quality of life. Earth's population began to increase rapidly. Although the rate of increase has begun to slow, the United Nations projects that Earth's population will reach 8 billion by 2028.

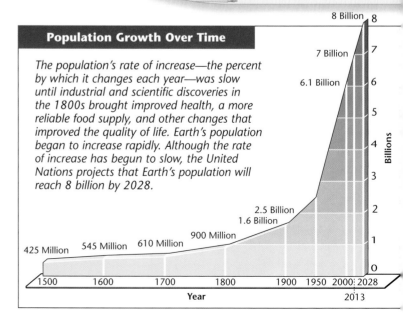

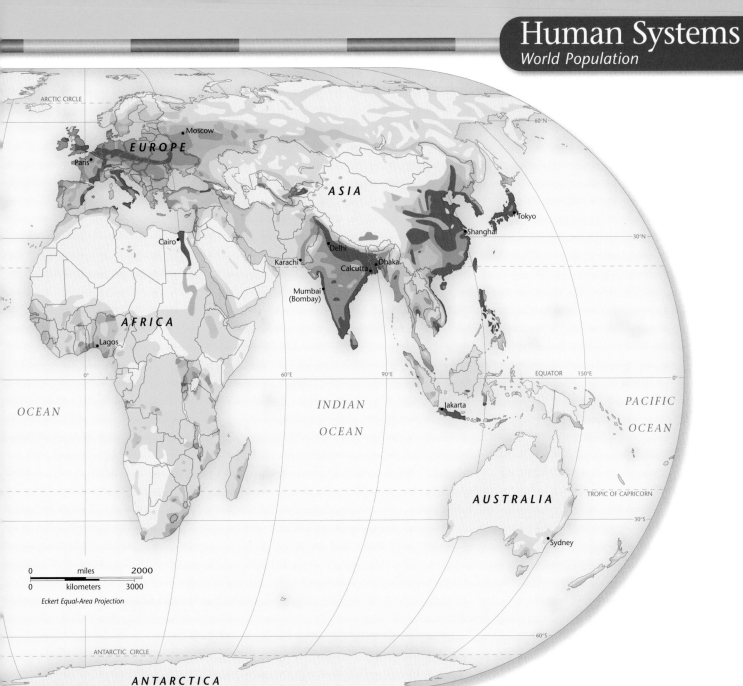

Eckert Equal-Area Projection

Three Population Pyramids

A population pyramid is a special type of bar graph that shows the distribution of a country's population by sex and age. Italy has a very narrow pyramid, which shows that most people are in middle age. Its population is said to be aging, meaning the median age is increasing. The United States also has a narrow pyramid, but one that shows some growth due to a median age of about 35 years and a young immigrant population. By contrast, Côte d'Ivoire's pyramid has a broad base, showing it has a young population. Almost half its people are younger than 15 years.

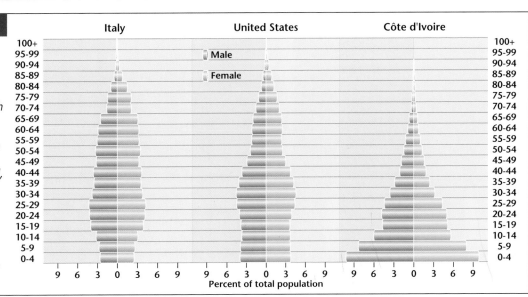

Italy | United States | Côte d'Ivoire

■ Male
■ Female

Percent of total population

WORLD CITIES

Throughout most of history, people have lived spread across the land, first as hunters and gatherers, later as farmers. But urban geographers—people who study cities—predict that sometime in the next decade more people will be living in urban areas than in rural areas. Urban areas include one or more cities and their surrounding suburbs. People living there are employed primarily in industry or in service-related jobs. Large urban areas are sometimes called metropolitan areas. In some countries, such as Belgium, almost all the population lives in cities. But throughout much of Africa south of the Sahara, less than one-third of the people live in urban areas. Even so, the world's fastest growing urban areas are in Africa and Asia, as shown in the graph below.

Web Link

NORTH AMERICA

Chicago
Toronto
New York
Los Angeles

TROPIC OF CANCER

México
Guatemala City

PACIFIC OCEAN

Bogotá

ATLANTIC

EQUATOR

SOUTH AMERICA

Lima

Belo Horizonte
Rio de Janeiro
São Paulo

Santiago
Buenos Aires

0 miles 2000
0 kilometers 3000

Winkel Tripel Projection

Most Populous Urban Areas

In 1950 New York topped a list of only 8 cities with populations of 5 million or greater. Just 50 years later, New York ranked fifth in a list of 41 cities with populations exceeding 5 million. By 2015, the list is projected to include 59 cities.

Cities with populations greater than five million for the years:

- 1950
- 2000
- 2015

	North America	South America	Europe	Africa	Asia	Australia/ Oceania
1950	1	1	4	0	2	0
2000	4	6	5	3	23	0
2015	6	7	5	6	35	0

Urban and Rural Populations

These graphs show the percentages of people living in urban and rural areas in various world regions. Only Asia and Africa are predominantly rural, although both are experiencing rapid urban growth. Asia, which had only 2 cities of five million or more people in 1950, now has 23.

United States & Canad

75% 25%

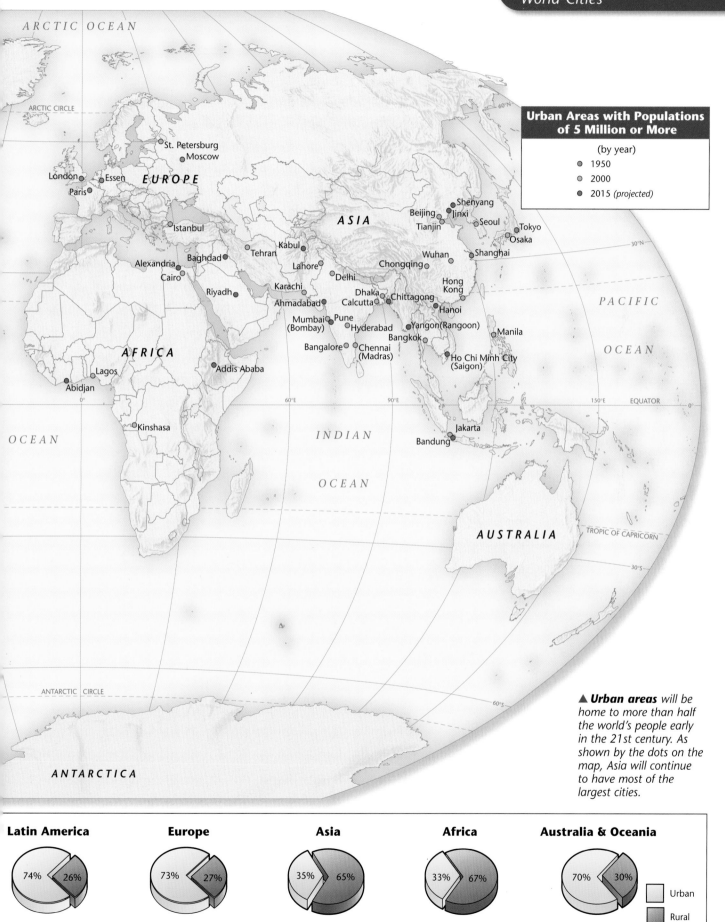

Urban Areas with Populations of 5 Million or More

(by year)
- 1950
- 2000
- 2015 (projected)

▲ **Urban areas** will be home to more than half the world's people early in the 21st century. As shown by the dots on the map, Asia will continue to have most of the largest cities.

Latin America
74% | 26%

Europe
73% | 27%

Asia
35% | 65%

Africa
33% | 67%

Australia & Oceania
70% | 30%

Urban
Rural

WORLD CULTURES

Culture is all the shared things that define the way a people live—customs and symbols, food and clothing preferences, housing styles, systems of government, music and art forms, language and belief systems. Tracing the diffusion, or movement, of culture traits, or characteristics, is one way that geographers understand how places are connected.

For example, English originated in western Europe, but its widespread use today reflects the far-reaching effects of 19th-century colonial empires. About 6,000 languages are spoken in the world today, many of which will probably become extinct as global trade, communications, and travel blur distinctions among cultures.

Some religions also have spread far from their areas of origin—Islam and Christianity from southwestern Asia and Buddhism from southern Asia.

Web Link

Major Language Families Today

- Afro-Asiatic
- Altaic
- Austro-Asiatic
- Austronesian
- Dravidian
- Indo-European
- Japanese/Korean
- Kam-Tai
- Niger-Congo
- Nilo-Saharan
- Sino-Tibetan
- Uralic
- Other

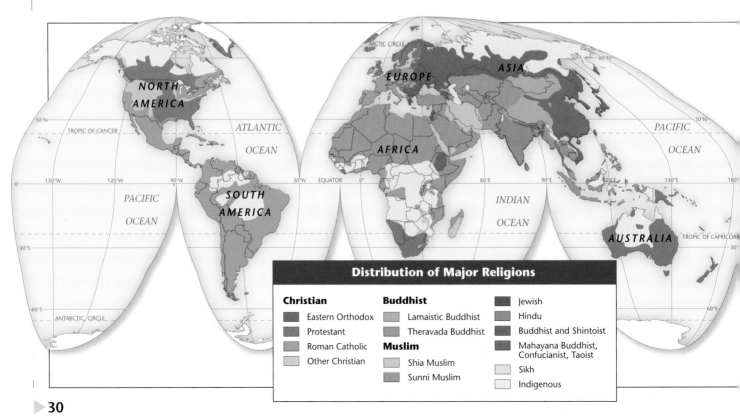

Distribution of Major Religions

Christian
- Eastern Orthodox
- Protestant
- Roman Catholic
- Other Christian

Buddhist
- Lamaistic Buddhist
- Theravada Buddhist

Muslim
- Shia Muslim
- Sunni Muslim

- Jewish
- Hindu
- Buddhist and Shintoist
- Mahayana Buddhist, Confucianist, Taoist
- Sikh
- Indigenous

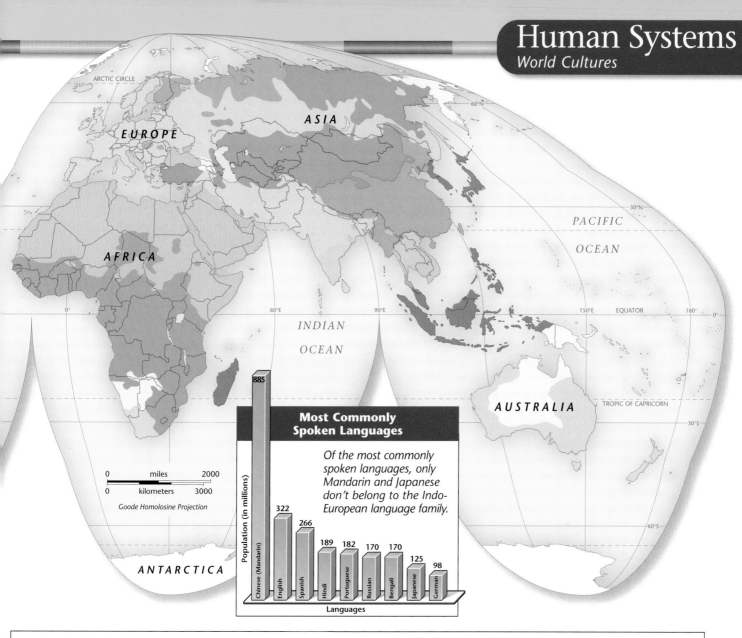

Most Commonly Spoken Languages

Of the most commonly spoken languages, only Mandarin and Japanese don't belong to the Indo-European language family.

Population (in millions) / Languages:

Language	Population
Chinese (Mandarin)	885
English	322
Spanish	266
Hindi	189
Portuguese	182
Russian	170
Bengali	170
Japanese	125
German	98

Goode Homolosine Projection

miles 0–2000
kilometers 0–3000

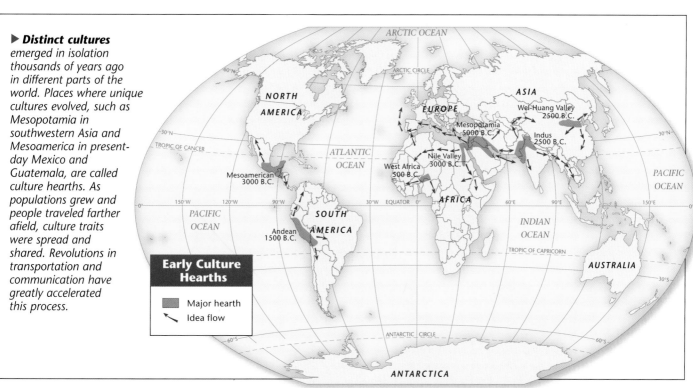

▶ **Distinct cultures** emerged in isolation thousands of years ago in different parts of the world. Places where unique cultures evolved, such as Mesopotamia in southwestern Asia and Mesoamerica in present-day Mexico and Guatemala, are called culture hearths. As populations grew and people traveled farther afield, culture traits were spread and shared. Revolutions in transportation and communication have greatly accelerated this process.

Early Culture Hearths
- Major hearth
- Idea flow

Mesoamerican 3000 B.C.
Andean 1500 B.C.
West Africa 500 B.C.
Nile Valley 3000 B.C.
Mesopotamia 5000 B.C.
Indus 2500 B.C.
Wei-Huang Valley 2500 B.C.

PREDOMINANT WORLD ECONOMIES

Economic activities are the many different ways that people create products and generate income to meet their needs and wants. Long ago most people lived by hunting and gathering. Today, most engage in a variety of other activities that are commonly grouped into the following categories. Primary activities: agriculture, fishing, forestry; secondary activities: manufacturing and processing industries; tertiary activities: services, such as finance, medicine, education; and quaternary activities: information exchange and e-commerce—buying and selling over the Internet. The more developed economies of the world have shifted from secondary activities toward tertiary and quaternary activities. Less developed economies continue to rely on primary activities. **Web Link**

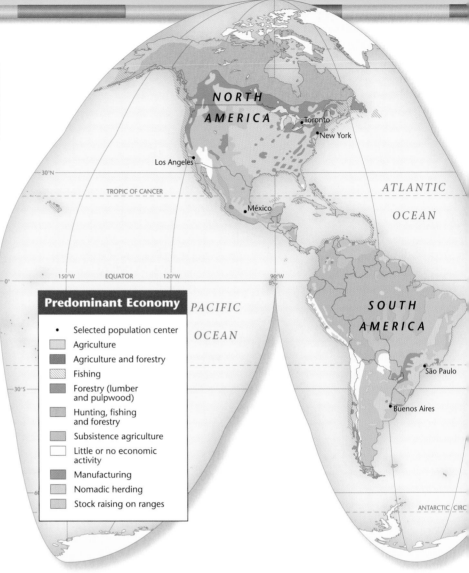

Predominant Economy

- • Selected population center
- Agriculture
- Agriculture and forestry
- Fishing
- Forestry (lumber and pulpwood)
- Hunting, fishing and forestry
- Subsistence agriculture
- Little or no economic activity
- Manufacturing
- Nomadic herding
- Stock raising on ranges

▲ **Subsistence Agriculture.** Many people in developing countries, such as these farmers in Peru, use traditional methods to grow crops for their daily food requirements rather than for commercial sale.

◀ **Logging.** Workers ready logs to float down the Columbia River in Washington State. Processing plants will turn the logs into paper products or cut them into lumber for the construction industry.

▶ **Fishing.** Tuna is one of the chief commercial fishes as well as a favorite among big game fishermen. Japan is the world's leading harvester of tuna. Albacore, shown here, is one of the top commercial varieties.

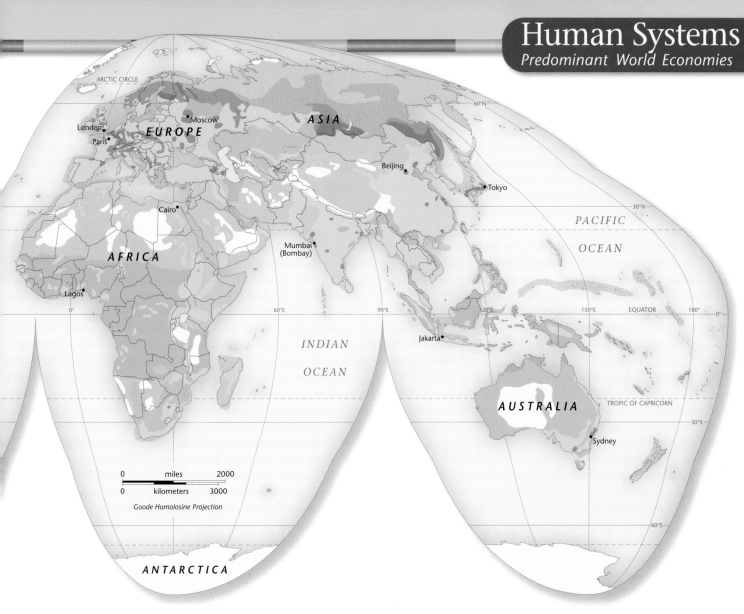

ARCTIC CIRCLE

London
Paris
EUROPE
Moscow
ASIA
60°N

Beijing
Tokyo
30°N

PACIFIC

OCEAN

Cairo

AFRICA

Mumbai
(Bombay)

60°E
90°E
120°E
150°E
EQUATOR
180°
0°

Lagos

0°

INDIAN

OCEAN

Jakarta

AUSTRALIA

TROPIC OF CAPRICORN

30°S

Sydney

0   miles   2000

0   kilometers   3000

Goode Homolosine Projection

60°S

ANTARCTICA

▶ **Education and Communications.** *These services combine to allow students to interact with scientists working in the field. Here students explore the underwater ecology of California's Monterey Bay as part of renowned ocean explorer Robert Ballard's JASON Project.*

▲ **Manufacturing.** *This mill in Slovakia processes raw materials—coal and iron ore—to make steel, which in turn is used by other industries to produce cars, machinery, and other kinds of manufactured goods.*

▶ **The Internet.** *This has opened a whole new way of exchanging information. E-mail connects people in places near and far, while e-commerce allows them to buy and sell products without ever leaving home.*

33 ◀

WORLD FOOD

As the 20th century drew to a close, the world's population surpassed six billion—six billion hungry mouths to feed. Productive cropland, though, like other natural resources, is unevenly distributed. In addition, access to modern farming methods and technology varies from country to country. Some countries produce large surpluses; others struggle to feed their populations. Grains such as rice, corn, and wheat provide 80 percent of the world's food energy supply.

Web Link

NORTH AMERICA

TROPIC OF CANCER

ATLANTIC OCEAN

30°N

150°W   EQUATOR   120°W   90°W

0°

PACIFIC OCEAN

SOUTH AMERICA

30°S

Major Types of Grain

- Corn
- Wheat
- Rice

60°S

ANTARCTIC CIRCL

▲ **Rice** is an important staple food crop, especially in eastern and southern Asia. Although China produces about one-third of the world's rice, it is also a major importer of rice to feed its population of more than a billion people.

▶ **Corn** originated in the Americas but was carried by Europeans to Europe, Asia, and Africa. Corn is an important food grain for both people and livestock.

◀ **Wheat** is the world's leading export grain. It is a main ingredient in bread and pasta and is grown on every inhabited continent. Each year trade in this grain exceeds 100 million tons.

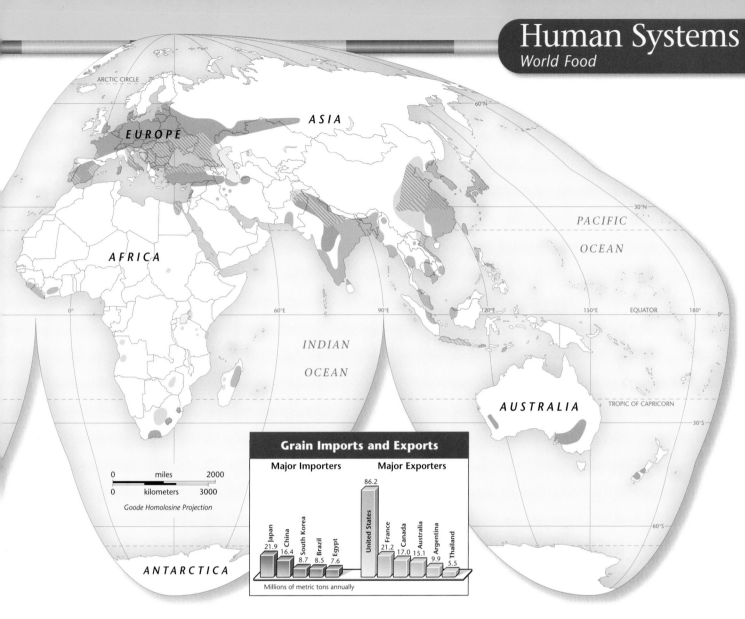

ASIA

EUROPE

PACIFIC OCEAN

30°N

AFRICA

60°E

90°E

120°E

150°E

EQUATOR

180°

INDIAN OCEAN

AUSTRALIA

TROPIC OF CAPRICORN

30°S

0   miles   2000
0   kilometers   3000
Goode Homolosine Projection

ANTARCTICA

60°S

Grain Imports and Exports

Major Importers

Japan	21.9
China	16.4
South Korea	8.7
Brazil	8.5
Egypt	7.6

Major Exporters

United States	86.2
France	21.2
Canada	17.0
Australia	15.1
Argentina	9.9
Thailand	5.5

Millions of metric tons annually

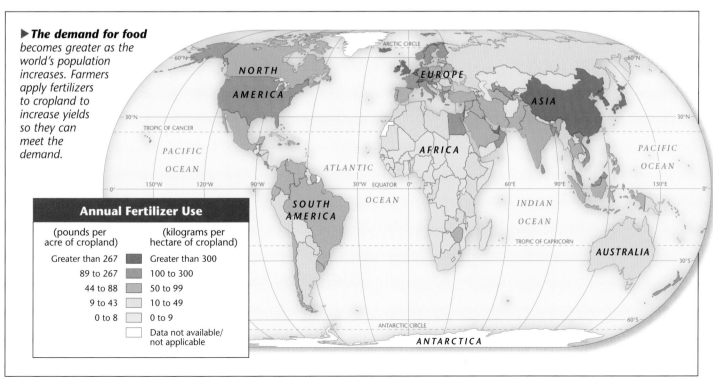

▶ **The demand for food** becomes greater as the world's population increases. Farmers apply fertilizers to cropland to increase yields so they can meet the demand.

NORTH AMERICA

EUROPE

ASIA

AFRICA

SOUTH AMERICA

AUSTRALIA

ARCTIC CIRCLE

TROPIC OF CANCER

PACIFIC OCEAN

ATLANTIC OCEAN

INDIAN OCEAN

PACIFIC OCEAN

TROPIC OF CAPRICORN

EQUATOR

ANTARCTIC CIRCLE

ANTARCTICA

Annual Fertilizer Use

(pounds per acre of cropland)	(kilograms per hectare of cropland)
Greater than 267	Greater than 300
89 to 267	100 to 300
44 to 88	50 to 99
9 to 43	10 to 49
0 to 8	0 to 9
	Data not available/ not applicable

Water is essential for life and is one of Earth's most valuable natural resources. It is even more important than food. More than 70 percent of Earth's surface is covered with water, but most of it—about 97 percent—is salty. Without treatment it is not usable for drinking or growing crops. The remaining 3 percent is fresh, but most of this is either trapped in glaciers or ice caps or lies too deep underground to be tapped economically.

Water is a renewable resource. We can use it over and over because the hydrologic, or water, cycle purifies water as it moves through the processes of evaporation, condensation, precipitation, runoff, and infiltration. But careless use can diminish the supply of usable fresh water. Water may become polluted as a result of runoff from industries, cultivated fields, and urban areas. In addition, water, like other natural resources, is unevenly distributed on Earth. Some countries have an abundance of water while others face serious water shortages, especially in parts of Asia and Africa. (Web Link)

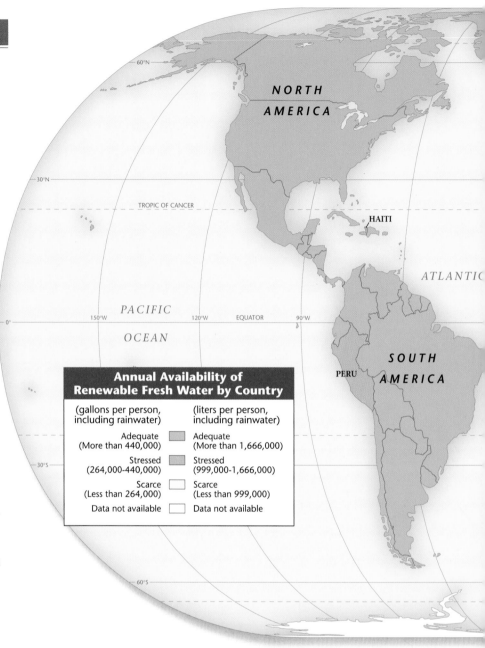

Annual Availability of Renewable Fresh Water by Country

(gallons per person, including rainwater)		(liters per person, including rainwater)
Adequate (More than 440,000)		Adequate (More than 1,666,000)
Stressed (264,000-440,000)		Stressed (999,000-1,666,000)
Scarce (Less than 264,000)		Scarce (Less than 999,000)
Data not available		Data not available

▲ **Domestic Water Use.** *In much of the less developed world, people haul water daily for household use, as in this village in Central America.*

▲ **Agricultural Water Use.** *Irrigation has made agriculture possible in dry areas such as the San Pedro Valley in Arizona, shown here.*

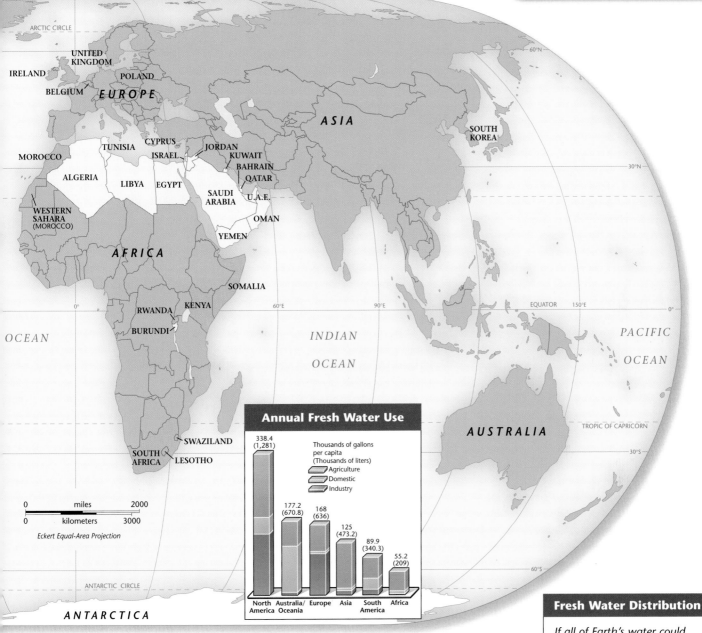

ARCTIC CIRCLE

60°N

UNITED
KINGDOM

IRELAND

BELGIUM

POLAND

EUROPE

ASIA

SOUTH
KOREA

MOROCCO

TUNISIA

CYPRUS

JORDAN

ISRAEL

KUWAIT

BAHRAIN

QATAR

30°N

ALGERIA

LIBYA

EGYPT

SAUDI
ARABIA

U.A.E.

OMAN

WESTERN
SAHARA
(MOROCCO)

YEMEN

AFRICA

SOMALIA

EQUATOR

150°E

0°

RWANDA

KENYA

0°

60°E

90°E

BURUNDI

OCEAN

INDIAN

OCEAN

PACIFIC

OCEAN

AUSTRALIA

TROPIC OF CAPRICORN

SWAZILAND

30°S

SOUTH
AFRICA

LESOTHO

miles 2000

0

kilometers 3000

Eckert Equal-Area Projection

60°S

ANTARCTIC CIRCLE

ANTARCTICA

Annual Fresh Water Use

Thousands of gallons
per capita
(Thousands of liters)

▨ Agriculture
▨ Domestic
▨ Industry

338.4
(1,281)

177.2
(670.8)

168
(636)

125
(473.2)

89.9
(340.3)

55.2
(209)

North America	Australia/ Oceania	Europe	Asia	South America	Africa

▲ *Industrial Water Use.* Hydroelectric projects, such as South America's Itaipú Dam, harness running water to generate electricity that powers industry.

▲ *Water Stress.* By using groundwater faster than it is renewed, agriculture in dry areas puts stress on limited water supplies.

Fresh Water Distribution

If all of Earth's water could fit into a gallon (4.5 liter) jug, only slightly more than a tablespoon of it would be available fresh water. This graph shows the sources of Earth's fresh water.

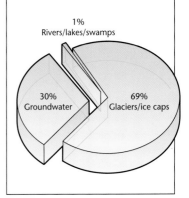

1%
Rivers/lakes/swamps

30%
Groundwater

69%
Glaciers/ice caps

WORLD ENERGY & MINERAL RESOURCES

Beginning in the 19th century, as the Industrial Revolution spread across Europe and around the world, the demand for energy and mineral resources skyrocketed. Fossil fuels—first coal, then oil—provided the energy that kept the wheels of industry turning. Minerals such as iron ore, which is essential for the production of steel, and copper, which is used for electrical wiring, became increasingly important.

Energy and minerals, like all non-renewable resources, are in limited supply and are unevenly distributed. Countries with major deposits play an important role in the global economy. For example, the Organization of Petroleum Exporting Countries (OPEC) influences the world supply of oil and, therefore, fuel prices. **Web Link**

Major fossil fuel deposits

- ▨ Coal
- ⬭ Natural gas
- ▪ Oil
- ▨ OPEC member

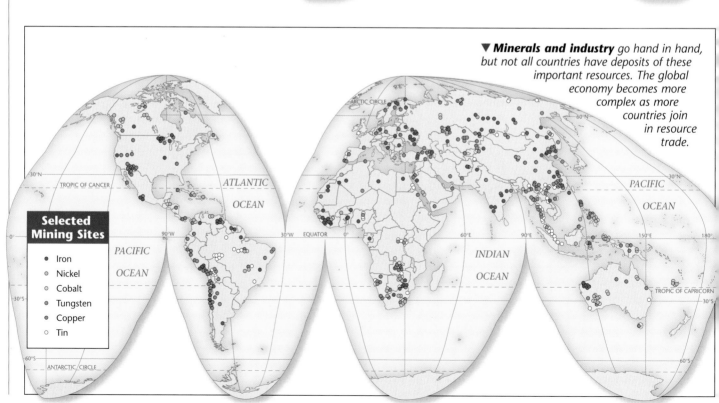

▼ **Minerals and industry** go hand in hand, but not all countries have deposits of these important resources. The global economy becomes more complex as more countries join in resource trade.

Selected Mining Sites

- ● Iron
- ◐ Nickel
- ○ Cobalt
- ◑ Tungsten
- ● Copper
- ○ Tin

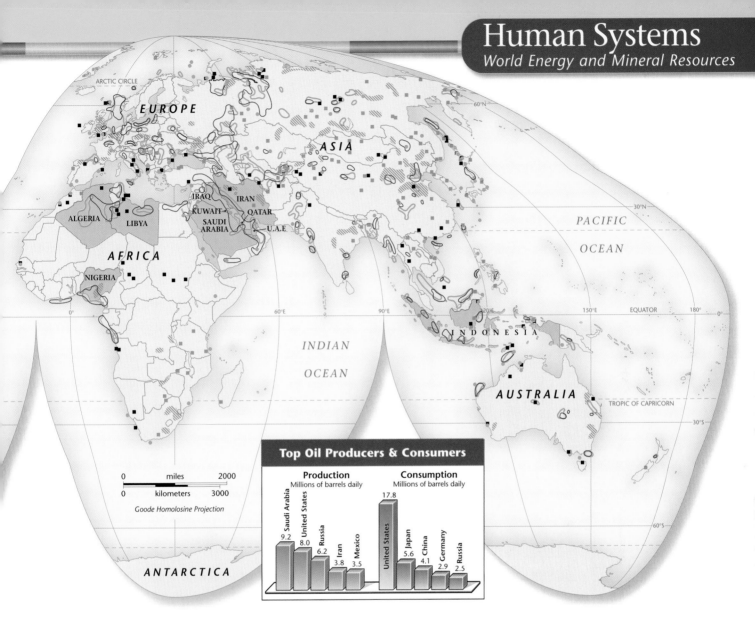

EUROPE

ASIA

PACIFIC

OCEAN

ARCTIC CIRCLE

60°N

30°N

IRAQ

IRAN

KUWAIT

QATAR

SAUDI
ARABIA

U.A.E

ALGERIA

LIBYA

AFRICA

NIGERIA

0°

60°E

90°E

EQUATOR

150°E

180°

0°

INDIAN

OCEAN

INDONESIA

AUSTRALIA

TROPIC OF CAPRICORN

30°S

60°S

ANTARCTICA

miles		2000
0		
kilometers		3000
0		

Goode Homolosine Projection

Top Oil Producers & Consumers

Production
Millions of barrels daily

Saudi Arabia 9.2
United States 8.0
Russia 6.2
Iran 3.8
Mexico 3.5

Consumption
Millions of barrels daily

United States 17.8
Japan 5.6
China 4.1
Germany 2.9
Russia 2.5

▶ **Reactors** near Sacramento, California, produce nuclear energy, and solar panels capture energy from the sun. These two sources of energy are important alternatives to nonrenewable fossil fuels.

▲ **A wind energy farm** near Tehachapi, California, uses windmills to capture the energy of winds blowing off the Pacific Ocean.

◀ **A geothermal power plant,** fueled by heat from deep within Earth, produces energy to heat homes in Iceland. Runoff creates a warm pool for bathers.

▼ **Dependence on oil** for motor vehicles, industries, and domestic power and heating makes the United States the world's leading consumer of this energy resource.

North America

Viewed from high above, North America stretches from the frozen expanses of the Arctic Ocean and Greenland to the lush green of Panama's tropical forests. Hudson Bay and the Great Lakes, fingerprints of long-departed glaciers, dominate the continent's east, while the brown landscapes of the west and southwest tell of dry lands where water is scarce.

Facts & Figures

▶ **Land area:** 9,449,500 sq mi (24,474,000 sq km)

▶ **Population:** 479,326,000

▶ **Highest point:** Mount McKinley (Denali), Alaska: 20,320 ft (6,194 m)

▶ **Lowest point:** Death Valley, California: 282 ft (86 m) below sea level

▶ **Longest river:** Mississippi-Missouri, United States: 3,710 mi (5,971 km)

▶ **Largest lake:** Lake Superior, U.S.-Canada: 31,701 sq mi (82,100 sq km)

▶ **Number of Independent countries:** 23

▶ **Largest country:** Canada: 3,849,670 sq mi (9,970,610 sq km)

▶ **Smallest country:** St. Kitts and Nevis: 101 sq mi (261 sq km)

▶ **Most populous country:** United States: Pop. 275,600,000

▶ **Least populous country:** St. Kitts and Nevis: Pop. 43,000

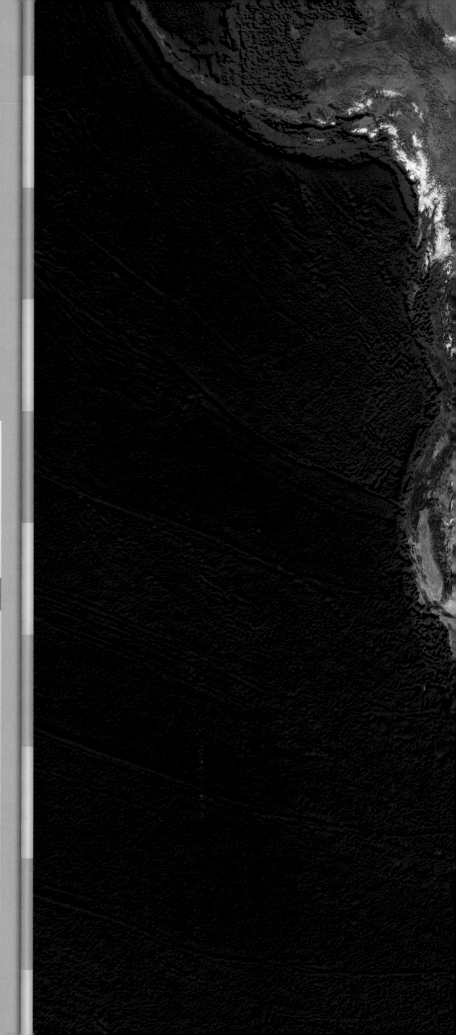

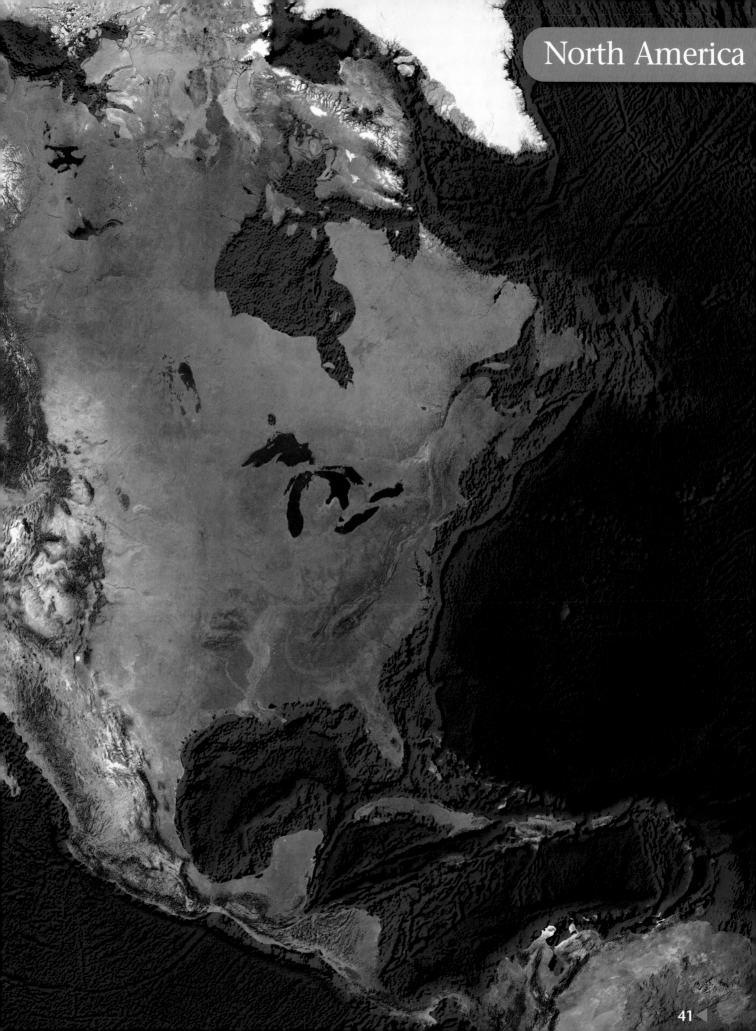

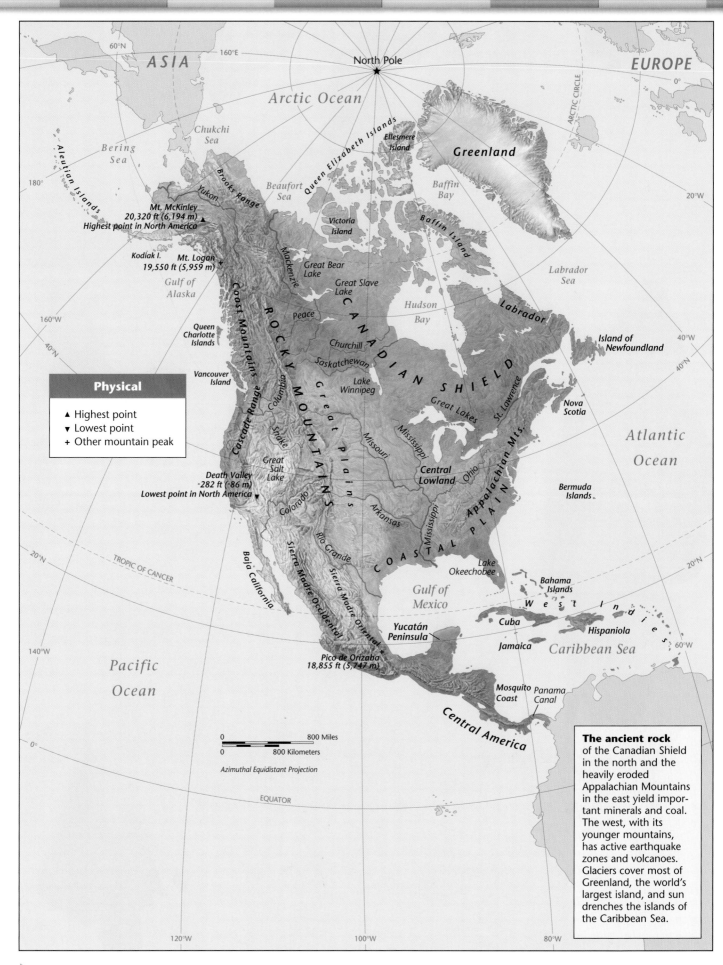

ASIA

EUROPE

North Pole

Arctic Ocean

ARCTIC CIRCLE

0°

60°N

160°E

Chukchi
Sea

Queen Elizabeth Islands

Ellesmere
Island

Greenland

Bering
Sea

Aleutian Islands

180°

Beaufort
Sea

Baffin
Bay

20°W

Brooks Range

Yukon

Victoria
Island

Baffin Island

Mt. McKinley
20,320 ft (6,194 m)
Highest point in North America

160°W

Kodiak I.

Mt. Logan
19,550 ft (5,959 m)

Gulf of
Alaska

Mackenzie

Great Bear
Lake

Great Slave
Lake

Hudson
Bay

Labrador

Labrador
Sea

40°W

Peace

Queen
Charlotte
Islands

Coast Mountains

ROCKY MOUNTAINS

CANADIAN SHIELD

Island of
Newfoundland

40°N

40°N

Churchill

Saskatchewan

Vancouver
Island

Columbia

Great Plains

Lake
Winnipeg

Great Lakes

St. Lawrence

Nova
Scotia

Physical

▲ Highest point
▼ Lowest point
+ Other mountain peak

Cascade Range

Snake

Missouri

Mississippi

Central
Lowland

Ohio

Appalachian Mts.

Atlantic
Ocean

Great
Salt
Lake

Death Valley
-282 ft (-86 m)
Lowest point in North America

Colorado

Arkansas

Mississippi

COASTAL PLAIN

Bermuda
Islands

20°N

Baja California

Sierra Madre Occidental

Rio Grande

Sierra Madre Oriental

TROPIC OF CANCER

Lake
Okeechobee

Bahama
Islands

West Indies

20°N

Gulf of
Mexico

Yucatán
Peninsula

Cuba

Hispaniola

140°W

Jamaica

Caribbean Sea

60°W

Pico de Orizaba
18,855 ft (5,747 m)

Pacific
Ocean

Mosquito
Coast

Panama
Canal

0°

Central America

0   800 Miles
0   800 Kilometers

Azimuthal Equidistant Projection

EQUATOR

120°W

100°W

80°W

The ancient rock of the Canadian Shield in the north and the heavily eroded Appalachian Mountains in the east yield important minerals and coal. The west, with its younger mountains, has active earthquake zones and volcanoes. Glaciers cover most of Greenland, the world's largest island, and sun drenches the islands of the Caribbean Sea.

North America

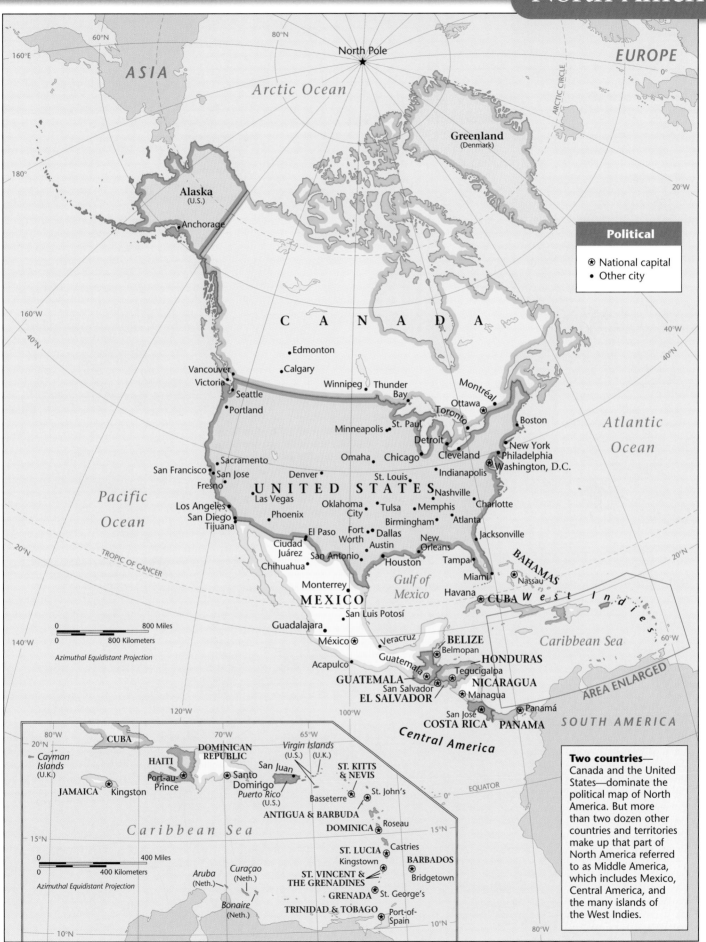

Political

⊛ National capital
• Other city

EUROPE

ASIA

North Pole

Arctic Ocean

Greenland
(Denmark)

Alaska
(U.S.)

• Anchorage

C A N A D A

• Edmonton
• Calgary

Vancouver
Victoria
Seattle
Portland

Winnipeg • Thunder
Bay

Montréal

Ottawa ⊛
Toronto

Boston

*Atlantic
Ocean*

Minneapolis • St. Paul

Detroit

New York
Cleveland Philadelphia
⊛ Washington, D.C.

Sacramento

San Francisco
San Jose
Fresno

Omaha • Chicago

Denver

St. Louis • Indianapolis

U N I T E D   S T A T E S

Nashville

Pacific

Ocean

Las Vegas

Los Angeles
San Diego
Tijuana

Phoenix

Oklahoma
City

Tulsa • Memphis

Charlotte

Birmingham Atlanta

El Paso

Ciudad
Juárez

San Antonio

Fort
Worth

Dallas

Austin

New
Orleans

Jacksonville

Chihuahua

Houston

Tampa

BAHAMAS

TROPIC OF CANCER

Monterrey

*Gulf of
Mexico*

Miami
• Nassau

⊛ CUBA   *W e s t   I n d i e s*

Havana

MEXICO

San Luis Potosí

Guadalajara

México ⊛   Veracruz

BELIZE
• Belmopan

Caribbean Sea

0   800 Miles
0   800 Kilometers

Azimuthal Equidistant Projection

Acapulco

Guatemala

HONDURAS

Tegucigalpa

AREA ENLARGED

GUATEMALA
San Salvador
EL SALVADOR

NICARAGUA
⊛ Managua

SOUTH AMERICA

San José

COSTA RICA

Panamá

PANAMA

Central America

CUBA

*Cayman
Islands*
(U.K.)

**DOMINICAN
REPUBLIC**

Virgin Islands
(U.S.) (U.K.)

HAITI

San Juan

**ST. KITTS
& NEVIS**

JAMAICA Kingston

Port-au-
Prince

Santo
Domingo

Puerto Rico
(U.S.)

Basseterre

St. John's

Caribbean Sea

ANTIGUA & BARBUDA

EQUATOR

DOMINICA Roseau

0   400 Miles
0   400 Kilometers

Azimuthal Equidistant Projection

ST. LUCIA Castries

Kingstown

BARBADOS

Aruba
(Neth.)

Curaçao
(Neth.)

**ST. VINCENT &
THE GRENADINES**

GRENADA St. George's

BARBADOS

Bridgetown

Bonaire
(Neth.)

TRINIDAD & TOBAGO

Port-of-
Spain

Two countries—
Canada and the United
States—dominate the
political map of North
America. But more
than two dozen other
countries and territories
make up that part of
North America referred
to as Middle America,
which includes Mexico,
Central America, and
the many islands of
the West Indies.

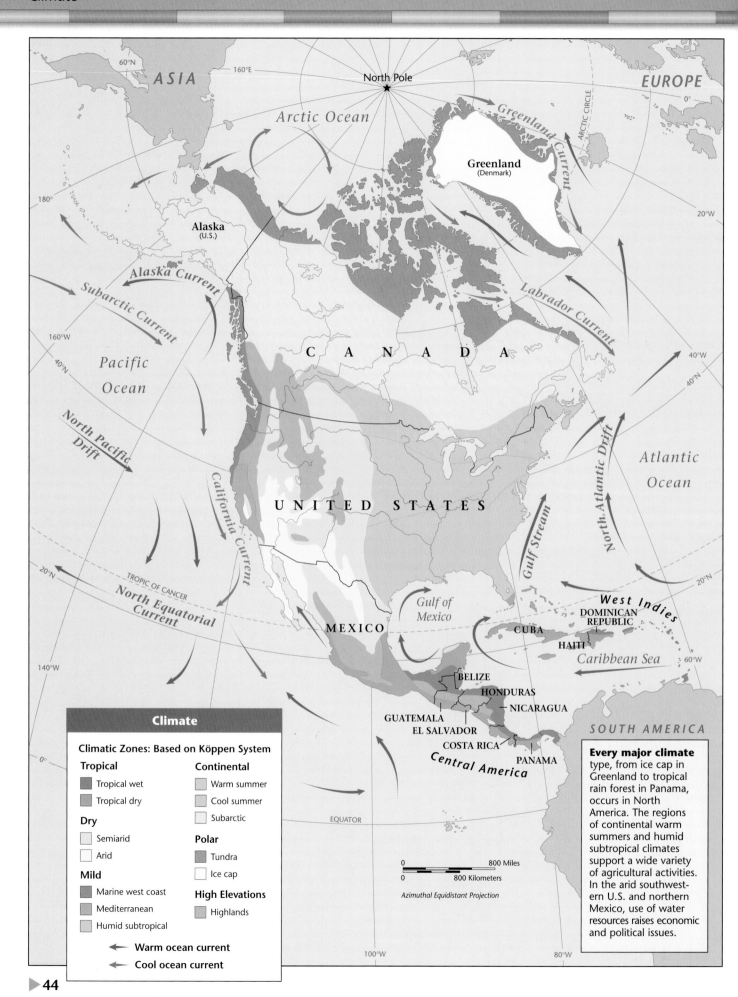

Climate

Climatic Zones: Based on Köppen System

Tropical
- Tropical wet
- Tropical dry

Dry
- Semiarid
- Arid

Mild
- Marine west coast
- Mediterranean
- Humid subtropical

Continental
- Warm summer
- Cool summer
- Subarctic

Polar
- Tundra
- Ice cap

High Elevations
- Highlands

← Warm ocean current
← Cool ocean current

0   800 Miles
0   800 Kilometers

Azimuthal Equidistant Projection

Every major climate type, from ice cap in Greenland to tropical rain forest in Panama, occurs in North America. The regions of continental warm summers and humid subtropical climates support a wide variety of agricultural activities. In the arid southwestern U.S. and northern Mexico, use of water resources raises economic and political issues.

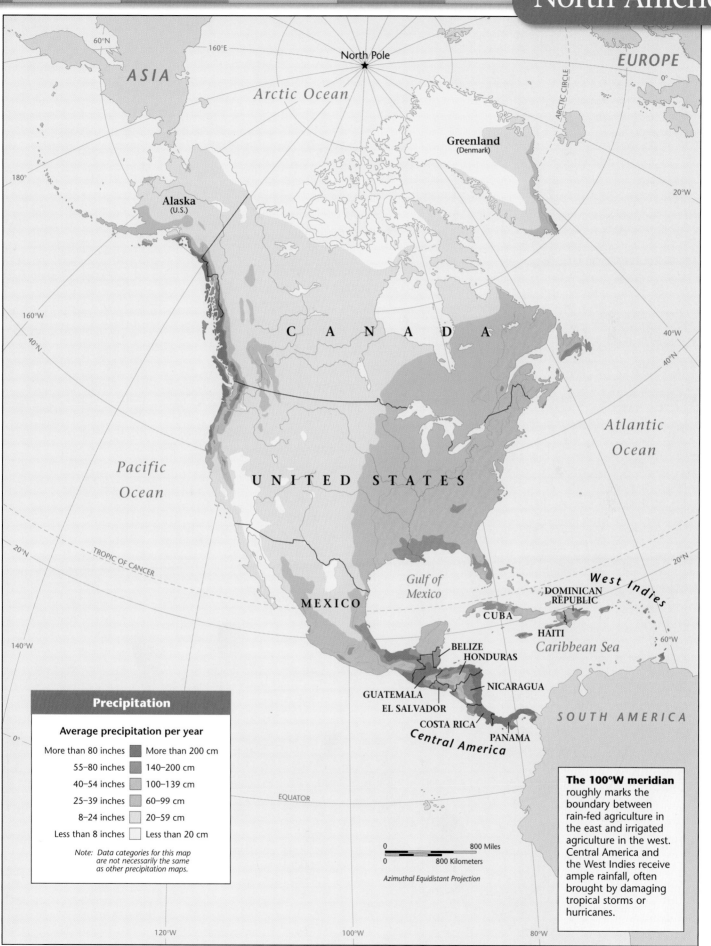

ASIA

North Pole

Arctic Ocean

EUROPE

0°

160°E

60°N

Greenland
(Denmark)

ARCTIC CIRCLE

180°

20°W

Alaska
(U.S.)

40°N

160°W

C A N A D A

40°W

40°N

Pacific
Ocean

U N I T E D   S T A T E S

Atlantic
Ocean

140°W

20°N

TROPIC OF CANCER

Gulf of
Mexico

20°N

West Indies

DOMINICAN
REPUBLIC

CUBA

MEXICO

HAITI

Caribbean Sea

60°W

BELIZE
HONDURAS

NICARAGUA

GUATEMALA
EL SALVADOR

SOUTH AMERICA

COSTA RICA

PANAMA

Central America

0°

EQUATOR

Precipitation

Average precipitation per year

More than 80 inches	More than 200 cm
55–80 inches	140–200 cm
40–54 inches	100–139 cm
25–39 inches	60–99 cm
8–24 inches	20–59 cm
Less than 8 inches	Less than 20 cm

Note: Data categories for this map are not necessarily the same as other precipitation maps.

0   800 Miles
0   800 Kilometers

Azimuthal Equidistant Projection

The 100°W meridian roughly marks the boundary between rain-fed agriculture in the east and irrigated agriculture in the west. Central America and the West Indies receive ample rainfall, often brought by damaging tropical storms or hurricanes.

120°W

100°W

80°W

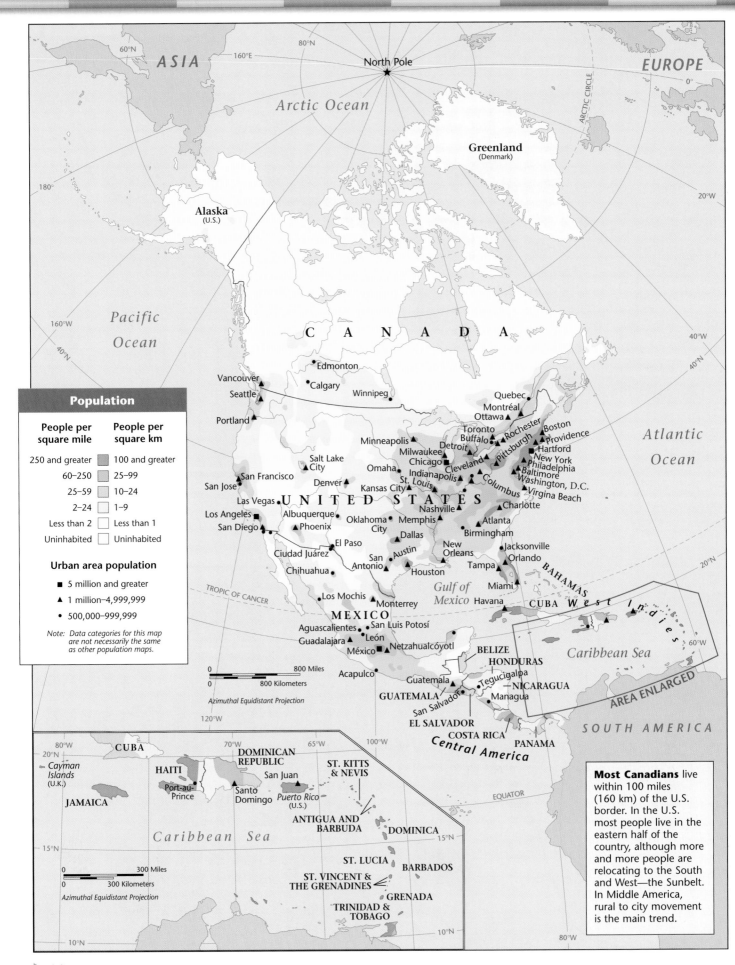

Population

People per square mile / People per square km

People per square mile	People per square km
250 and greater	100 and greater
60–250	25–99
25–59	10–24
2–24	1–9
Less than 2	Less than 1
Uninhabited	Uninhabited

Urban area population

- ■ 5 million and greater
- ▲ 1 million–4,999,999
- • 500,000–999,999

Note: Data categories for this map are not necessarily the same as other population maps.

Most Canadians live within 100 miles (160 km) of the U.S. border. In the U.S. most people live in the eastern half of the country, although more and more people are relocating to the South and West—the Sunbelt. In Middle America, rural to city movement is the main trend.

ASIA

North Pole

Arctic Ocean

Greenland
(Denmark)

Alaska
(U.S.)

EUROPE

Pacific Ocean

C A N A D A

Atlantic Ocean

Edmonton
Calgary
Winnipeg
Vancouver
Seattle
Portland

Quebec
Montréal
Ottawa
Toronto
Rochester
Boston
Buffalo
Pittsburgh
Providence
Hartford
New York
Philadelphia
Baltimore
Washington, D.C.
Virgina Beach

Minneapolis
Milwaukee
Chicago
Detroit
Cleveland
Omaha
Indianapolis
Columbus
St. Louis
Salt Lake City
Denver
Kansas City
San Francisco
San Jose
Las Vegas
U N I T E D   S T A T E S
Nashville
Charlotte
Albuquerque
Oklahoma City
Memphis
Atlanta
Los Angeles
San Diego
Phoenix
Dallas
Birmingham
Jacksonville
El Paso
New Orleans
Orlando
Ciudad Juárez
San Antonio
Austin
Houston
Tampa
Chihuahua
Miami
Havana
CUBA
BAHAMAS
West Indies
Caribbean Sea

Los Mochis
Monterrey
Gulf of Mexico
M E X I C O
Aguascalientes
San Luis Potosí
Guadalajara
León
México
Netzahualcóyotl
BELIZE
HONDURAS
Tegucigalpa
NICARAGUA
Managua
Acapulco
Guatemala
GUATEMALA
San Salvador
EL SALVADOR
COSTA RICA
PANAMA
Central America
SOUTH AMERICA
AREA ENLARGED

TROPIC OF CANCER

0   800 Miles
0   800 Kilometers

Azimuthal Equidistant Projection

CUBA
Cayman Islands (U.K.)
HAITI
Port-au-Prince
JAMAICA
DOMINICAN REPUBLIC
Santo Domingo
San Juan
Puerto Rico (U.S.)
ST. KITTS & NEVIS
ANTIGUA AND BARBUDA
DOMINICA
Caribbean Sea
ST. LUCIA
BARBADOS
ST. VINCENT & THE GRENADINES
GRENADA
TRINIDAD & TOBAGO
EQUATOR

0   300 Miles
0   300 Kilometers

Azimuthal Equidistant Projection

North America

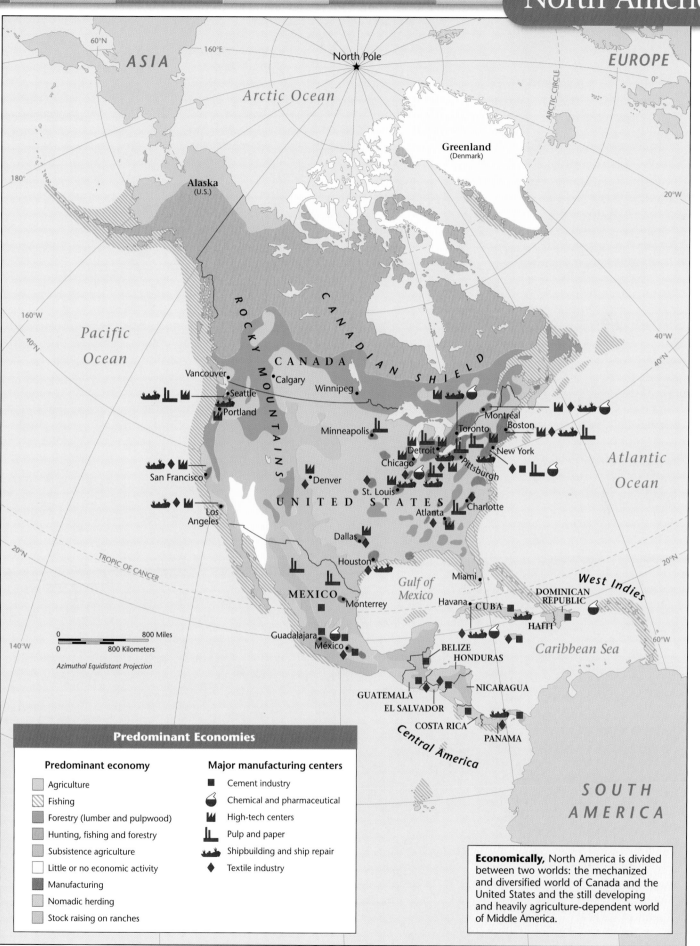

ASIA

EUROPE

North Pole

Arctic Ocean

Greenland
(Denmark)

Alaska
(U.S.)

Pacific
Ocean

CANADA

CANADIAN SHIELD

ROCKY MOUNTAINS

Vancouver
•Calgary
Winnipeg
Seattle
Portland
Minneapolis
Montréal
Boston
Toronto
New York
Detroit
Chicago
Pittsburgh
San Francisco
Denver
St. Louis
Charlotte
UNITED STATES
Atlanta
Los Angeles
Dallas

Atlantic
Ocean

TROPIC OF CANCER

Houston
Miami
Gulf of
Mexico
MEXICO
Monterrey
Havana
CUBA
DOMINICAN REPUBLIC
HAITI
West Indies
Guadalajara
México
BELIZE
HONDURAS
Caribbean Sea
GUATEMALA
EL SALVADOR
NICARAGUA
COSTA RICA
PANAMA
Central America

SOUTH
AMERICA

800 Miles
800 Kilometers
Azimuthal Equidistant Projection

Predominant Economies

Predominant economy

- Agriculture
- Fishing
- Forestry (lumber and pulpwood)
- Hunting, fishing and forestry
- Subsistence agriculture
- Little or no economic activity
- Manufacturing
- Nomadic herding
- Stock raising on ranches

Major manufacturing centers

- Cement industry
- Chemical and pharmaceutical
- High-tech centers
- Pulp and paper
- Shipbuilding and ship repair
- Textile industry

Economically, North America is divided between two worlds: the mechanized and diversified world of Canada and the United States and the still developing and heavily agriculture-dependent world of Middle America.

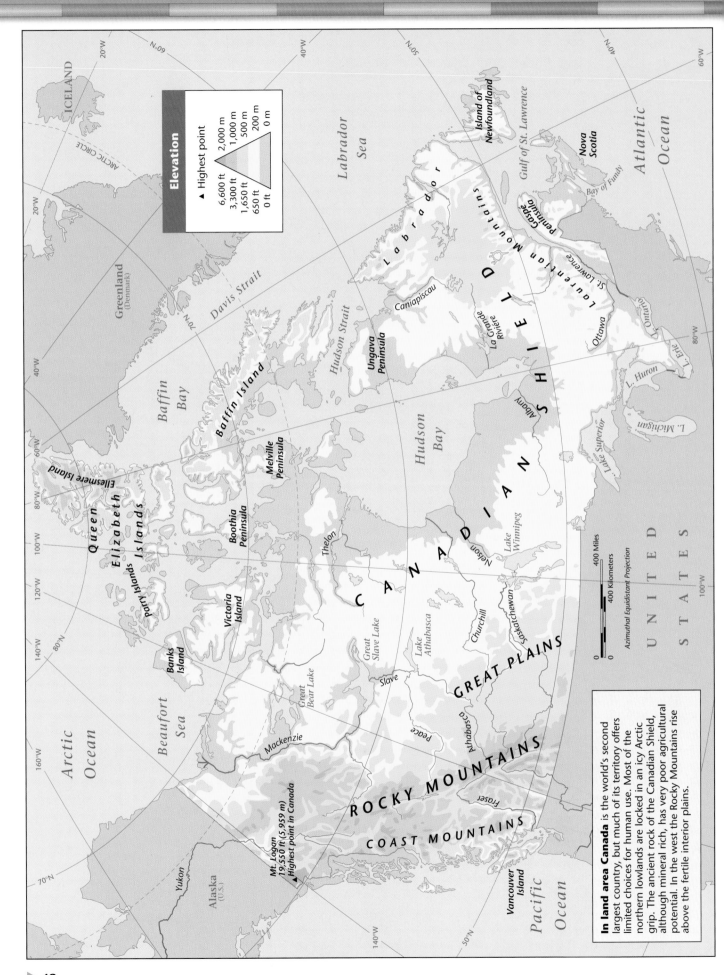

Elevation

▲ Highest point

6,600 ft — 2,000 m
3,300 ft — 1,000 m
1,650 ft — 500 m
650 ft — 200 m
0 ft — 0 m

ICELAND

ARCTIC CIRCLE

Greenland
(Denmark)

Davis Strait

Baffin
Bay

Labrador
Sea

Island of
Newfoundland

Gulf of St. Lawrence

Nova
Scotia

Atlantic
Ocean

Bay of Fundy

Gaspé
Peninsula

St. Lawrence

Laurentian Mountains

Labrador

Caniapiscau

Ungava
Peninsula

La Grande
Rivière

Ottawa

Ottawa

Hudson Strait

Baffin Island

Ellesmere Island

Queen
Elizabeth
Islands

Parry Islands

Melville
Peninsula

Boothia
Peninsula

Victoria
Island

Banks
Island

Beaufort
Sea

Arctic
Ocean

Alaska
(U.S.)

Yukon

Mt. Logan
19,550 ft (5,959 m)
▲ Highest point in Canada

Mackenzie

Great
Bear Lake

Thelon

Great
Slave Lake

Slave

Lake
Athabasca

Peace

Athabasca

Churchill

Nelson

Lake
Winnipeg

Saskatchewan

Albany

Hudson
Bay

Lake Superior

L. Michigan

L. Huron

L. Erie

C A N A D I A N   S H I E L D

GREAT PLAINS

ROCKY MOUNTAINS

COAST MOUNTAINS

Fraser

Vancouver
Island

Pacific
Ocean

UNITED
STATES

0   400 Miles
0   400 Kilometers
Azimuthal Equidistant Projection

In land area Canada is the world's second largest country, but much of its territory offers limited choices for human use. Most of the northern lowlands are locked in an icy Arctic grip. The ancient rock of the Canadian Shield, although mineral rich, has very poor agricultural potential. In the west the Rocky Mountains rise above the fertile interior plains.

North America
Canada

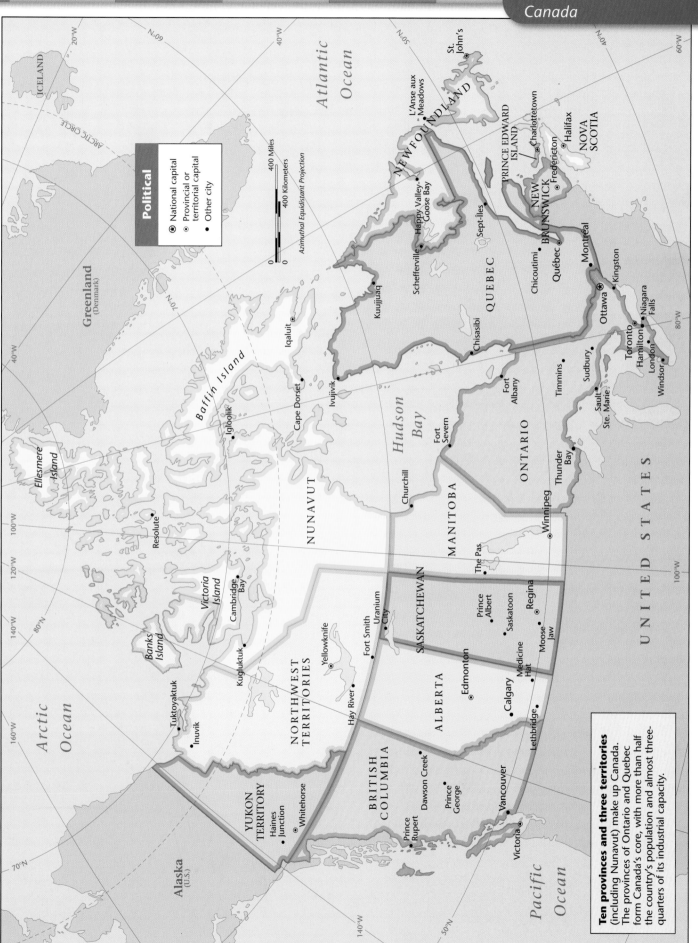

Political
- ✳ National capital
- ◉ Provincial or territorial capital
- • Other city

400 Miles
400 Kilometers
Azimuthal Equidistant Projection

ICELAND

Greenland
(Denmark)

ARCTIC CIRCLE

Atlantic
Ocean

St. John's

L'Anse aux Meadows

NEWFOUNDLAND

PRINCE EDWARD ISLAND

Charlottetown

Halifax
NOVA SCOTIA

Fredericton

NEW BRUNSWICK

Happy Valley-Goose Bay

Sept-Îles

Montréal

Scefferville

QUEBEC

Chicoutimi

Québec

Kingston

Kuujjuaq

Chisasibi

Ottawa

Niagara Falls

Iqaluit

Toronto
Hamilton
London
Windsor

Baffin Island

Cape Dorset

Ivujivik

Fort Albany

Sudbury

Sault Ste. Marie

Igloolik

Hudson
Bay

Fort Severn

Timmins

ONTARIO

Ellesmere Island

Thunder Bay

Resolute

NUNAVUT

Churchill

Victoria Island

Cambridge Bay

MANITOBA

The Pas

Winnipeg

Banks Island

Uranium City

SASKATCHEWAN

Kugluktuk

Fort Smith

Prince Albert

Saskatoon

Regina

Yellowknife

Tuktoyaktuk

NORTHWEST TERRITORIES

Hay River

Edmonton

Medicine Hat

Moose Jaw

Inuvik

ALBERTA

Calgary

Lethbridge

UNITED STATES

YUKON TERRITORY

Haines Junction

Whitehorse

BRITISH COLUMBIA

Dawson Creek

Prince George

Vancouver

Victoria

Prince Rupert

Alaska
(U.S.)

Arctic
Ocean

Pacific
Ocean

Ten provinces and three territories (including Nunavut) make up Canada. The provinces of Ontario and Quebec form Canada's core, with more than half the country's population and almost three-quarters of its industrial capacity.

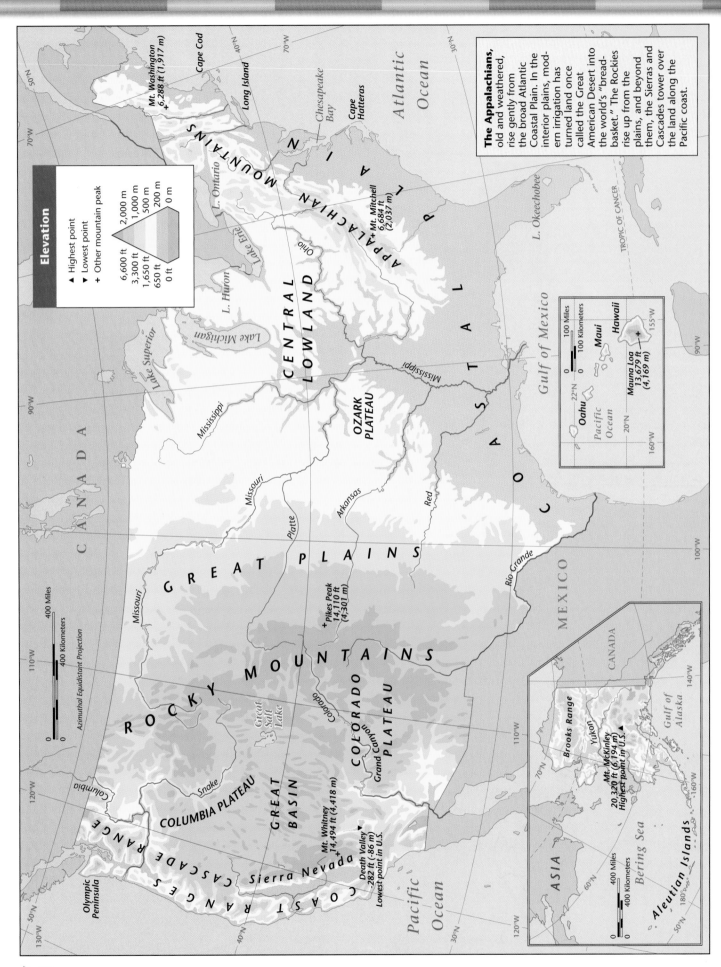

Elevation

▲ Highest point
▼ Lowest point
+ Other mountain peak

6,600 ft	2,000 m
3,300 ft	1,000 m
1,650 ft	500 m
650 ft	200 m
0 ft	0 m

The Appalachians, old and weathered, rise gently from the broad Atlantic Coastal Plain. In the interior plains, modern irrigation has turned land once called the Great American Desert into the world's "breadbasket." The Rockies rise up from the plains, and beyond them, the Sierras and Cascades tower over the land along the Pacific coast.

Mt. Washington 6,288 ft (1,917 m)
Cape Cod
Long Island
Chesapeake Bay
Cape Hatteras

Atlantic Ocean

APPALACHIAN MOUNTAINS

+ Mt. Mitchell 6,684 ft (2,037 m)

L. Ontario
Lake Erie
L. Huron
Lake Superior
Lake Michigan
Ohio

CENTRAL LOWLAND

OZARK PLATEAU

Mississippi

C O A S T A L   P L A I N

L. Okeechobee

Gulf of Mexico

TROPIC OF CANCER

Hawaii
Maui
Oahu
Mauna Loa 13,679 ft (4,169 m)
Pacific Ocean
100 Miles
100 Kilometers
22°N
20°N
160°W
155°W

Mississippi
Missouri
Arkansas
Red
Platte

G R E A T   P L A I N S

Rio Grande

MEXICO

Pikes Peak 14,110 ft (4,301 m)

R O C K Y   M O U N T A I N S

Great Salt Lake
Colorado

COLORADO PLATEAU
Grand Canyon

GREAT BASIN

COLUMBIA PLATEAU

Snake
Columbia

C O A S T   R A N G E S   C A S C A D E   R A N G E

Olympic Peninsula

Sierra Nevada

Mt. Whitney 14,494 ft (4,418 m)
Death Valley -282 ft (-86 m) Lowest point in U.S.

Pacific Ocean

CANADA

400 Miles
400 Kilometers
Azimuthal Equidistant Projection

ASIA

CANADA

Brooks Range
Yukon

Mt. McKinley 20,320 ft (6,194 m) Highest point in U.S. ▲

Gulf of Alaska

Bering Sea
Aleutian Islands

400 Miles
400 Kilometers

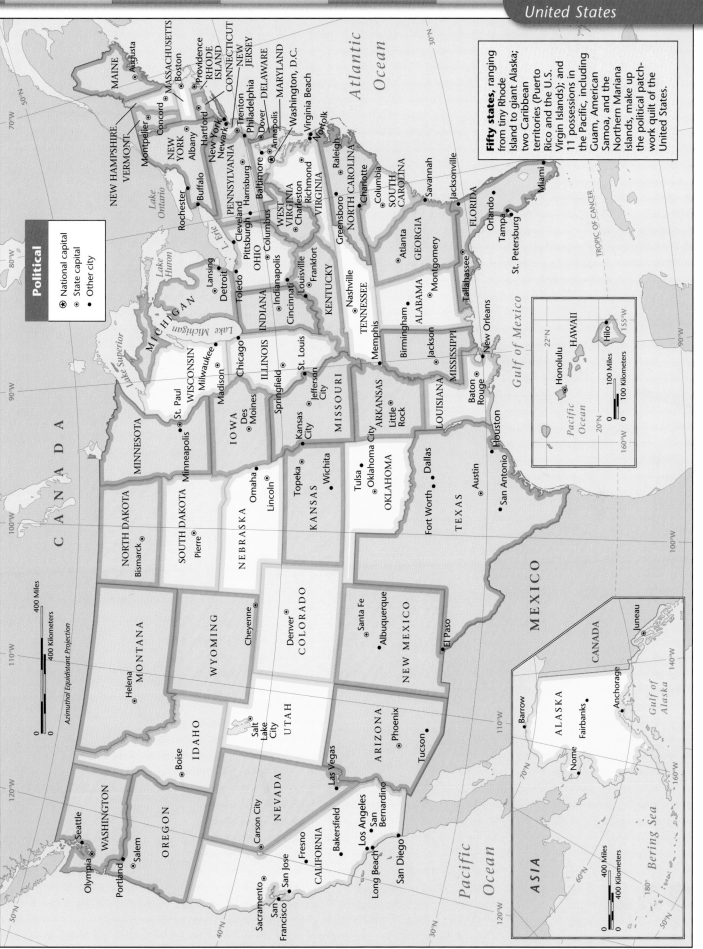

Political
- ⊗ National capital
- ⊙ State capital
- • Other city

Fifty states, ranging from tiny Rhode Island to giant Alaska; two Caribbean territories (Puerto Rico and the U.S. Virgin Islands); and 11 possessions in the Pacific, including Guam, American Samoa, and the Northern Mariana Islands, make up the political patchwork quilt of the United States.

MAINE
NEW HAMPSHIRE
VERMONT
Augusta
Montpelier
Concord
MASSACHUSETTS
Boston
Providence
RHODE ISLAND
CONNECTICUT
NEW JERSEY
DELAWARE
MARYLAND
Washington, D.C.
NEW YORK
Albany
Hartford
New York
Newark
Trenton
Philadelphia
Dover
Annapolis
Virginia Beach
Norfolk
Buffalo
Rochester
PENNSYLVANIA
Harrisburg
Baltimore
Raleigh
Richmond
VIRGINIA
WEST VIRGINIA
Charleston
Greensboro
NORTH CAROLINA
Charlotte
Columbia
SOUTH CAROLINA
Cleveland
Pittsburgh
Columbus
OHIO
Lansing
Detroit
Toledo
Indianapolis
Cincinnati
Louisville
Frankfort
KENTUCKY
Nashville
TENNESSEE
Memphis
Atlanta
GEORGIA
Savannah
Jacksonville
FLORIDA
Orlando
Tampa
St. Petersburg
Miami
MICHIGAN
INDIANA
ILLINOIS
Chicago
Springfield
St. Louis
MISSOURI
Jefferson City
Birmingham
ALABAMA
Montgomery
Jackson
MISSISSIPPI
Tallahassee
New Orleans
Baton Rouge
LOUISIANA
Houston
WISCONSIN
Milwaukee
Madison
St. Paul
MINNESOTA
Minneapolis
IOWA
Des Moines
KANSAS
Topeka
Wichita
Kansas City
ARKANSAS
Little Rock
OKLAHOMA
Tulsa
Oklahoma City
Omaha
Lincoln
NEBRASKA
SOUTH DAKOTA
Pierre
NORTH DAKOTA
Bismarck
Dallas
Fort Worth
Austin
San Antonio
TEXAS
Santa Fe
Albuquerque
NEW MEXICO
El Paso
Denver
COLORADO
Cheyenne
WYOMING
MONTANA
Helena
IDAHO
Boise
UTAH
Salt Lake City
ARIZONA
Phoenix
Tucson
Las Vegas
NEVADA
Carson City
Sacramento
San Francisco
San Jose
Fresno
Bakersfield
CALIFORNIA
Los Angeles
San Bernardino
Long Beach
San Diego
WASHINGTON
Seattle
Olympia
Portland
Salem
OREGON

CANADA
MEXICO

Atlantic Ocean
Pacific Ocean
Gulf of Mexico

Lake Superior
Lake Michigan
Lake Huron
Lake Ontario
L. Erie

TROPIC OF CANCER

HAWAII
Honolulu
Hilo
Pacific Ocean
22°N
20°N
160°W
155°W
0 100 Miles
0 100 Kilometers

ALASKA
Barrow
Fairbanks
Nome
Anchorage
Juneau
CANADA
Gulf of Alaska
ASIA
Bering Sea
70°N
60°N
180°
160°W
140°W

400 Miles
400 Kilometers
0

Azimuthal Equidistant Projection

400 Miles
400 Kilometers

70°W
80°W
90°W
100°W
110°W
120°W
30°N
40°N
50°N

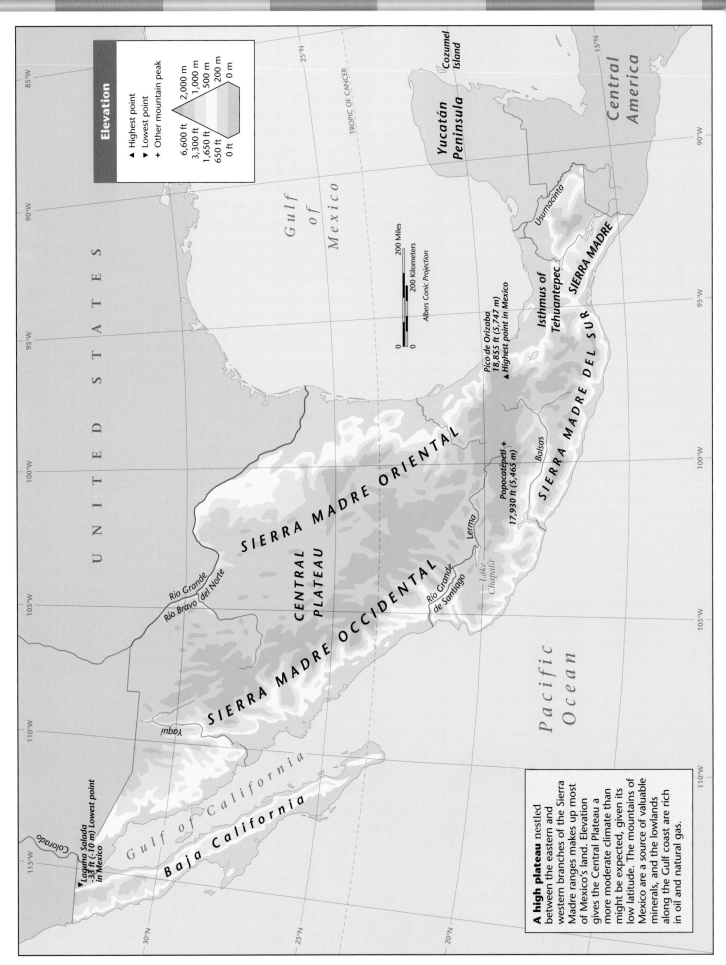

Elevation

▲ Highest point
▼ Lowest point
+ Other mountain peak

6,600 ft	2,000 m
3,300 ft	1,000 m
1,650 ft	500 m
650 ft	200 m
0 ft	0 m

85°W
90°W
95°W
100°W
105°W
110°W
115°W

25°N
TROPIC OF CANCER

15°N

Cozumel Island

Yucatán Peninsula

Central America

Gulf of Mexico

UNITED STATES

200 Miles
200 Kilometers
Albers Conic Projection

Usumacinta

Isthmus of Tehuantepec

SIERRA MADRE

Pico de Orizaba
18,855 ft (5,747 m)
▲ Highest point in Mexico

SIERRA MADRE ORIENTAL

CENTRAL PLATEAU

Popocatépetl +
17,930 ft (5,465 m)

Balsas

SIERRA MADRE DEL SUR

Lerma

SIERRA MADRE OCCIDENTAL

Río Grande de Santiago

Lake Chapala

Río Grande
Río Bravo del Norte

Yaqui

Pacific Ocean

Gulf of California

Baja California

Colorado

▼ Laguna Salada
-33 ft (-10 m) Lowest point in Mexico

30°N
25°N
20°N

A high plateau nestled between the eastern and western branches of the Sierra Madre ranges makes up most of Mexico's land. Elevation gives the Central Plateau a more moderate climate than might be expected, given its low latitude. The mountains of Mexico are a source of valuable minerals, and the lowlands along the Gulf coast are rich in oil and natural gas.

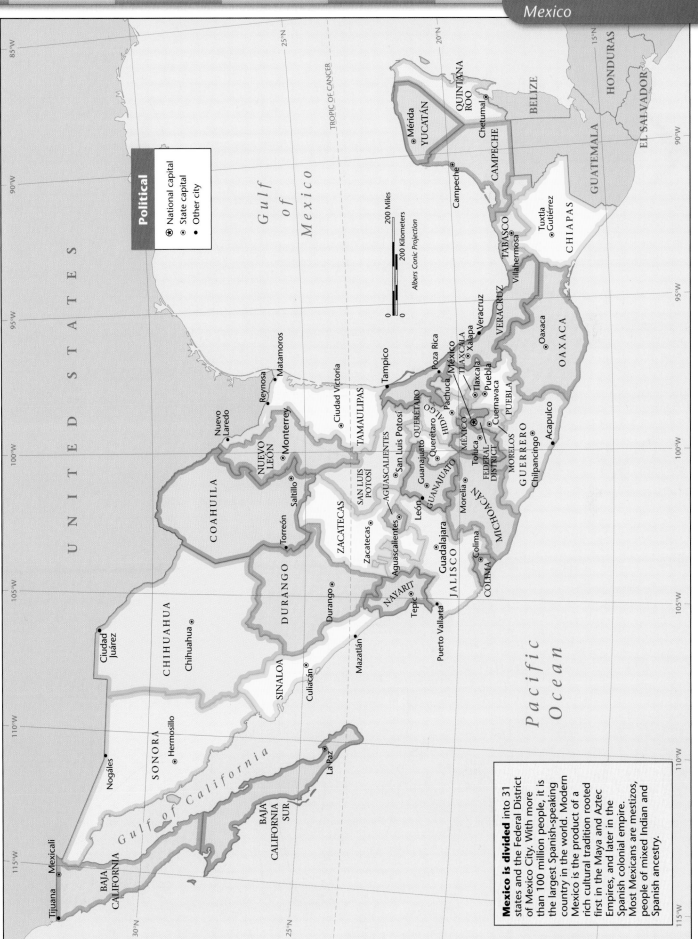

Political
⊗ National capital
⊙ State capital
• Other city

Gulf of Mexico

UNITED STATES

TROPIC OF CANCER

200 Miles
200 Kilometers
Albers Conic Projection

HONDURAS

EL SALVADOR

GUATEMALA

BELIZE

Chetumal

QUINTANA ROO

Mérida
YUCATÁN

Campeche

CAMPECHE

Tuxtla Gutiérrez

CHIAPAS

TABASCO

Villahermosa

VERACRUZ

Veracruz

Xalapa

OAXACA

Oaxaca

Poza Rica

México
TLAXCALA
Tlaxcala
Pachuca
Puebla
PUEBLA
Cuernavaca

Matamoros

Reynosa

Nuevo Laredo

Monterrey
NUEVO LEÓN

Ciudad Victoria

TAMAULIPAS

Tampico

SAN LUIS POTOSÍ

San Luis Potosí

QUERÉTARO
Querétaro
HIDALGO

MÉXICO
⊗

Toluca
FEDERAL DISTRICT
MORELOS

GUERRERO
Chilpancingo

Acapulco

COAHUILA

Saltillo

ZACATECAS

Zacatecas

AGUASCALIENTES
Aguascalientes

GUANAJUATO
Guanajuato
León

Morelia

MICHOACÁN

Colima
COLIMA

Guadalajara
JALISCO

DURANGO

Torreón

Durango

NAYARIT
Tepic

Puerto Vallarta

SINALOA

Culiacán

Mazatlán

CHIHUAHUA

Chihuahua

Ciudad Juárez

SONORA

Hermosillo

Nogáles

La Paz

BAJA CALIFORNIA SUR

Gulf of California

Pacific Ocean

Tijuana

Mexicali

BAJA CALIFORNIA

Mexico is divided into 31 states and the Federal District of Mexico City. With more than 100 million people, it is the largest Spanish-speaking country in the world. Modern Mexico is the product of a rich cultural tradition rooted first in the Maya and Aztec Empires, and later in the Spanish colonial empire. Most Mexicans are mestizos, people of mixed Indian and Spanish ancestry.

Hurricanes
This list names North America's eight strongest recorded hurricanes. In other parts of the world hurricanes are called cyclones and typhoons.

1980 Allen: 165 mph/265 kmph*

1979 Camille: 165 mph/265 kmph

1950 Dog: 160 mph/257 kmph

1988 Gilbert: 160 mph/257 kmph

1977 Anita: 150 mph/241 kmph

1961 Carla: 150 mph/241 kmph

1979 David: 150 mph/241 kmph

1955 Janet: 150 mph//241 kmph
*maximum wind speed recorded

Tornadoes
The following states had the highest average annual number of tornadoes from 1961 to 1990.

Texas: 137

Florida: 52

Oklahoma: 47

Kansas: 36

Nebraska: 36

Iowa: 35

South Dakota: 28

Illinois: 27

Louisiana: 27

Missouri: 27

Earthquakes
This list shows the number of earthquakes in North America in the 20th century that had a magnitude of 8.0 to 9.9 on the Richter scale.

Mexico: 8

Alaska (U.S.): 7

Guatemala: 2

British Columbia (Canada): 1

California (U.S.): 1

Dominican Republic: 1
(see map page 43)

Panama: 1

FOCUS ON

Natural Hazards

The forces of nature inspire awe. They can also bring damage and destruction, especially when people locate homes and businesses in places that are at risk of experiencing violent storms, earthquakes, volcanoes, floods, wildfires, or other natural hazards.

Tornadoes, violent, swirling storms with winds that can exceed 200 miles (300 km) per hour, strike the U.S. more than 800 times each year. Hurricanes, massive low-pressure storms that form over warm ocean waters, bring destructive winds and rain primarily to the Gulf of Mexico and the southeastern mainland. Melting spring snows and heavy rains trigger flooding; periods of drought make other regions vulnerable to wildfires. These and other hazards of nature are not limited to this continent. Natural hazards pose serious threats to lives and property wherever people live.

▼ **Wildfires.** *Putting lives and property at great risk, wildfires destroy millions of acres of forest each year. At the same time, fires help renew ecosystems by removing debris and encouraging seedling growth.*

▲ **Volcanoes.** *From deep inside Earth, molten rock, called magma, rises and breaks through the surface, sometimes quietly, but more often violently, shooting billowing ash clouds as shown here at Mount St. Helens, in Washington State.*

▶ **Floods.** *Towns and farmland that occupy fertile plains along rivers are always in danger from floods. In 1993 the great Mississippi River floods devastated millions of people in the midwestern United States.*

Web Link for information on natural hazards: www.cindi.usgs.gov

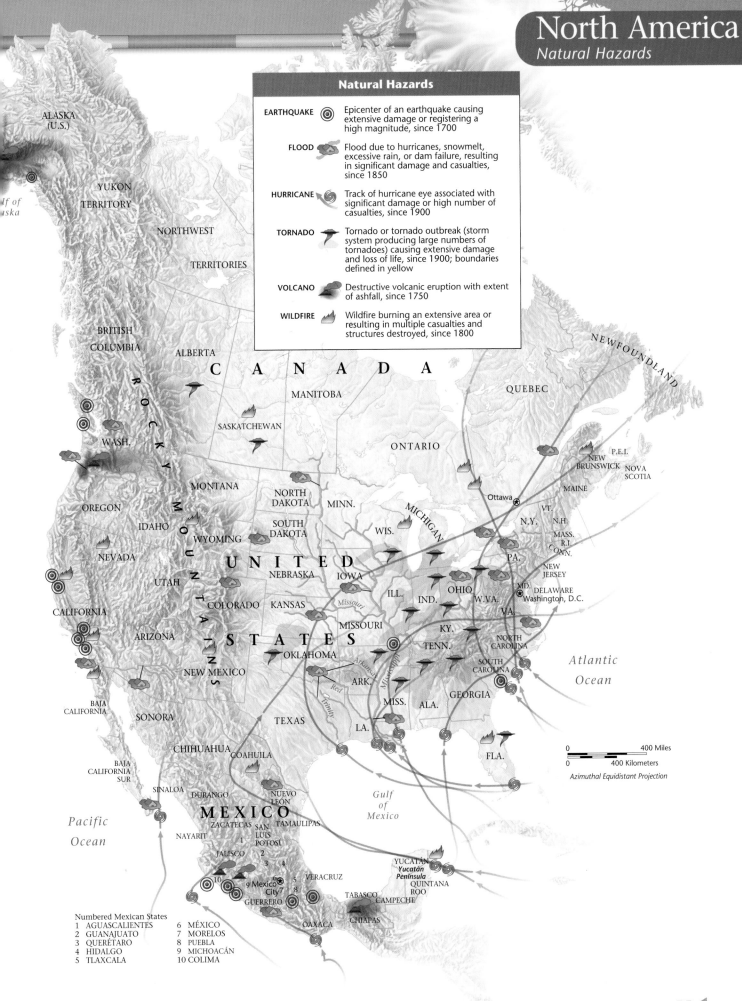

Natural Hazards

EARTHQUAKE — Epicenter of an earthquake causing extensive damage or registering a high magnitude, since 1700

FLOOD — Flood due to hurricanes, snowmelt, excessive rain, or dam failure, resulting in significant damage and casualties, since 1850

HURRICANE — Track of hurricane eye associated with significant damage or high number of casualties, since 1900

TORNADO — Tornado or tornado outbreak (storm system producing large numbers of tornadoes) causing extensive damage and loss of life, since 1900; boundaries defined in yellow

VOLCANO — Destructive volcanic eruption with extent of ashfall, since 1750

WILDFIRE — Wildfire burning an extensive area or resulting in multiple casualties and structures destroyed, since 1800

ALASKA (U.S.)

YUKON TERRITORY

NORTHWEST TERRITORIES

BRITISH COLUMBIA

ALBERTA

C A N A D A

MANITOBA

SASKATCHEWAN

ONTARIO

QUEBEC

NEWFOUNDLAND

WASH.

OREGON

IDAHO

MONTANA

WYOMING

NORTH DAKOTA

SOUTH DAKOTA

MINN.

WIS.

MICHIGAN

Ottawa

MAINE

P.E.I.

NEW BRUNSWICK

NOVA SCOTIA

NEVADA

CALIFORNIA

UTAH

ROCKY MOUNTAINS

U N I T E D

NEBRASKA

IOWA

ILL.

IND.

OHIO

PA.

N.Y.

VT.

N.H.

MASS.

R.I.

CONN.

NEW JERSEY

W.VA.

MD.

DELAWARE

Washington, D.C.

ARIZONA

S T A T E S

COLORADO

KANSAS

Missouri

MISSOURI

OKLAHOMA

KY.

TENN.

VA.

NORTH CAROLINA

SOUTH CAROLINA

Atlantic Ocean

NEW MEXICO

Arkansas

Red

Trinity

ARK.

MISS.

Mississippi

ALA.

GEORGIA

BAJA CALIFORNIA

SONORA

TEXAS

LA.

FLA.

CHIHUAHUA

COAHUILA

BAJA CALIFORNIA SUR

SINALOA

DURANGO

NUEVO LEÓN

TAMAULIPAS

Gulf of Mexico

Pacific Ocean

M E X I C O

ZACATECAS

SAN LUIS POTOSÍ

NAYARIT

JALISCO

1

2

3

4

5

6

7

8

9 Mexico City

10

GUERRERO

VERACRUZ

YUCATÁN

Yucatán Peninsula

QUINTANA ROO

TABASCO

CAMPECHE

CHIAPAS

OAXACA

0   400 Miles
0   400 Kilometers

Azimuthal Equidistant Projection

Numbered Mexican States
1 AGUASCALIENTES
2 GUANAJUATO
3 QUERÉTARO
4 HIDALGO
5 TLAXCALA
6 MÉXICO
7 MORELOS
8 PUEBLA
9 MICHOACÁN
10 COLIMA

Gulf of Alaska

South America

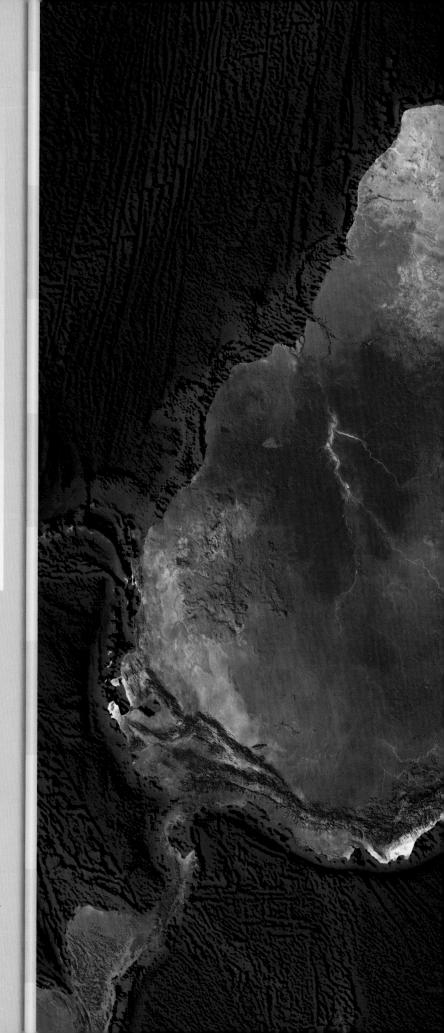

From the towering, snow-capped Andes in the west to the steamy rain forest of the Amazon Basin in the north, and from the fertile grasslands of the Pampas to the arid Atacama Desert along the Pacific coast, South America is a continent of extremes. North to south the continent extends from the tropical waters of the Caribbean Sea to the windblown islands of Tierra del Fuego. Its longest river, the Amazon, carries more water than any other river in the world.

Facts & Figures

- **Land area:** 6,880,500 sq mi (17,819,000 sq km)
- **Population:** 344,790,000
- **Highest point:** Aconcagua, Argentina: 22,834 ft (6,960 m)
- **Lowest point:** Valdés Peninsula, Argentina: 131 ft (40 m) below sea level
- **Longest river:** Amazon: 4,000 mi (6,437 km)
- **Largest lake:** Lake Titicaca, Bolivia-Peru: 3,200 sq mi (8,287 sq km)
- **Number of independent countries:** 12
- **Largest country:** Brazil: 3,286,488 sq mi (8,511,965 sq km)
- **Smallest country:** Suriname: 63,037 sq mi (163,265 sq km)
- **Most populous country:** Brazil: Pop. 170,115,000
- **Least populous country:** Suriname: Pop. 434,000

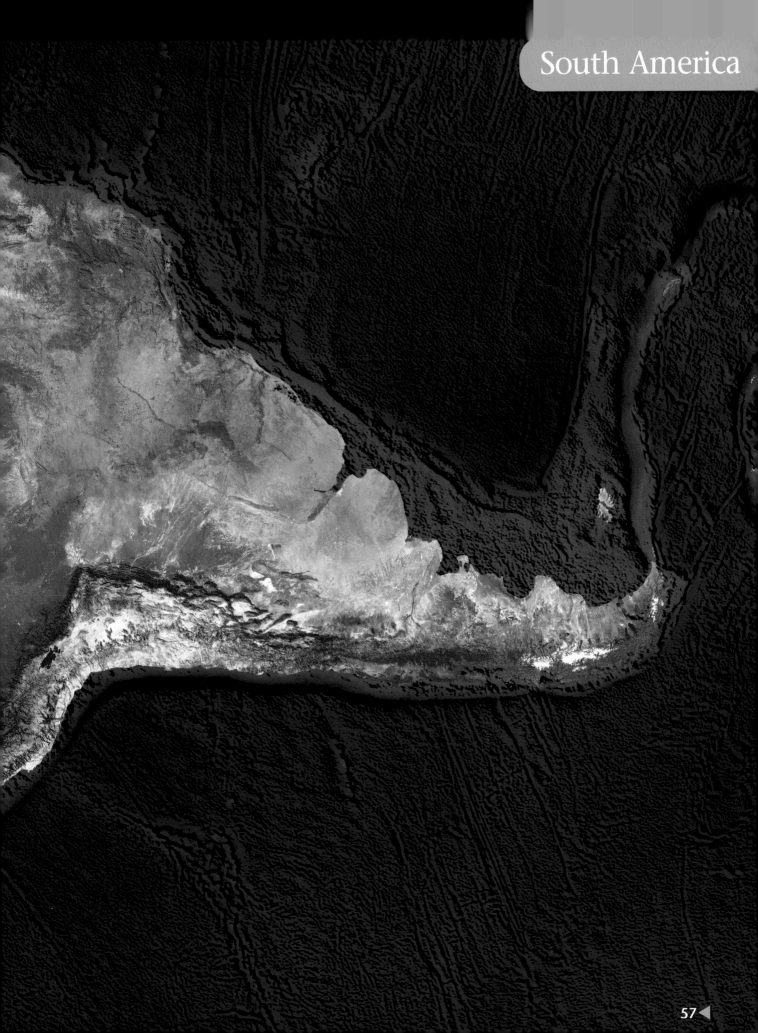

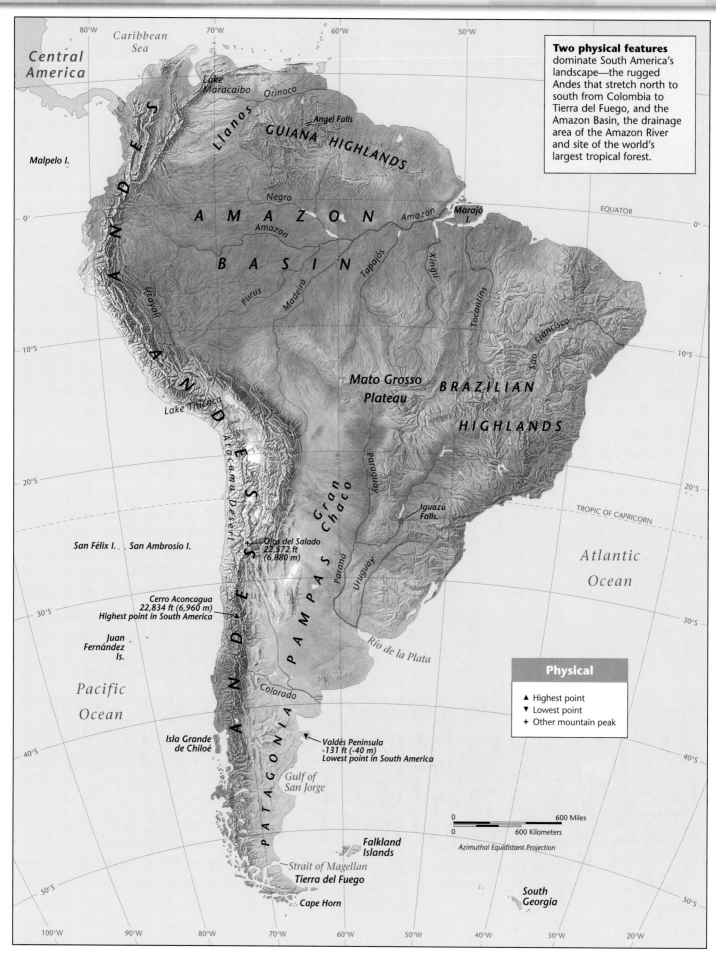

Caribbean Sea

Central America

Malpelo I.

Lake Maracaibo

Orinoco

Llanos

GUIANA HIGHLANDS

Angel Falls

ANDES

Negro

A M A Z O N

Amazon

Amazon

Marajó I.

EQUATOR

0°

0°

B A S I N

Purus

Madeira

Tapajós

Xingu

Tocantins

São Francisco

Utayali

10°S

10°S

Lake Titicaca

Mato Grosso Plateau

BRAZILIAN

HIGHLANDS

A N D E S

Atacama Desert

San Félix I.   San Ambrosio I.

Ojos del Salado
22,572 ft
(6,880 m)

Gran Chaco

paraguay

Iguazú Falls

TROPIC OF CAPRICORN

20°S

20°S

PAMPAS

Paraná

Uruguay

Cerro Aconcagua
22,834 ft (6,960 m)
Highest point in South America

Juan Fernández Is.

Río de la Plata

Atlantic Ocean

30°S

30°S

Colorado

Pacific Ocean

Physical

▲ Highest point
▼ Lowest point
+ Other mountain peak

Isla Grande de Chiloé

PATAGONIA

Valdés Peninsula
-131 ft (-40 m)
Lowest point in South America

40°S

40°S

Gulf of San Jorge

0   600 Miles
0   600 Kilometers

Azimuthal Equidistant Projection

Falkland Islands

Strait of Magellan

Tierra del Fuego

South Georgia

50°S

50°S

Cape Horn

100°W   90°W   80°W   70°W   60°W   50°W   40°W   30°W   20°W

Two physical features dominate South America's landscape—the rugged Andes that stretch north to south from Colombia to Tierra del Fuego, and the Amazon Basin, the drainage area of the Amazon River and site of the world's largest tropical forest.

South America

Twelve countries and one French territory (French Guiana) make up South America. The continent was under mainly Spanish and Portuguese control from the 16th to the 19th century. Colonial influence is still evident in the use of Spanish and Portuguese languages and in the widespread presence of the Roman Catholic church.

Central America

Caribbean Sea

Barranquilla
Maracaibo
Caracas
Valencia
Barquisimeto

VENEZUELA

Georgetown
Paramaribo
Cayenne

GUYANA
SURINAME
French Guiana
(France)

Medellín
Bogotá
Cali

COLOMBIA

Quito
ECUADOR
Guayaquil

Manaus

Belém

Fortaleza

Natal

Recife

EQUATOR

PERU

Callao
Lima

BOLIVIA
La Paz

Santa Cruz
Sucre

BRAZIL

Salvador
(Bahia)

Goiânia
Brasília

Belo
Horizonte

PARAGUAY

Asunción

Nova Iguaçu
São Paulo
Santos
Rio de Janeiro
Curitiba

CHILE

San Miguel
de Tucumán

Pôrto Alegre

Atlantic
Ocean

TROPIC OF CAPRICORN

Córdoba
Rosario

Santa
Fe

URUGUAY

Valparaíso
Santiago

Buenos Aires
La Plata
Montevideo

ARGENTINA

Mar del Plata

Pacific
Ocean

Political

⊛ National capital
• Other city

Stanley
Falkland Islands
(U.K.)

South
Georgia
(U.K.)

0   600 Miles
0   600 Kilometers

Azimuthal Equidistant Projection

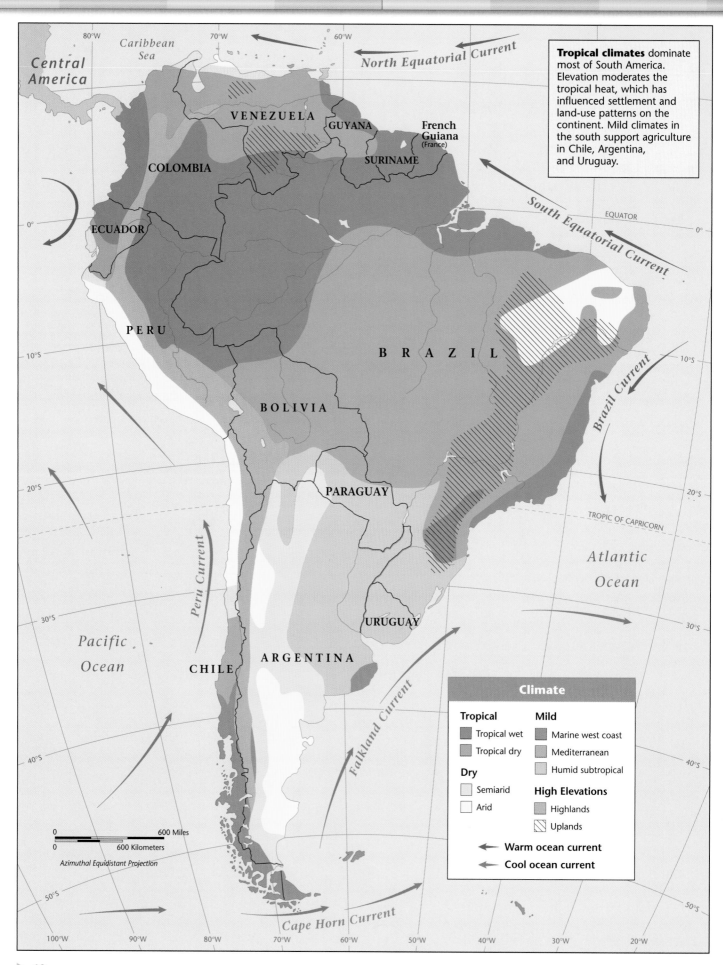

Central America

Caribbean Sea

North Equatorial Current

Tropical climates dominate most of South America. Elevation moderates the tropical heat, which has influenced settlement and land-use patterns on the continent. Mild climates in the south support agriculture in Chile, Argentina, and Uruguay.

VENEZUELA

GUYANA

SURINAME

French Guiana (France)

COLOMBIA

South Equatorial Current

EQUATOR

ECUADOR

0°

PERU

10°S

B R A Z I L

Brazil Current

10°S

BOLIVIA

20°S

PARAGUAY

TROPIC OF CAPRICORN

20°S

Atlantic Ocean

Peru Current

30°S

URUGUAY

30°S

Pacific Ocean

CHILE

ARGENTINA

Falkland Current

40°S

40°S

0   600 Miles
0   600 Kilometers

Azimuthal Equidistant Projection

Climate

Tropical
■ Tropical wet
■ Tropical dry

Dry
□ Semiarid
□ Arid

Mild
■ Marine west coast
■ Mediterranean
■ Humid subtropical

High Elevations
■ Highlands
▨ Uplands

← Warm ocean current
← Cool ocean current

Cape Horn Current

50°S

50°S

100°W   90°W   80°W   70°W   60°W   50°W   40°W   30°W   20°W

South America

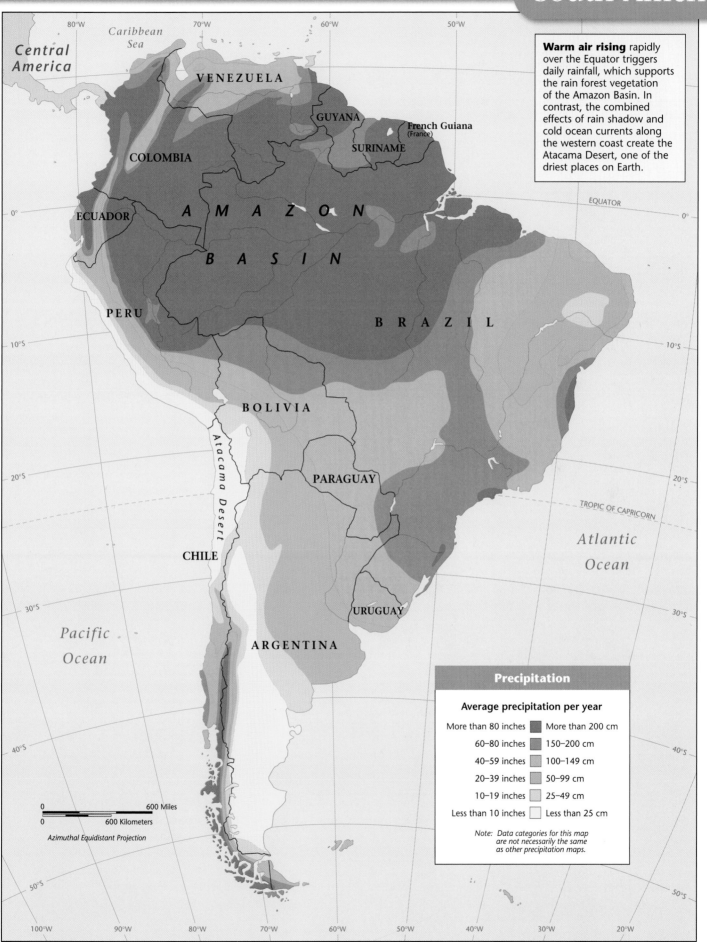

Warm air rising rapidly over the Equator triggers daily rainfall, which supports the rain forest vegetation of the Amazon Basin. In contrast, the combined effects of rain shadow and cold ocean currents along the western coast create the Atacama Desert, one of the driest places on Earth.

Central America

Caribbean Sea

VENEZUELA

GUYANA

French Guiana (France)

SURINAME

COLOMBIA

ECUADOR

A M A Z O N

EQUATOR

B A S I N

PERU

B R A Z I L

BOLIVIA

PARAGUAY

Atacama Desert

TROPIC OF CAPRICORN

Atlantic Ocean

CHILE

URUGUAY

Pacific Ocean

ARGENTINA

0   600 Miles
0   600 Kilometers

Azimuthal Equidistant Projection

Precipitation

Average precipitation per year

More than 80 inches	More than 200 cm
60–80 inches	150–200 cm
40–59 inches	100–149 cm
20–39 inches	50–99 cm
10–19 inches	25–49 cm
Less than 10 inches	Less than 25 cm

Note: Data categories for this map are not necessarily the same as other precipitation maps.

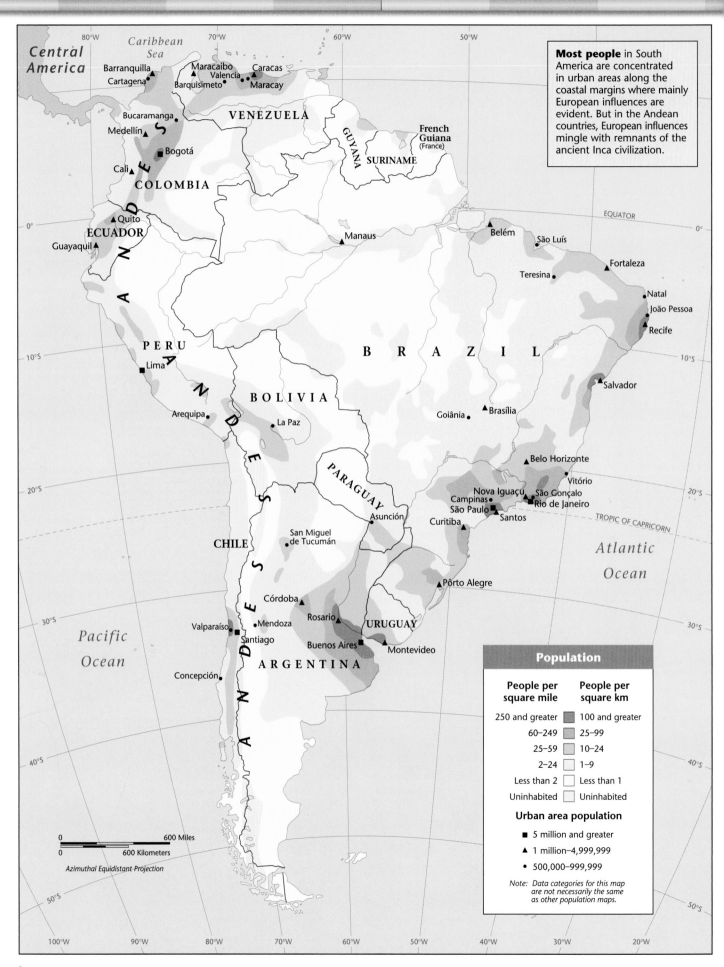

Central America

Caribbean Sea

Barranquilla
Cartagena
Maracaibo
Valencia
Caracas
Barquisimeto
Maracay

VENEZUELA

GUYANA
SURINAME
French Guiana (France)

Bucaramanga
Medellín
Bogotá
Cali

COLOMBIA

Quito
ECUADOR
Guayaquil

EQUATOR

Manaus
Belém
São Luís
Fortaleza
Teresina
Natal
João Pessoa
Recife

PERU
Lima

B R A Z I L

Salvador

A N D E S

Arequipa
La Paz

BOLIVIA

Goiânia
Brasília

Belo Horizonte
Vitório

PARAGUAY

Asunción

Nova Iguaçu
São Gonçalo
Campinas
Rio de Janeiro
São Paulo
Santos
Curitiba

TROPIC OF CAPRICORN

Atlantic Ocean

San Miguel de Tucumán

CHILE

Pôrto Alegre

Córdoba
Rosario
URUGUAY

Valparaíso
Mendoza
Santiago
Buenos Aires
Montevideo

Pacific Ocean

Concepción

A R G E N T I N A

Most people in South America are concentrated in urban areas along the coastal margins where mainly European influences are evident. But in the Andean countries, European influences mingle with remnants of the ancient Inca civilization.

0   600 Miles
0   600 Kilometers
Azimuthal Equidistant Projection

Population	
People per square mile	People per square km
250 and greater	100 and greater
60–249	25–99
25–59	10–24
2–24	1–9
Less than 2	Less than 1
Uninhabited	Uninhabited

Urban area population

■ 5 million and greater
▲ 1 million–4,999,999
● 500,000–999,999

Note: Data categories for this map are not necessarily the same as other population maps.

South America

Plantation agriculture, livestock raising, and mining are the base for much of South America's economy, although people in large areas of the Amazon Basin and the Andes still practice subsistence agriculture. Manufacturing centers have emerged near major cities.

Central America

Caribbean Sea

Cartagena
Maracaibo
Caracas
VENEZUELA
GUYANA
SURINAME
French Guiana (France)
Bogotá
Cali
COLOMBIA
Quito
ECUADOR
Guayaquil
PERU
A N D E S
AMAZON
BASIN
BRAZIL
Belém
EQUATOR
Lima
BOLIVIA
La Paz
PARAGUAY
Rio de Janeiro
São Paulo
TROPIC OF CAPRICORN
CHILE
Atlantic Ocean
Pacific Ocean
Santiago
Rosario
URUGUAY
Buenos Aires
Montevideo
ARGENTINA
Concepción
P A T A G O N I A
A N D E S

0   600 Miles
0   600 Kilometers
Azimuthal Equidistant Projection

Predominant Economies

Predominant economy

- Agriculture
- Fishing
- Forestry (lumber and pulpwood)
- Subsistence agriculture
- Little or no economic activity
- Manufacturing
- Stock raising on ranges

Major manufacturing centers

- Cement industry
- Chemical and pharmaceutical
- High-tech centers
- Pulp and paper
- Shipbuilding and ship repair
- Textile industry

Amazon Rain Forest

AREA ENLARGED

SOUTH AMERICA

The Amazon rain forest, which covers approximately 2.7 million square miles (7 million sq km), is the world's largest tropical forest. Located mainly in Brazil, the Amazon rain forest accounts for more than 20 percent of all the world's tropical forests. Known in Brazil as the selva, the rain forest is a vast storehouse of biological diversity, filled with plants and animals both familiar and exotic. According to estimates, at least half of all species are found in tropical forests, but many of these species have not yet been identified.

Tropical forests contain many valuable resources, including cacao (chocolate), nuts, spices, rare hardwoods, and plant extracts used to make medicines. Some drugs used in treating cancer and heart disease come from plants found only in tropical forests. But human intervention—logging, mining, and clearing land for crops and grazing—has put tropical forests at great risk. In Brazil, roads cut into the rain forest have opened the way for settlers, who clear away the forest only to discover soil too poor in nutrients to sustain agriculture for more than a few years. Land usually is cleared by a method called slash-and-burn, which contributes to global warming by releasing great amounts of carbon dioxide into the atmosphere.

▶ **Tropical rain forests** grow in parts of every continent except Europe and Antarctica. Together, the tropical forests of South America and Africa make up three-quarters of the world's total. Brazil alone has more than 300 million acres (120 million hectares)—more than any other country.

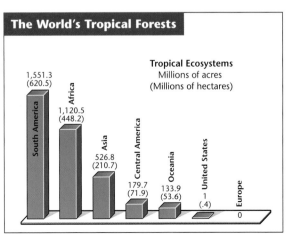

The World's Tropical Forests

Tropical Ecosystems
Millions of acres
(Millions of hectares)

Region	Millions of acres (Millions of hectares)
South America	1,551.3 (620.5)
Africa	1,120.5 (448.2)
Asia	526.8 (210.7)
Central America	179.7 (71.9)
Oceania	133.9 (53.6)
United States	1 (.4)
Europe	0

Price of Progress

CLEARING TREES to make way for expanding economic activities leads to widespread environmental destruction. Slash-and-burn agriculture exposes fragile soils to heat and torrential rains, and the runoff from mining operations pollutes streams and rivers. In an effort to reverse this trend, some countries and international organizations have set up national parks, reserves, and other protected areas.

Web Link for information on rain forests: www.wri.org

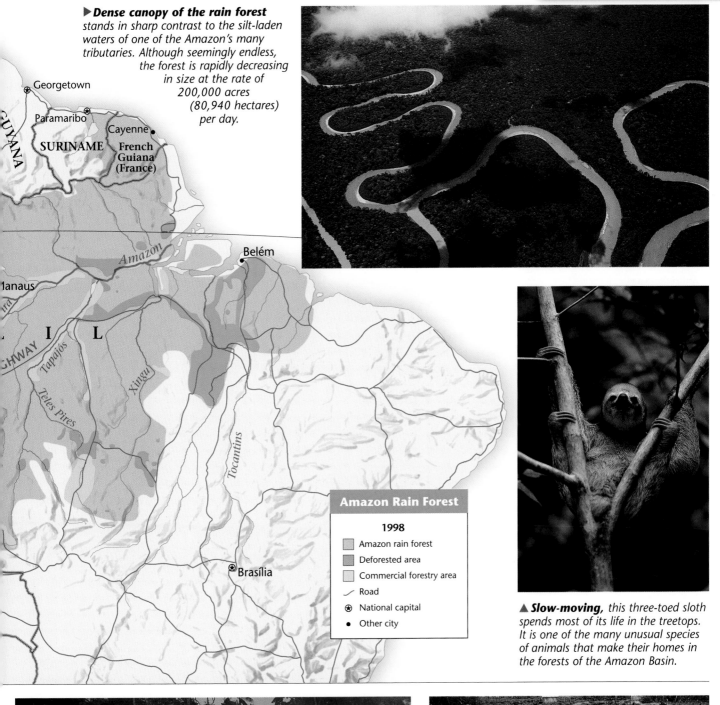

▶ **Dense canopy of the rain forest** stands in sharp contrast to the silt-laden waters of one of the Amazon's many tributaries. Although seemingly endless, the forest is rapidly decreasing in size at the rate of 200,000 acres (80,940 hectares) per day.

Georgetown
Paramaribo
Cayenne
SURINAME
French Guiana (France)
GUYANA
Amazon
Belém
Manaus
B R A Z I L
Tapajós
Xingu
Teles Pires
HIGHWAY
Tocantins
⊛ Brasília

Amazon Rain Forest

1998
- Amazon rain forest
- Deforested area
- Commercial forestry area
- Road
- ⊛ National capital
- • Other city

▲ **Slow-moving,** this three-toed sloth spends most of its life in the treetops. It is one of the many unusual species of animals that make their homes in the forests of the Amazon Basin.

▲ **Slash-and-burn** is a method used in the tropics for clearing land for farms. But the soil is poor in nutrients, and good yields are short-lived.

▲ **Mining operations,** such as this tin mine, remove forests to gain access to mineral deposits.

Europe

Smaller than every other continent except Australia, Europe is a mosaic of islands and peninsulas. In fact, Europe itself is one big peninsula, jutting westward from the huge land-mass of Asia and nearly touching Africa to the south. Europe's ragged coastline measures more than one and a half times the length of the Equator—37,877 miles (60,955 km) to be exact—giving 30 of its 43 countries direct access to the sea.

Facts & Figures

▶ **Land area:** 3,837,400 sq mi (9,938,000 sq km)

▶ **Population:** 727,758,000

▶ **Highest point:** Mount El'brus, Russia: 18,510 ft (5,642 m)

▶ **Lowest point:** Caspian Sea: 92 ft (28 m) below sea level

▶ **Longest river:** Volga, Russia: 2,290 mi (3,685 km)

▶ **Largest lake entirely in Europe:** Ladoga, Russia: 6,853 sq mi (17,703 sq km)

▶ **Number of independent countries:** 43 (including Russia)

▶ **Largest country entirely in Europe:** Ukraine 233,206 sq mi (604,001 sq km)

▶ **Smallest country:** Vatican City: 0.2 sq mi (0.4 sq km)

▶ **Most populous country entirely in Europe:** Germany: Pop. 82,141,000

▶ **Least populous country:** Vatican City: Pop. 1,000

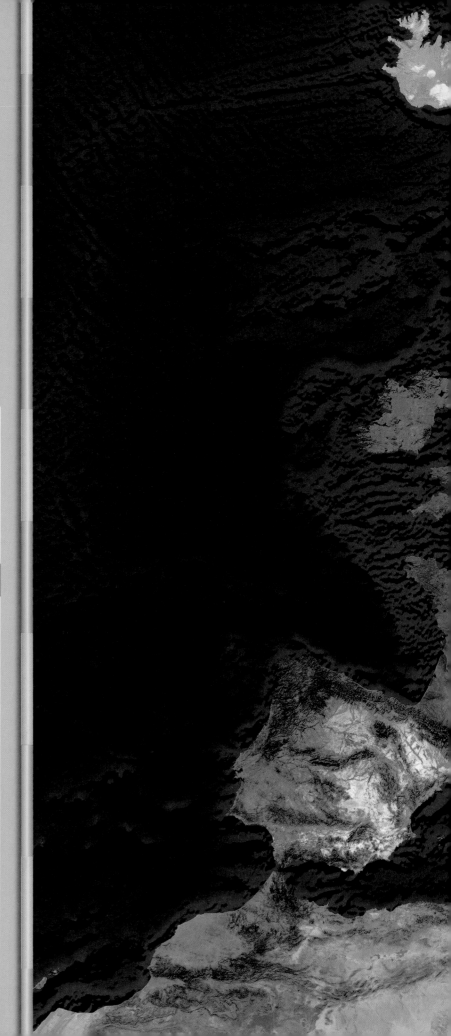

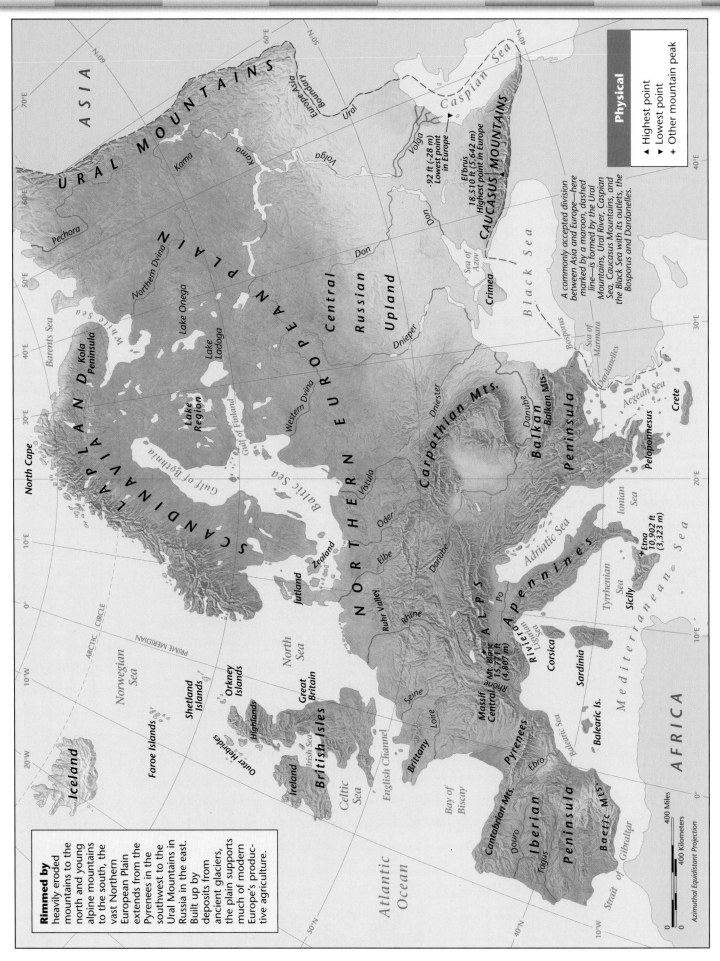

Physical
▲ Highest point
▼ Lowest point
+ Other mountain peak

A commonly accepted division between Asia and Europe—here marked by a maroon, dashed line—is formed by the Ural Mountains, Ural River, Caspian Sea, Caucasus Mountains, and the Black Sea with its outlets, the Bosporus and Dardanelles.

ASIA

URAL MOUNTAINS

Europe-Asia Boundary

Ural

Kama

Kama

Pechora

Volga

Volga

Don

Don

Dnieper

Dniester

Caspian Sea

-92 ft (-28 m) Lowest point in Europe ▼

Elbrus 18,510 ft (5,642 m) Highest point in Europe ▲

CAUCASUS MOUNTAINS

Crimea

Sea of Azov

Black Sea

Bosporus

Sea of Marmara

Dardanelles

Barents Sea

White Sea

Kola Peninsula

Northern Dvina

Lake Onega

Lake Ladoga

Western Dvina

Lake Region

Gulf of Finland

NORTHERN EUROPEAN PLAIN

Central Russian Upland

Carpathian Mts.

Danube

Balkan Mts.

Balkan Peninsula

Aegean Sea

Crete

Peloponnesus

North Cape

S C A N D I N A V I A N   U P L A N D

Gulf of Bothnia

Baltic Sea

Vistula

Oder

Elbe

Danube

Adriatic Sea

Ionian Sea

ARCTIC CIRCLE

PRIME MERIDIAN

Norwegian Sea

Iceland

Faroe Islands

Shetland Islands

Orkney Islands

Outer Hebrides

Highlands

Great Britain

British Isles

Ireland

North Sea

Irish Sea

Celtic Sea

English Channel

Zealand

Jutland

Ruhr Valley

Rhine

Seine

Loire

Brittany

Bay of Biscay

Atlantic Ocean

Massif Central

Mt. Blanc 15,771 ft (4,807 m)

ALPS

Rhône

Rhône

Po

Riviera

Ligurian Sea

Apennines

Corsica

Sardinia

Tyrrhenian Sea

Sicily

+ Etna 10,902 ft (3,323 m)

Mediterranean Sea

AFRICA

Pyrenees

Balearic Is.

Balearic Sea

Cantabrian Mts.

Douro

Tagus

Iberian Peninsula

Ebro

Baetic Mts.

Strait of Gibraltar

Rimmed by heavily eroded mountains to the north and young alpine mountains to the south, the vast Northern European Plain extends from the Pyrenees in the southwest to the Ural Mountains in Russia in the east. Built up by deposits from ancient glaciers, the plain supports much of modern Europe's productive agriculture.

400 Miles
400 Kilometers

Azimuthal Equidistant Projection

Europe

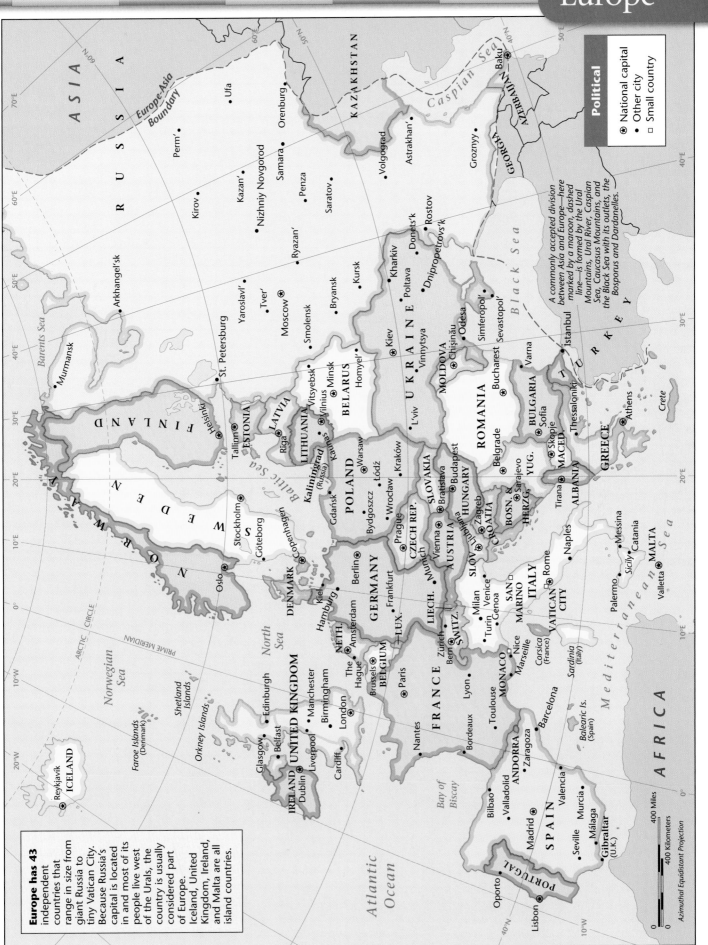

A commonly accepted division between Asia and Europe—here marked by a maroon, dashed line—is formed by the Ural Mountains, Ural River, Caspian Sea, Caucasus Mountains, and the Black Sea with its outlets, the Bosporus and Dardanelles.

Europe has 43 independent countries that range in size from giant Russia to tiny Vatican City. Because Russia's capital is located in and most of its people live west of the Urals, the country is usually considered part of Europe. Iceland, United Kingdom, Ireland, and Malta are all island countries.

ASIA

Europe-Asia Boundary

KAZAKHSTAN

R U S S I A

• Ufa

• Perm'

• Orenburg

• Arkhangel'sk

• Kirov

• Kazan'

• Samara

Caspian Sea

⊛ Baku

AZERBAIJAN

GEORGIA

• Astrakhan'

• Volgograd

• Grozny

• Nizhniy Novgorod

• Penza

• Saratov

• Ryazan'

Barents Sea

• Murmansk

• Yaroslavl'

• Tver'

⊛ Moscow

• Smolensk

• Bryansk

• Kursk

• Rostov

• Donets'k

• Dnipropetrovs'k

• Kharkiv

⊛ Kiev

Black Sea

• Poltava

U K R A I N E

⊛ Chişinău

• Vinnytsya

MOLDOVA

• Odesa

• Simferopol'

• Sevastopol'

⊛ St. Petersburg

F I N L A N D

⊛ Helsinki

ESTONIA

⊛ Tallinn

• Riga

LATVIA

LITHUANIA

⊛ Vilnius

• Kaunas

⊛ Minsk

• Homyel'

BELARUS

• Vitsyebsk

• L'viv

ROMANIA

⊛ Bucharest

⊛ Belgrade

• Varna

BULGARIA

⊛ Sofia

⊛ Skopje

MACED.

• Thessaloníki

TURKEY

⊛ Istanbul

GREECE

⊛ Athens

Crete

N O R W A Y

S W E D E N

• Stockholm

• Göteborg

Baltic Sea

Kaliningrad
(Russia)

• Gdańsk

POLAND

⊛ Warsaw

• Łódź

• Wrocław

• Kraków

• Bydgoszcz

CZECH REP.

⊛ Prague

SLOVAKIA

⊛ Bratislava

⊛ Budapest

HUNGARY

SLOV.

⊛ Ljubljana

CROATIA

⊛ Zagreb

BOSN. &
HERZG.

⊛ Sarajevo

YUG.

⊛ Tirana

ALBANIA

⊛ Oslo

DENMARK

⊛ Copenhagen

• Kiel

• Hamburg

⊛ Berlin

GERMANY

• Frankfurt

• Munich

LIECH.

⊛ Vienna

AUSTRIA

SWITZ.

⊛ Bern

⊛ Zürich

• Milan

• Turin

• Venice

• Genoa

SAN
MARINO □

ITALY

⊛ Rome

VATICAN
CITY ⊛

• Naples

• Messina

Sicily

• Palermo

• Catania

MALTA

⊛ Valletta

Mediterranean Sea

Arctic Circle

Prime Meridian

Faroe Islands
(Denmark)

Shetland
Islands

Orkney Islands

ICELAND

⊛ Reykjavík

Norwegian
Sea

North
Sea

IRELAND

⊛ Dublin

• Belfast

UNITED KINGDOM

• Glasgow

• Edinburgh

• Manchester

• Liverpool

• Birmingham

• Cardiff

⊛ London

NETH.

⊛ Amsterdam

The
Hague

BELGIUM

⊛ Brussels

LUX.

FRANCE

⊛ Paris

• Nantes

• Bordeaux

• Toulouse

• Lyon

• Marseille

• Nice

MONACO ⊛

ANDORRA ⊛

Corsica
(France)

Sardinia
(Italy)

Balearic Is.
(Spain)

• Barcelona

• Zaragoza

• Valencia

S P A I N

⊛ Madrid

• Valladolid

• Bilbao

• Seville

• Murcia

• Málaga

Gibraltar
(U.K.)

PORTUGAL

• Oporto

⊛ Lisbon

Bay of
Biscay

Atlantic
Ocean

AFRICA

400 Miles

400 Kilometers

Azimuthal Equidistant Projection

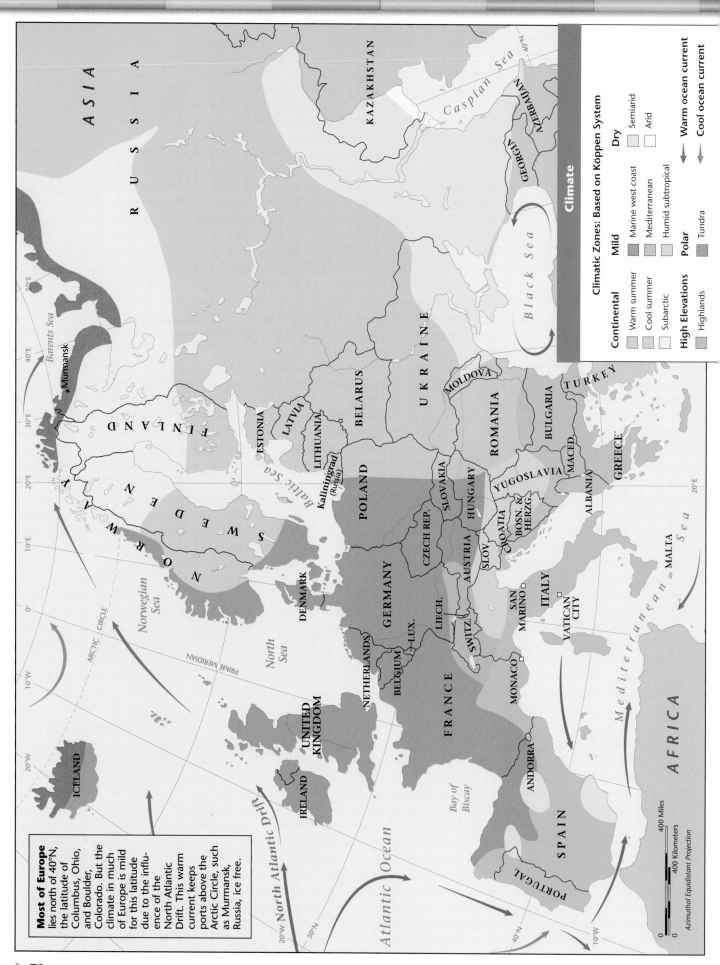

Most of Europe lies north of 40°N, the latitude of Columbus, Ohio, and Boulder, Colorado. But the climate in much of Europe is mild for this latitude due to the influence of the North Atlantic Drift. This warm current keeps ports above the Arctic Circle, such as Murmansk, Russia, ice free.

Climate

Climatic Zones: Based on Köppen System

Continental
- Warm summer
- Cool summer
- Subarctic

High Elevations
- Highlands

Mild
- Marine west coast
- Mediterranean
- Humid subtropical

Polar
- Tundra

Dry
- Semiarid
- Arid

→ Warm ocean current
→ Cool ocean current

Europe

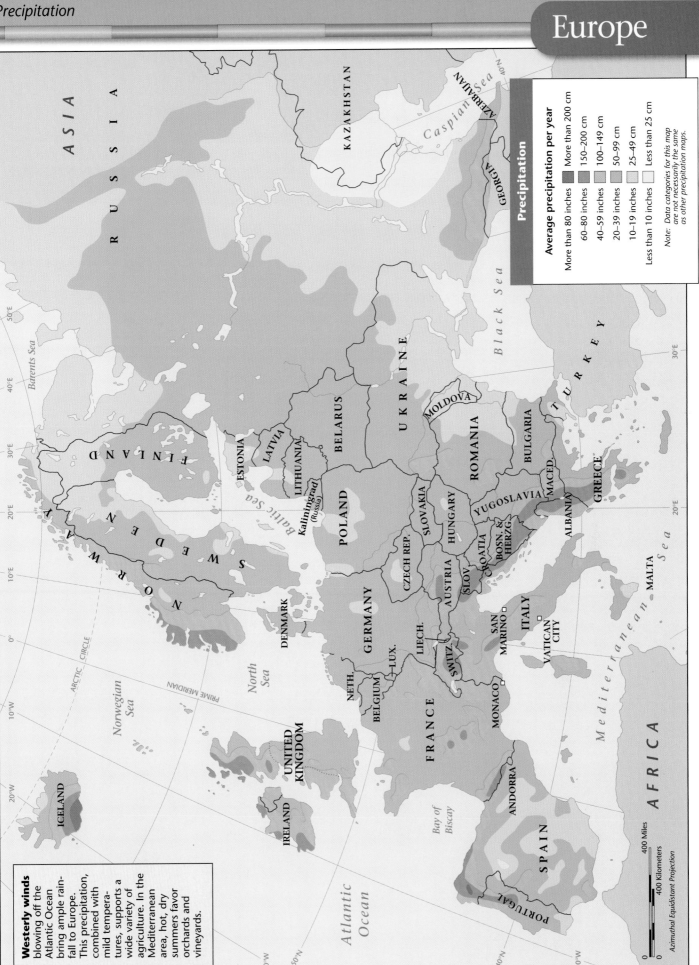

Westerly winds blowing off the Atlantic Ocean bring ample rainfall to Europe. This precipitation, combined with mild temperatures, supports a wide variety of agriculture. In the Mediterranean area, hot, dry summers favor orchards and vineyards.

Precipitation

Average precipitation per year

More than 80 inches	More than 200 cm
60–80 inches	150–200 cm
40–59 inches	100–149 cm
20–39 inches	50–99 cm
10–19 inches	25–49 cm
Less than 10 inches	Less than 25 cm

Note: Data categories for this map are not necessarily the same as other precipitation maps.

ASIA

RUSSIA

KAZAKHSTAN

Caspian Sea

AZERBAIJAN

GEORGIA

Black Sea

TURKEY

Barents Sea

FINLAND

ESTONIA

LATVIA

LITHUANIA

Kaliningrad (Russia)

BELARUS

UKRAINE

MOLDOVA

ROMANIA

BULGARIA

MACED.

GREECE

ALBANIA

YUGOSLAVIA

Baltic Sea

POLAND

SLOVAKIA

HUNGARY

CROATIA

BOSN. & HERZG.

SWEDEN

NORWAY

DENMARK

GERMANY

CZECH REP.

AUSTRIA

SLOV.

LIECH.

SWITZ.

SAN MARINO

ITALY

VATICAN CITY

MALTA

Mediterranean Sea

NETH.

BELGIUM

LUX.

FRANCE

MONACO

ANDORRA

SPAIN

PORTUGAL

North Sea

Norwegian Sea

Bay of Biscay

UNITED KINGDOM

IRELAND

ICELAND

Atlantic Ocean

AFRICA

ARCTIC CIRCLE

PRIME MERIDIAN

400 Miles

400 Kilometers

Azimuthal Equidistant Projection

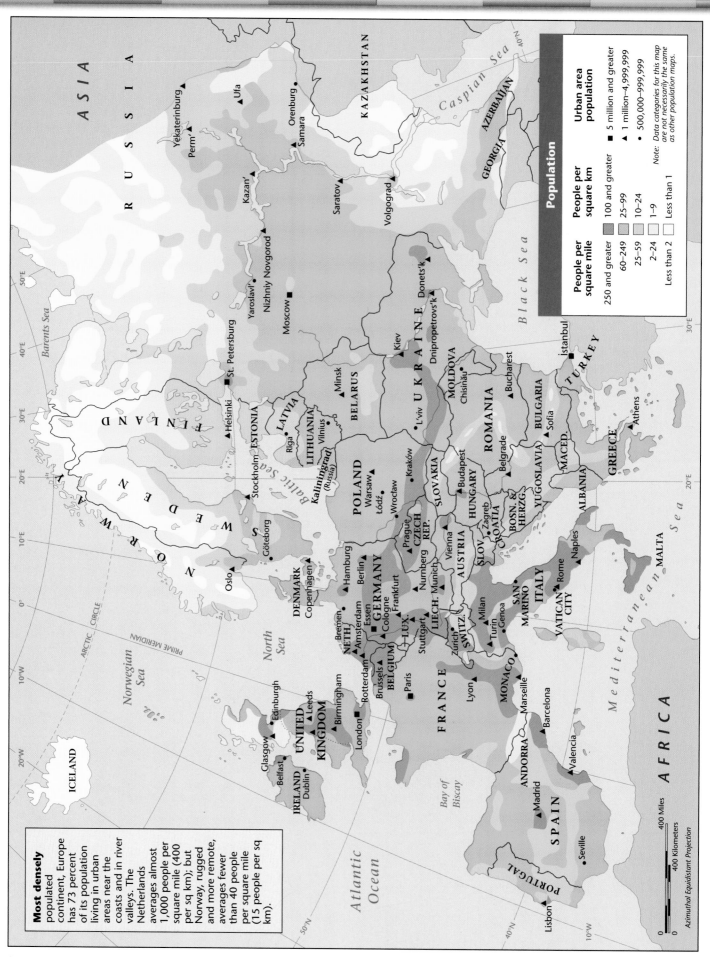

Most densely populated continent, Europe has 73 percent of its population living in urban areas near the coasts and in river valleys. The Netherlands averages almost 1,000 people per square mile (400 per sq km); but Norway, rugged and more remote, averages fewer than 40 people per square mile (15 people per sq km).

Population

People per square mile	People per square km
250 and greater	100 and greater
60–249	25–99
25–59	10–24
2–24	1–9
Less than 2	Less than 1

Urban area population
■ 5 million and greater
▲ 1 million–4,999,999
● 500,000–999,999

Note: Data categories for this map are not necessarily the same as other population maps.

Azimuthal Equidistant Projection

0   400 Miles
0   400 Kilometers

Europe

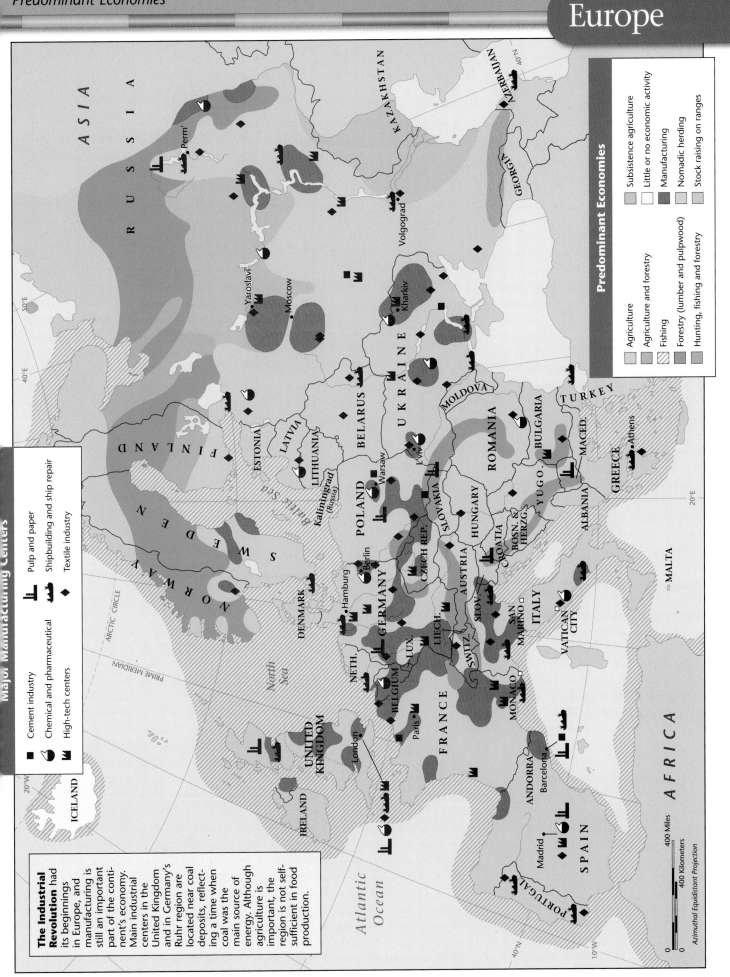

Predominant Economies

	Subsistence agriculture
	Little or no economic activity
	Manufacturing
	Nomadic herding
	Stock raising on ranges

	Agriculture
	Agriculture and forestry
	Fishing
	Forestry (lumber and pulpwood)
	Hunting, fishing and forestry

Major Manufacturing Centers

- ■ Cement industry
- ◗ Chemical and pharmaceutical
- ⚒ High-tech centers
- ⊓ Pulp and paper
- ⚓ Shipbuilding and ship repair
- ◆ Textile industry

The Industrial Revolution had its beginnings in Europe, and manufacturing is still an important part of the continent's economy. Main industrial centers in the United Kingdom and in Germany's Ruhr region are located near coal deposits, reflecting a time when coal was the main source of energy. Although agriculture is important, the region is not self-sufficient in food production.

ASIA

RUSSIA

Perm'

Yaroslavl'

Moscow

Volgograd

KAZAKHSTAN

GEORGIA

AZERBAIJAN

Kharkiv

TURKEY

UKRAINE

MOLDOVA

ROMANIA

BULGARIA

MACED.

GREECE

Athens

Lviv

SLOVAKIA

HUNGARY

YUGO.

ALBANIA

BOSN. & HERZ.

CROATIA

SLOV.

AUSTRIA

SAN MARINO

ITALY

VATICAN CITY

MALTA

FINLAND

ESTONIA

LATVIA

LITHUANIA

Kaliningrad (Russia)

BELARUS

POLAND

Warsaw

CZECH REP.

LIECH.

SWITZ.

MONACO

ANDORRA

Barcelona

SPAIN

Madrid

PORTUGAL

SWEDEN

NORWAY

ARCTIC CIRCLE

PRIME MERIDIAN

ICELAND

DENMARK

Hamburg

Berlin

GERMANY

NETH.

BELGIUM

LUX.

FRANCE

Paris

UNITED KINGDOM

London

IRELAND

North Sea

Baltic Sea

Atlantic Ocean

AFRICA

Azimuthal Equidistant Projection

0   400 Miles
0   400 Kilometers

1950 Union of Europe's coal and steel industries proposed by Robert Schuman of France

1951 European Coal and Steel Community (ECSC) established—composed of Belgium, Italy, Netherlands, Luxembourg, France, and West Germany

1957 European Economic Community (EEC) established to oversee economic integration of European nations

1965 European Community (EC) formed from EEC and other European organizations

1973 Denmark, Republic of Ireland, and United Kingdom became members of EC

1979 European Monetary System (EMS) initiated

1981 Greece became a member

1986 Spain and Portugal became members

1989 Plan for an Economic and Monetary Union (EMU) endorsed

1990 Former East Germany admitted as part of reunited Germany

1993 Maastricht Treaty created European Union (EU) after ratification by member countries

1995 Austria, Finland, and Sweden became members of EU

1998–99 Membership talks opened with 12 countries in eastern and southern Europe, looking toward enlargement of the EU early in the 21st century

1999 Euro introduced as an accounting currency in 11 EMU member countries

2002 Euro to begin circulating, replacing national currencies in all EMU member countries

FOCUS ON

European Union

In the years following World War II, the countries of Europe looked for ways to restore political stability to the continent while rebuilding their war-ravaged economies. The first step toward the European Union was taken in 1950 when France proposed creating common institutions to govern coal and steel production in Europe jointly. In 1951 France, West Germany, Italy, Belgium, Netherlands, and Luxembourg created the European Coal and Steel Community with the goal of bringing former adversaries together. In 1965 that organization became the European Community (EC).

The Maastricht Treaty took effect in 1993, establishing today's European Union (EU) and paving the way for a common foreign policy and a single European currency. The treaty also laid plans for the open flow of people, products, and services among the member countries. Since 1993, three more countries have joined the EU, bringing the total number of members to 15 (see map). As of the year 2000, 12 other countries were actively seeking admission: Bulgaria, Cypress, Czech Republic, Estonia, Hungary, Latvia, Lithuania, Poland, Romania, Slovakia, Slovenia, and Turkey.

▲ ***Main trade outlet*** *for Germany's heavily industrialized Ruhr Valley, the port of Rotterdam in the Netherlands accommodates massive supertankers and container ships.*

Web Link for information on the European Union: www.europa.eu.int

European Union

- Member country
- Other European country
- 1957 Year of admission

ARCTIC CIRCLE

Norwegian Sea

FINLAND
1995

SWEDEN
1995

North
Sea

Baltic Sea

IRELAND
1973

UNITED
KINGDOM
1973

DENMARK
1973

NETHERLANDS
1957

Atlantic
Ocean

English Channel

BELGIUM
1957

GERMANY
(WEST) (EAST)
1957 1990

E U R O P E

LUXEMBOURG
1957

Bay of
Biscay

FRANCE
1957

AUSTRIA
1995

PORTUGAL
1986

ITALY
1957

Adriatic Sea

SPAIN
1986

Aegean
Sea

ASIA

GREECE
1981

Mediterranean Sea

AFRICA

0   400 Miles
0   400 Kilometers

Azimuthal Equidistant Projection

Symbols of New Unity

THE FLAG of the Council of Europe, a circle of gold stars on a field of blue, was adopted as a symbol of unity first by the EC and then by the EU. Another important step toward European unity came in 1999 with the introduction of a common currency—the euro—which is scheduled to begin circulating in January 2002.

European Union's Share of World Trade

Acting as a trade bloc, the European Union is a major player in the global economy. With only a little more than six percent of the world's population, the EU accounts for about twice the trade of the U.S. and Canada combined or of Asia. The three regions together account for more than 80 percent of world trade in both products and services.

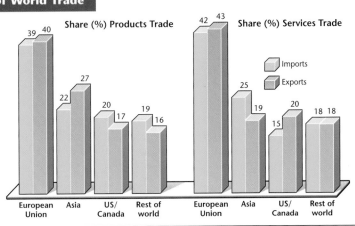

Share (%) Products Trade

	Imports	Exports
European Union	39	40
Asia	22	27
US/Canada	20	17
Rest of world	19	16

Share (%) Services Trade

	Imports	Exports
European Union	42	43
Asia	25	19
US/Canada	15	20
Rest of world	18	18

Africa

From space, Africa appears divided into three regions: the northern third, dominated by the vast Sahara, largest hot desert in the world; a central green band of rain forests and tropical grasslands; and more dry lands to the south. Africa itself may be dividing literally: The Great Rift Valley, which runs from the Red Sea through the volcanic Afar Triangle to the lake district in the south (see map page 85), eventually may split apart the continent.

Facts & Figures

▶ **Land area:** 11,609,000 sq mi (30,065,000 sq km)

▶ **Population:** 800,245,000

▶ **Highest point:** Mount Kilimanjaro, Tanzania: 19,340 ft (5,895 m)

▶ **Lowest point:** Lake Assal, Djibouti: 512 ft (156 m) below sea level

▶ **Longest river:** Nile: 4,241 mi (6,825 km)

▶ **Largest Lake:** Victoria: 26,836 sq mi (69,500 sq km)

▶ **Number of independent countries:** 53

▶ **Largest country:** Sudan: 963,600 sq mi (2,495,712 sq km)

▶ **Smallest country:** Seychelles: 175 sq mi (453 sq km)

▶ **Most populous country:** Nigeria: Pop. 123,338,000

▶ **Least populous country:** Seychelles: Pop. 82,000

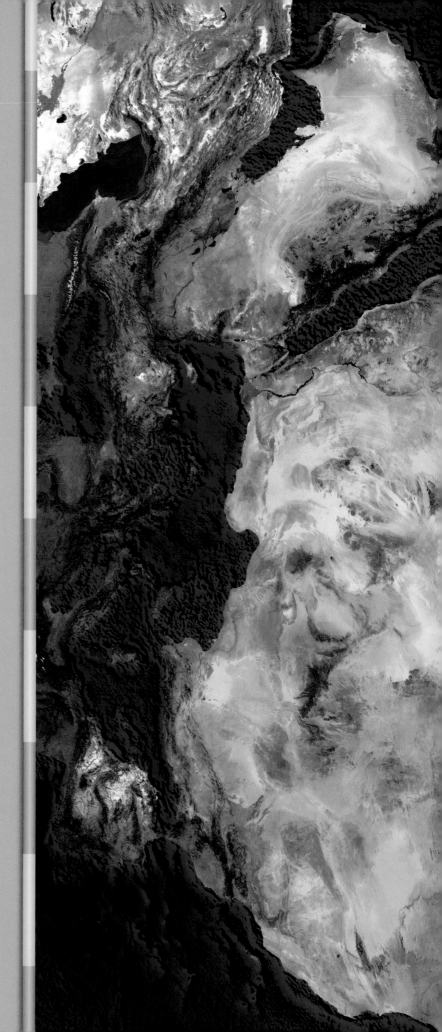

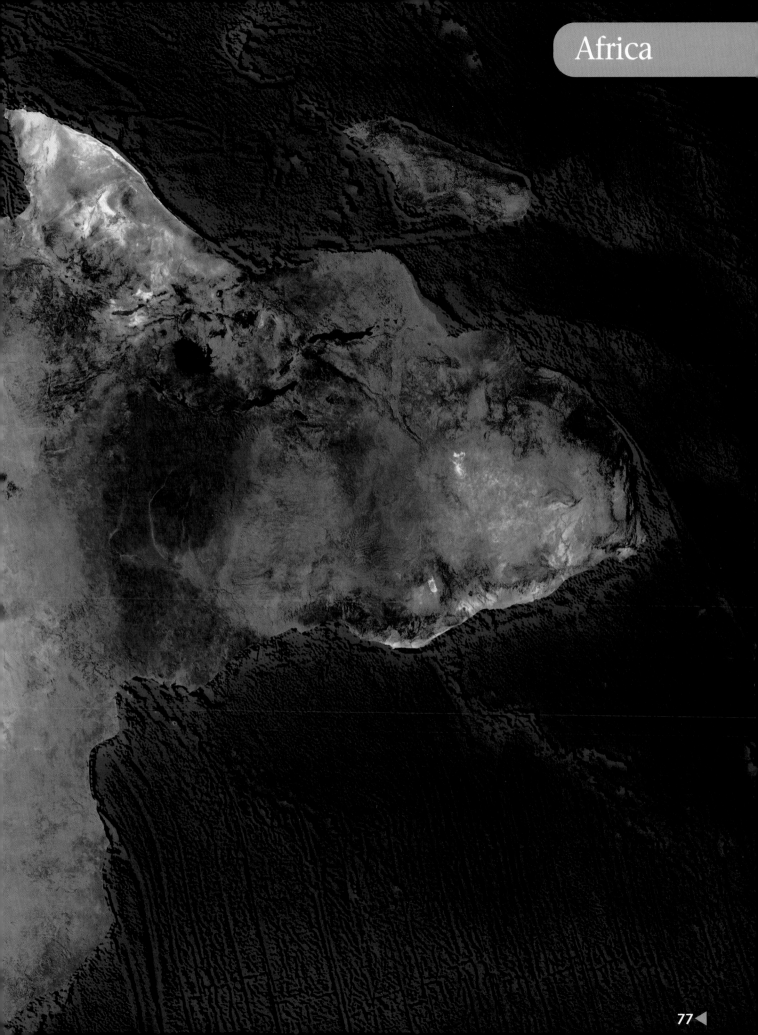

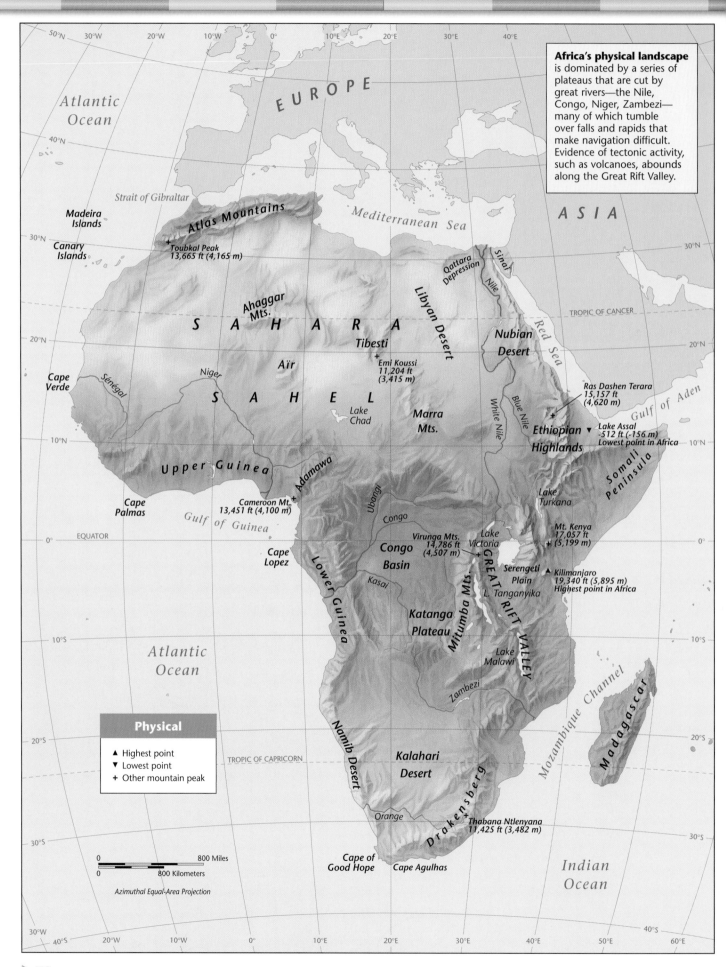

Africa's physical landscape is dominated by a series of plateaus that are cut by great rivers—the Nile, Congo, Niger, Zambezi— many of which tumble over falls and rapids that make navigation difficult. Evidence of tectonic activity, such as volcanoes, abounds along the Great Rift Valley.

EUROPE

ASIA

Atlantic Ocean

Madeira Islands

Canary Islands

Strait of Gibraltar

Atlas Mountains

Toubkal Peak 13,665 ft (4,165 m)

Mediterranean Sea

Qattara Depression

Sinai

Nile

TROPIC OF CANCER

Cape Verde

Ahaggar Mts.

S A H A R A

Tibesti

Aïr

S A H E L

Niger

Sénégal

Lake Chad

Emi Koussi 11,204 ft (3,415 m)

Libyan Desert

Nubian Desert

Marra Mts.

White Nile

Blue Nile

Red Sea

Ras Dashen Terara 15,157 ft (4,620 m)

Gulf of Aden

Ethiopian Highlands

Lake Assal -512 ft (-156 m) Lowest point in Africa

Somali Peninsula

Cape Palmas

Upper Guinea

Adamawa

Cameroon Mt. 13,451 ft (4,100 m)

Gulf of Guinea

Ubangi

Congo

Lake Turkana

Mt. Kenya 17,057 ft (5,199 m)

EQUATOR

Cape Lopez

Lower Guinea

Congo Basin

Kasai

Virunga Mts. 14,786 ft (4,507 m)

Lake Victoria

Serengeti Plain

L. Tanganyika

GREAT RIFT VALLEY

Kilimanjaro 19,340 ft (5,895 m) Highest point in Africa

Katanga Plateau

Mitumba Mts.

Lake Malawi

Atlantic Ocean

Zambezi

Mozambique Channel

Madagascar

Physical

▲ Highest point
▼ Lowest point
+ Other mountain peak

Namib Desert

TROPIC OF CAPRICORN

Kalahari Desert

Drakensberg

Orange

Thabana Ntlenyana 11,425 ft (3,482 m)

Cape of Good Hope

Cape Agulhas

Indian Ocean

0   800 Miles
0   800 Kilometers

Azimuthal Equal-Area Projection

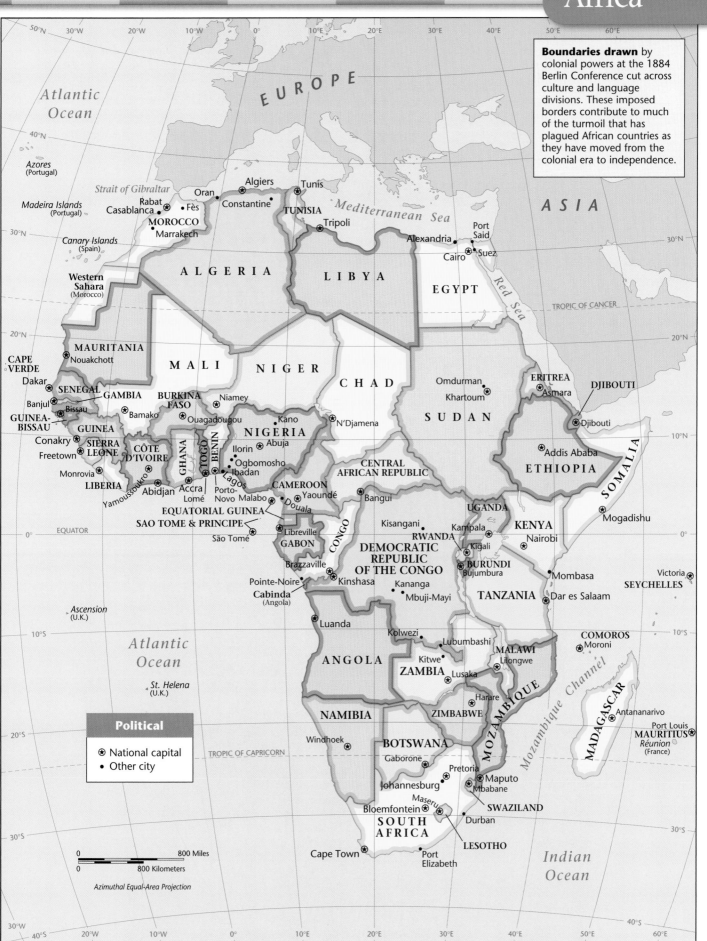

Boundaries drawn by colonial powers at the 1884 Berlin Conference cut across culture and language divisions. These imposed borders contribute to much of the turmoil that has plagued African countries as they have moved from the colonial era to independence.

Political

⊛ National capital
• Other city

Azimuthal Equal-Area Projection

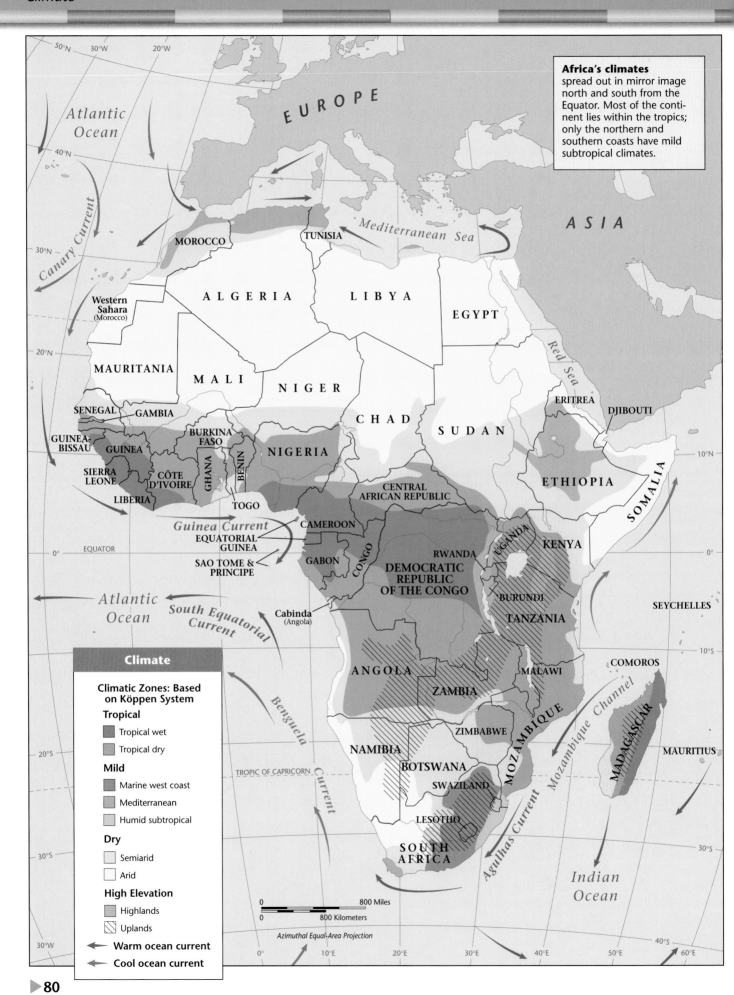

Africa's climates
spread out in mirror image north and south from the Equator. Most of the continent lies within the tropics; only the northern and southern coasts have mild subtropical climates.

EUROPE

ASIA

Atlantic Ocean

Mediterranean Sea

50°N
30°W
20°W
40°N
30°N
20°N

Canary Current

MOROCCO
TUNISIA

Western Sahara (Morocco)

ALGERIA
LIBYA
EGYPT

Red Sea

MAURITANIA
MALI
NIGER
CHAD
SUDAN

SENEGAL
GAMBIA
GUINEA-BISSAU
GUINEA
SIERRA LEONE
LIBERIA
CÔTE D'IVOIRE
GHANA
BURKINA FASO
BENIN
TOGO
NIGERIA

ERITREA
DJIBOUTI
ETHIOPIA
SOMALIA

10°N

CENTRAL AFRICAN REPUBLIC

Guinea Current

CAMEROON
EQUATORIAL GUINEA
SAO TOME & PRINCIPE
GABON
CONGO
DEMOCRATIC REPUBLIC OF THE CONGO
RWANDA
BURUNDI
UGANDA
KENYA
TANZANIA

EQUATOR
0°

Atlantic Ocean

South Equatorial Current

Cabinda (Angola)

SEYCHELLES

10°S

ANGOLA
ZAMBIA
MALAWI
COMOROS

Benguela Current

ZIMBABWE
MOZAMBIQUE
MADAGASCAR
MAURITIUS

NAMIBIA
BOTSWANA
SWAZILAND
LESOTHO
SOUTH AFRICA

TROPIC OF CAPRICORN

Mozambique Channel

Agulhas Current

Indian Ocean

20°S
30°S
40°S

Climate

Climatic Zones: Based on Köppen System

Tropical
- Tropical wet
- Tropical dry

Mild
- Marine west coast
- Mediterranean
- Humid subtropical

Dry
- Semiarid
- Arid

High Elevation
- Highlands
- Uplands

→ Warm ocean current
→ Cool ocean current

0   800 Miles
0   800 Kilometers

Azimuthal Equal-Area Projection

0°
10°E
20°E
30°E
40°E
50°E
60°E
30°W

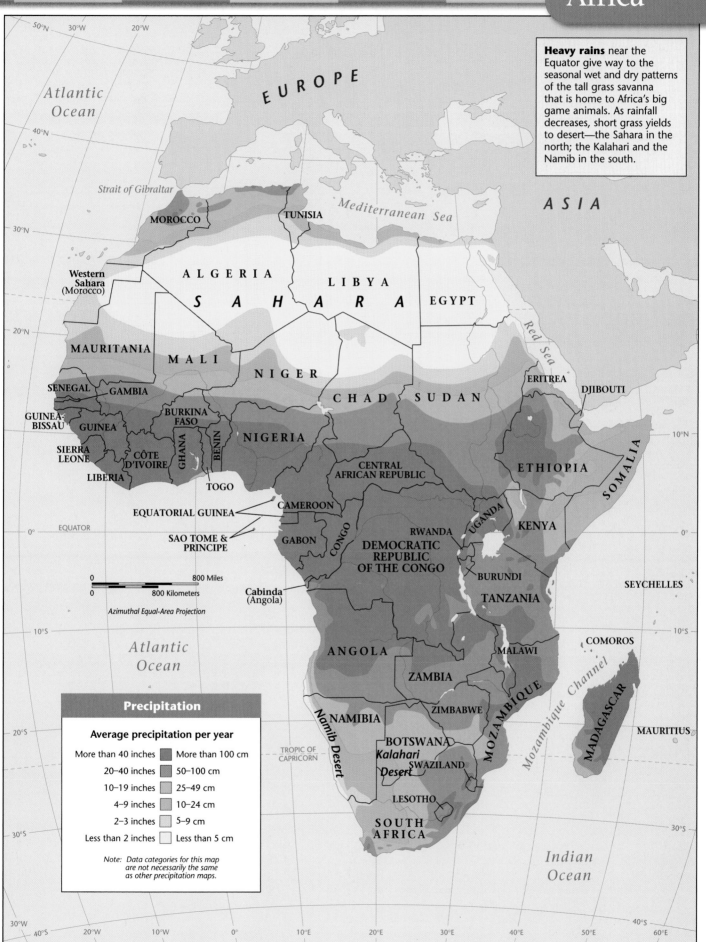

Heavy rains near the Equator give way to the seasonal wet and dry patterns of the tall grass savanna that is home to Africa's big game animals. As rainfall decreases, short grass yields to desert—the Sahara in the north; the Kalahari and the Namib in the south.

EUROPE

ASIA

Atlantic Ocean

Strait of Gibraltar

Mediterranean Sea

MOROCCO

TUNISIA

ALGERIA

LIBYA

EGYPT

SAHARA

Western Sahara (Morocco)

MAURITANIA

MALI

NIGER

Red Sea

SENEGAL

GAMBIA

CHAD

SUDAN

ERITREA

DJIBOUTI

GUINEA-BISSAU

GUINEA

BURKINA FASO

SIERRA LEONE

CÔTE D'IVOIRE

GHANA

BENIN

NIGERIA

CENTRAL AFRICAN REPUBLIC

ETHIOPIA

SOMALIA

LIBERIA

TOGO

CAMEROON

EQUATORIAL GUINEA

SAO TOME & PRINCIPE

GABON

CONGO

DEMOCRATIC REPUBLIC OF THE CONGO

RWANDA

UGANDA

KENYA

BURUNDI

TANZANIA

EQUATOR

SEYCHELLES

Cabinda (Angola)

0   800 Miles
0   800 Kilometers

Azimuthal Equal-Area Projection

ANGOLA

ZAMBIA

MALAWI

COMOROS

Mozambique Channel

ZIMBABWE

MOZAMBIQUE

MADAGASCAR

MAURITIUS

NAMIBIA

Namib Desert

BOTSWANA

Kalahari Desert

SWAZILAND

LESOTHO

SOUTH AFRICA

TROPIC OF CAPRICORN

Atlantic Ocean

Indian Ocean

Precipitation

Average precipitation per year

More than 40 inches	More than 100 cm
20–40 inches	50–100 cm
10–19 inches	25–49 cm
4–9 inches	10–24 cm
2–3 inches	5–9 cm
Less than 2 inches	Less than 5 cm

Note: Data categories for this map are not necessarily the same as other precipitation maps.

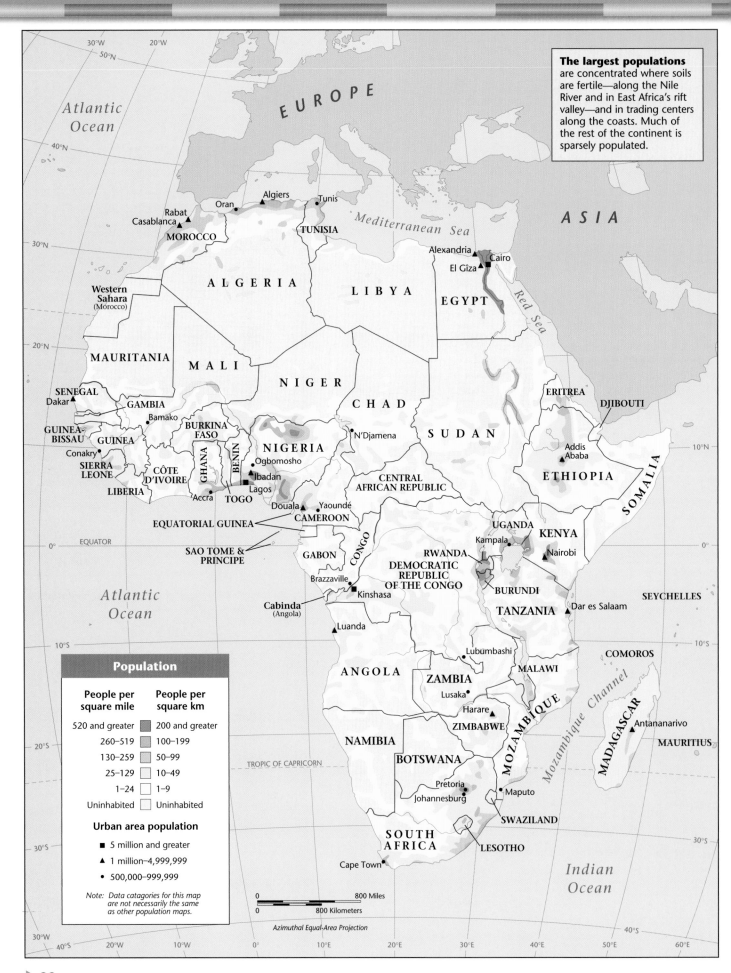

The largest populations are concentrated where soils are fertile—along the Nile River and in East Africa's rift valley—and in trading centers along the coasts. Much of the rest of the continent is sparsely populated.

Population

People per square mile	People per square km
520 and greater	200 and greater
260–519	100–199
130–259	50–99
25–129	10–49
1–24	1–9
Uninhabited	Uninhabited

Urban area population

■ 5 million and greater
▲ 1 million–4,999,999
• 500,000–999,999

Note: Data catagories for this map are not necessarily the same as other population maps.

Azimuthal Equal-Area Projection

0   800 Miles
0   800 Kilometers

Africa

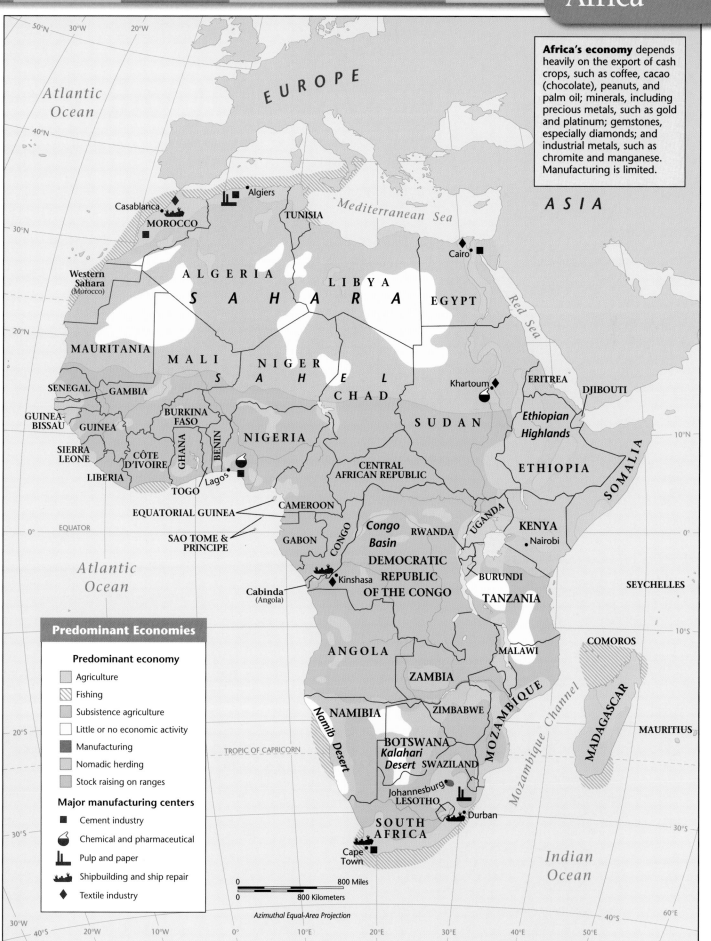

Africa's economy depends heavily on the export of cash crops, such as coffee, cacao (chocolate), peanuts, and palm oil; minerals, including precious metals, such as gold and platinum; gemstones, especially diamonds; and industrial metals, such as chromite and manganese. Manufacturing is limited.

Predominant Economies

Predominant economy
- Agriculture
- Fishing
- Subsistence agriculture
- Little or no economic activity
- Manufacturing
- Nomadic herding
- Stock raising on ranges

Major manufacturing centers
- Cement industry
- Chemical and pharmaceutical
- Pulp and paper
- Shipbuilding and ship repair
- Textile industry

0   800 Miles
0   800 Kilometers

Azimuthal Equal-Area Projection

EUROPE

Atlantic Ocean

Casablanca
MOROCCO
Algiers
TUNISIA

Western Sahara (Morocco)

ALGERIA
SAHARA
LIBYA
EGYPT

Mediterranean Sea

ASIA

Red Sea

Cairo

MAURITANIA
MALI
SAHEL
NIGER
CHAD
SUDAN
Khartoum
ERITREA
DJIBOUTI

SENEGAL
GAMBIA
GUINEA-BISSAU
GUINEA
BURKINA FASO
GHANA
BENIN
NIGERIA
Ethiopian Highlands

SIERRA LEONE
CÔTE D'IVOIRE
LIBERIA
TOGO
Lagos

CENTRAL AFRICAN REPUBLIC
ETHIOPIA
SOMALIA

EQUATORIAL GUINEA
SAO TOME & PRINCIPE
CAMEROON
GABON
CONGO
Congo Basin
RWANDA
UGANDA
KENYA
Nairobi

EQUATOR

Atlantic Ocean

Cabinda (Angola)
Kinshasa
DEMOCRATIC REPUBLIC OF THE CONGO
BURUNDI
TANZANIA

SEYCHELLES

ANGOLA
ZAMBIA
MALAWI
COMOROS

NAMIBIA
ZIMBABWE
MOZAMBIQUE
Mozambique Channel
MADAGASCAR
MAURITIUS

Namib Desert
BOTSWANA
Kalahari Desert
SWAZILAND

TROPIC OF CAPRICORN

Johannesburg
LESOTHO
Durban
SOUTH AFRICA

Cape Town

Indian Ocean

FOCUS ON

The Great Rift Valley

More than a hundred million years ago, Gondwana, the southern part of the supercontinent Pangaea, began to break apart. Landmasses that we know today as South America, Antarctica, Australia, and the Indian subcontinent slowly moved away, propelled by tectonic forces originating deep within Earth (see map page 14). The part of Gondwana that was left behind is what we know as Africa.

The forces that tore apart Gondwana continue today, especially in East Africa where the Great Rift Valley marks the boundary of what many earth scientists believe eventually will be a new sea that will separate part of eastern and southern Africa from the rest of the continent.

30 million years before present

The Arabian Peninsula and Africa were joined as one landmass 30 million years ago.

7 million years before present

ASIA

AFRICA

Fiery-hot magma rising from within Earth caused rifting that began to push apart the land along what is now the Red Sea.

30 million years in the future

ASIA

AFRICA

Long, narrow lakes could become a single channel if rifting continues and causes the Somali Plate to break away.

► **Volcanic cones,** in the tiny country of Djibouti, mark the area where active tectonic rifting may someday result in the formation of a new ocean.

▼ **Colorful flamingos** are attracted to rift valley lakes, where high evaporation rates help create alkaline waters. The birds feed on brine shrimp and various kinds of algae.

► **Subsistence farmers,** many of them women, grow staple crops of maize (corn) and beans in the fertile volcanic soils. Large commercial farms produce cash crops, such as coffee and sisal.

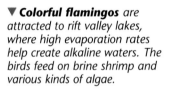

Web Link for information on the Great Rift: www.robinsonresearch.com/AFRICA/THE_LAND/Rift_Val.htm

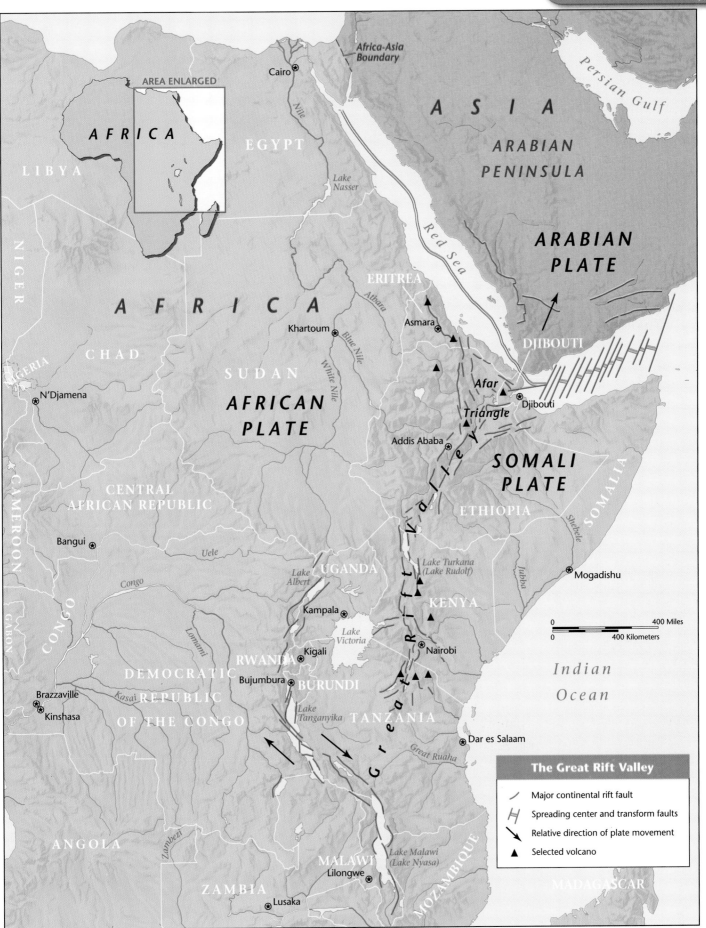

Africa-Asia
Boundary

Cairo

AREA ENLARGED

AFRICA

LIBYA

EGYPT

NIGER

Lake
Nasser

A S I A

ARABIAN
PENINSULA

Persian Gulf

Red Sea

ARABIAN
PLATE

A F R I C A

CHAD

Khartoum

ERITREA

Asmara

DJIBOUTI

N'Djamena

SUDAN

AFRICAN
PLATE

Blue Nile

White Nile

Athara

Afar

Djibouti

Addis Ababa

Triangle

SOMALI
PLATE

CENTRAL
AFRICAN REPUBLIC

Bangui

Uele

ETHIOPIA

Shebele

SOMALIA

CAMEROON

Congo

UGANDA

Lake
Albert

Lake Turkana
(Lake Rudolf)

KENYA

Jubba

Mogadishu

GABON

Lomami

Kampala

Lake
Victoria

Nairobi

400 Miles

400 Kilometers

CONGO

RWANDA

Kigali

Indian
Ocean

DEMOCRATIC

Brazzaville

Kinshasa

Kasai

REPUBLIC

Bujumbura

BURUNDI

Great Rift Valley

OF THE CONGO

Lake
Tanganyika

TANZANIA

Great Ruaha

Dar es Salaam

ANGOLA

Zambezi

MALAWI

Lake Malawi
(Lake Nyasa)

MOZAMBIQUE

MADAGASCAR

ZAMBIA

Lilongwe

Lusaka

The Great Rift Valley

/	Major continental rift fault
⊢	Spreading center and transform faults
↗	Relative direction of plate movement
▲	Selected volcano

Asia

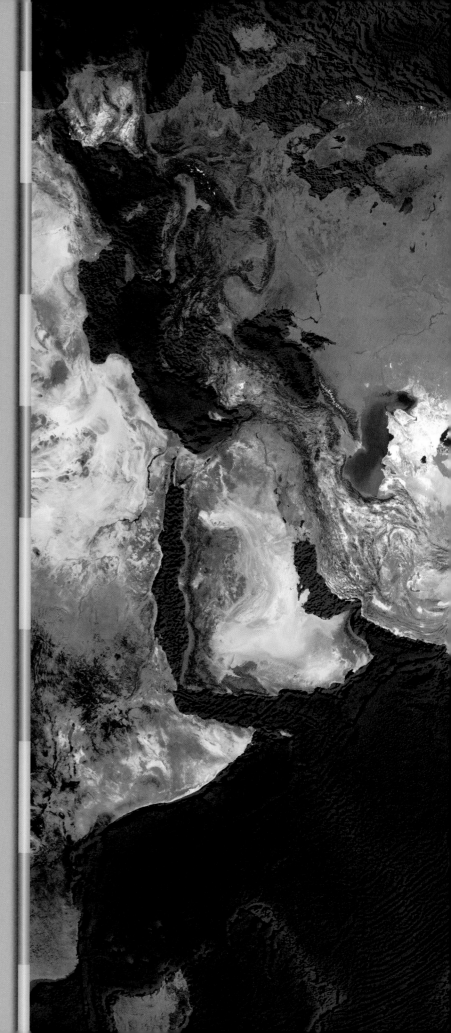

From the frozen shores of the Arctic Ocean to the equatorial islands of Indonesia, Asia stretches across 90 degrees of latitude. From the Ural Mountains to the Pacific Ocean it covers more than 150 degrees of longitude. Here, three of history's great culture hearths emerged in the valleys of the Tigris-Euphrates, the Indus, and the Yellow (Huang) Rivers. Today, Asia is home to more than 60 percent of Earth's people and some of the world's fastest growing economies.

Facts & Figures

▶ **Land area:** 17,213,300 sq mi (44,579,000 sq km)

▶ **Population:** 3,684,490,000

▶ **Highest point:** Mount Everest, China-Nepal: 29,035 ft (8,850 m)

▶ **Lowest point:** Dead Sea, Israel-Jordan: 1,349 ft (411 m) below sea level

▶ **Longest river:** Yangtze (Chang), China: 3,964 mi (6,380 km)

▶ **Largest lake entirely in Asia:** Baikal, Russia: 12,163 sq mi (31,500 sq km)

▶ **Number of independent countries:** 46 (excluding Russia)

▶ **Largest country entirely in Asia:** China: 3,705,820 sq mi (9,598,032 sq km)

▶ **Smallest country:** Maldives: 115 sq mi (298 sq km)

▶ **Most populous country:** China: Pop. 1,264,536,000

▶ **Least populous country:** Maldives: Pop. 286,000

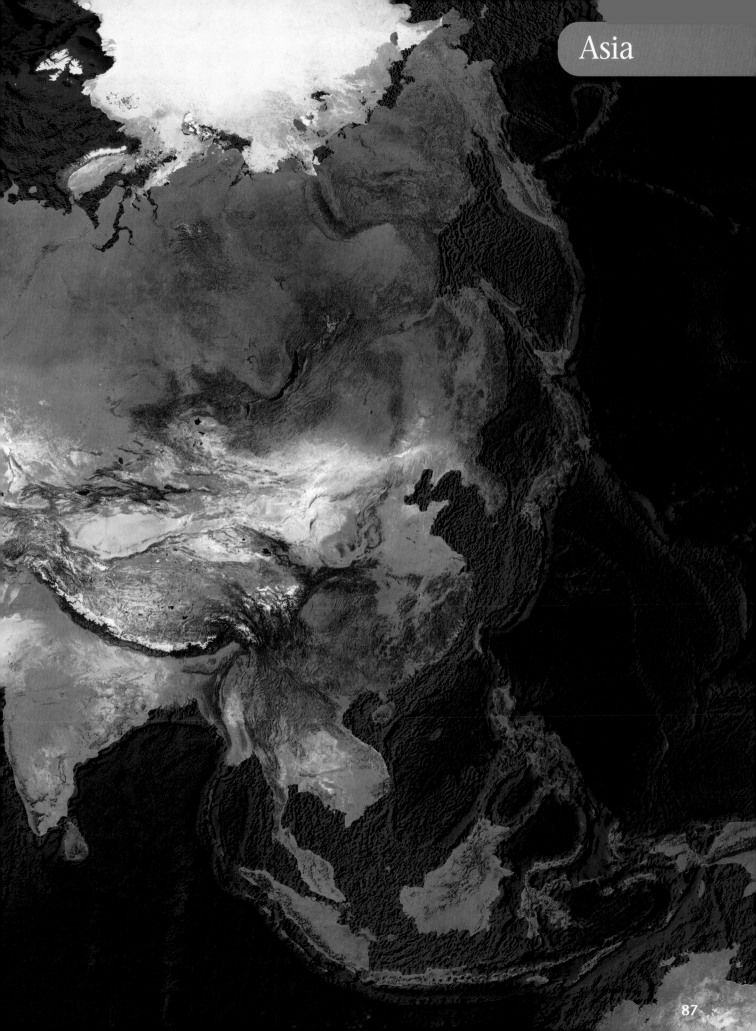

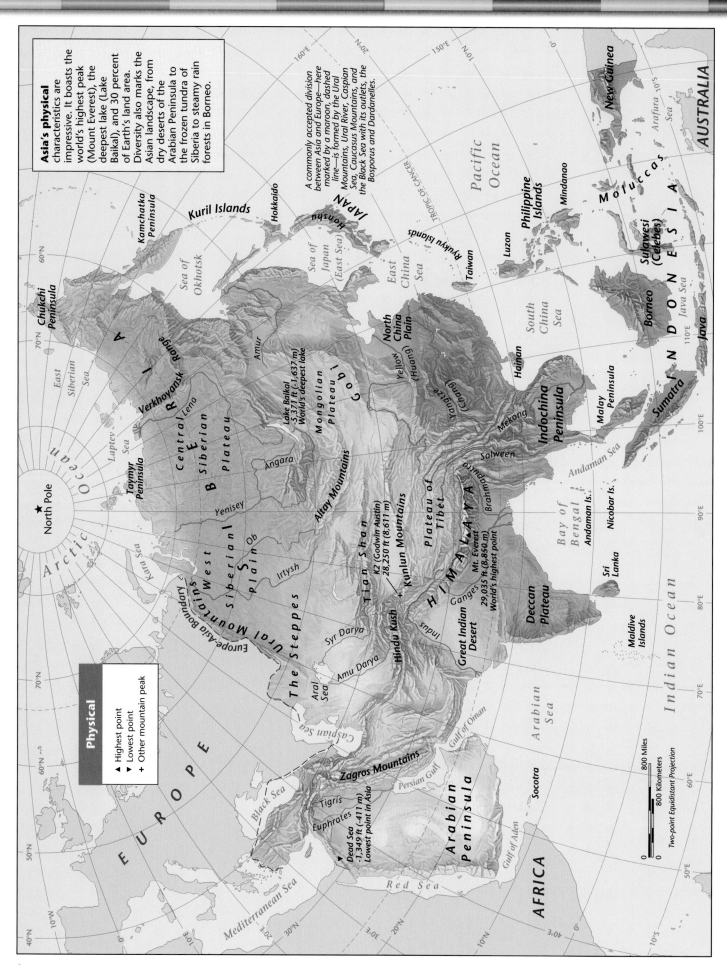

Asia's physical
characteristics are
impressive. It boasts the
world's highest peak
(Mount Everest), the
deepest lake (Lake
Baikal), and 30 percent
of Earth's land area.
Diversity also marks the
Asian landscape, from
dry deserts of the
Arabian Peninsula to
the frozen tundra of
Siberia to steamy rain
forests in Borneo.

A commonly accepted division
between Asia and Europe—here
marked by a maroon, dashed
line—is formed by the Ural
Mountains, Ural River, Caspian
Sea, Caucasus Mountains, and
the Black Sea with its outlets, the
Bosporus and Dardanelles.

Physical

▲ Highest point
▼ Lowest point
+ Other mountain peak

North Pole

Arctic Ocean

Chukchi Peninsula

East Siberian Sea

Laptev Sea

Kara Sea

Taymyr Peninsula

Kamchatka Peninsula

Kuril Islands

Hokkaido

Sea of Okhotsk

JAPAN

Honshu

Sea of Japan (East Sea)

EUROPE

Europe-Asia Boundary

Ural Mountains

West Siberian Plain

The Steppes

Central Siberian Plateau

Verkhoyansk Range

Lena

Angara

Yenisey

Ob

Irtysh

Amur

Syr Darya

Amu Darya

Aral Sea

Caspian Sea

Black Sea

Zagros Mountains

Tigris

Euphrates

Dead Sea
-1,349 ft (-411 m)
Lowest point in Asia

Mediterranean Sea

Red Sea

Gulf of Aden

Socotra

AFRICA

Arabian Peninsula

Persian Gulf

Gulf of Oman

Arabian Sea

Altay Mountains

Mongolian Plateau

Gobi

Lake Baikal
-5,371 ft (-1,637 m)
World's deepest lake

Tian Shan

K2 (Godwin Austin)
28,250 ft (8,611 m)

Kunlun Mountains

Plateau of Tibet

Hindu Kush

HIMALAYA

Mt. Everest
29,035 ft (8,850 m)
World's highest point

Ganges

Indus

Great Indian Desert

Brahmaputra

Salween

Mekong

Yangtze (Chang)

Yellow (Huang)

North China Plain

East China Sea

TROPIC OF CANCER

Ryukyu Islands

Taiwan

Hainan

South China Sea

Pacific Ocean

Philippine Islands

Luzon

Mindanao

Moluccas

Sulawesi (Celebes)

Borneo

Java Sea

INDONESIA

Java

Sumatra

Malay Peninsula

Indochina Peninsula

Andaman Sea

Bay of Bengal

Andaman Is.

Nicobar Is.

Sri Lanka

Maldive Islands

Deccan Plateau

Indian Ocean

New Guinea

Arafura Sea

AUSTRALIA

800 Miles

800 Kilometers

Two-point Equidistant Projection

Asia

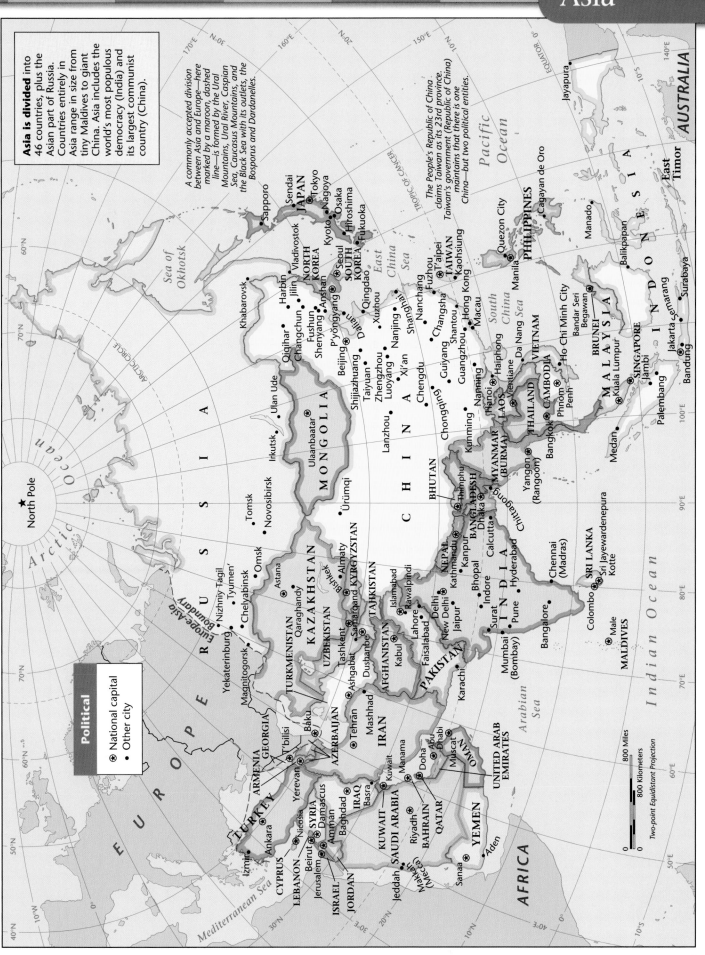

Asia is divided into 46 countries, plus the Asian part of Russia. Countries entirely in Asia range in size from tiny Maldives to giant China. Asia includes the world's most populous democracy (India) and its largest communist country (China).

A commonly accepted division between Asia and Europe—here marked by a maroon, dashed line—is formed by the Ural Mountains, Ural River, Caspian Sea, Caucasus Mountains, and the Black Sea with its outlets, the Bosporus and Dardanelles.

The People's Republic of China claims Taiwan as its 23rd province. Taiwan's government (Republic of China) maintains that there is one China—but two political entities.

Political
⊗ National capital
• Other city

Two-point Equidistant Projection

800 Miles

800 Kilometers

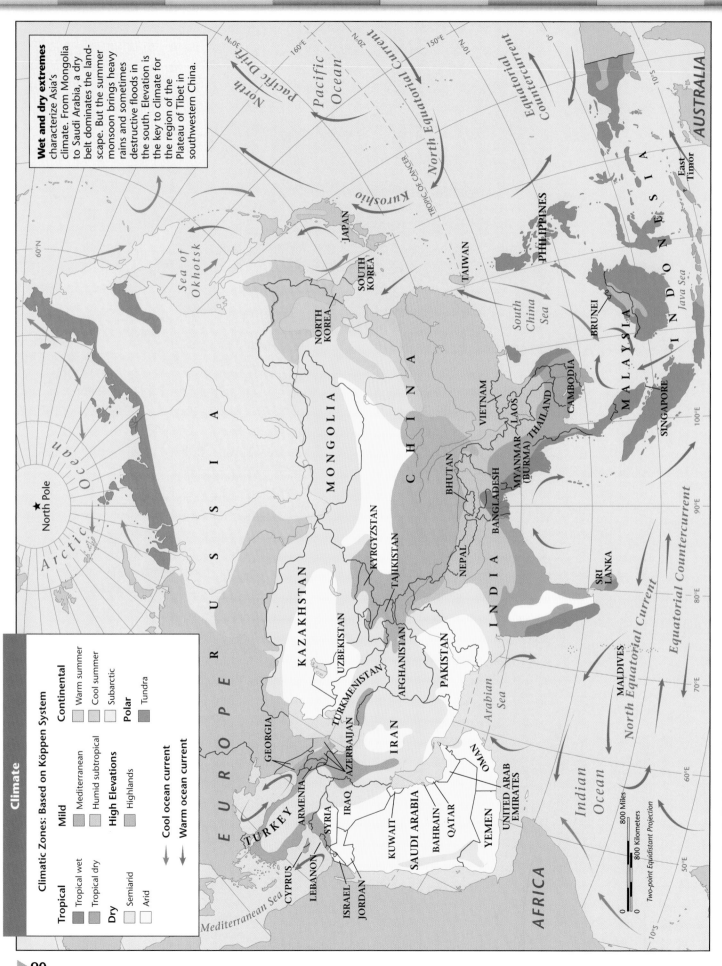

Climate

Climatic Zones: Based on Köppen System

Tropical
- Tropical wet
- Tropical dry

Dry
- Semiarid
- Arid

Mild
- Mediterranean
- Humid subtropical

Continental
- Warm summer
- Cool summer
- Subarctic

Polar
- Tundra

High Elevations
- Highlands

→ Cool ocean current
→ Warm ocean current

Wet and dry extremes characterize Asia's climate. From Mongolia to Saudi Arabia, a dry belt dominates the landscape. But the summer monsoon brings heavy rains and sometimes destructive floods in the south. Elevation is the key to climate for the region of the Plateau of Tibet in southwestern China.

Asia

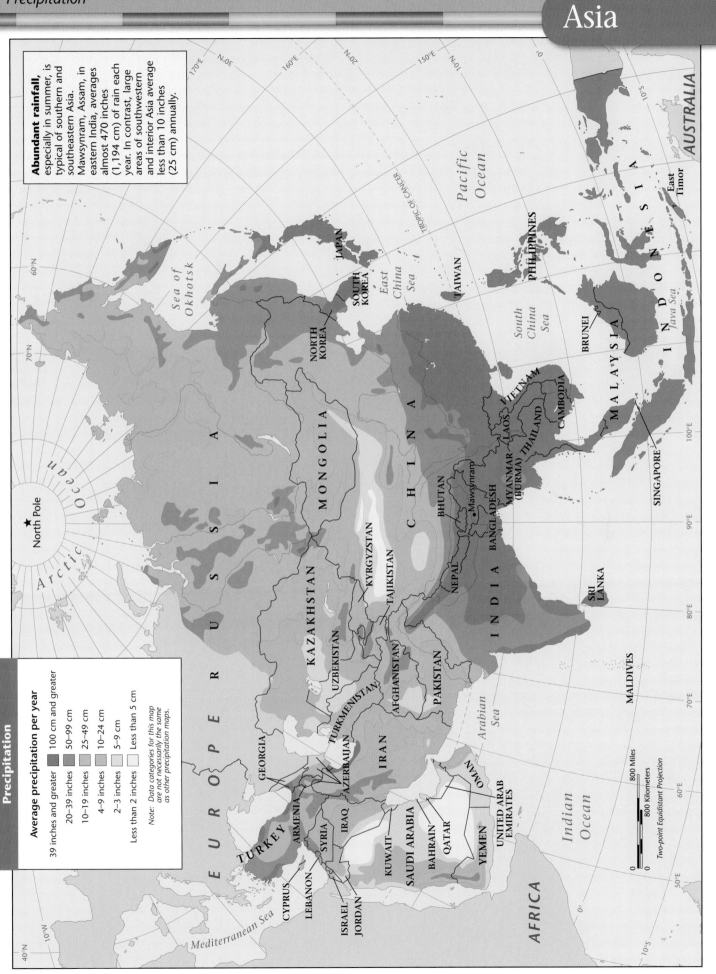

Abundant rainfall, especially in summer, is typical of southern and southeastern Asia. Mawsynram, Assam, in eastern India, averages almost 470 inches (1,194 cm) of rain each year. In contrast, large areas of southwestern and interior Asia average less than 10 inches (25 cm) annually.

Average precipitation per year

- 39 inches and greater — 100 cm and greater
- 20–39 inches — 50–99 cm
- 10–19 inches — 25–49 cm
- 4–9 inches — 10–24 cm
- 2–3 inches — 5–9 cm
- Less than 2 inches — Less than 5 cm

Note: Data categories for this map are not necessarily the same as other precipitation maps.

North Pole

Arctic Ocean

EUROPE

RUSSIA

Sea of Okhotsk

JAPAN

SOUTH KOREA

NORTH KOREA

East China Sea

TAIWAN

Pacific Ocean

TROPIC OF CANCER

South China Sea

PHILIPPINES

BRUNEI

MALAYSIA

INDONESIA

Java Sea

East Timor

AUSTRALIA

SINGAPORE

MONGOLIA

CHINA

VIETNAM

LAOS

CAMBODIA

MYANMAR (BURMA)

THAILAND

KAZAKHSTAN

UZBEKISTAN

KYRGYZSTAN

TAJIKISTAN

TURKMENISTAN

AFGHANISTAN

PAKISTAN

NEPAL

BHUTAN

BANGLADESH

INDIA

Mawsynram

SRI LANKA

MALDIVES

Arabian Sea

Indian Ocean

GEORGIA

AZERBAIJAN

ARMENIA

IRAN

IRAQ

SYRIA

TURKEY

CYPRUS

LEBANON

ISRAEL

JORDAN

KUWAIT

SAUDI ARABIA

BAHRAIN

QATAR

YEMEN

OMAN

UNITED ARAB EMIRATES

AFRICA

Mediterranean Sea

800 Miles

800 Kilometers

Two-point Equidistant Projection

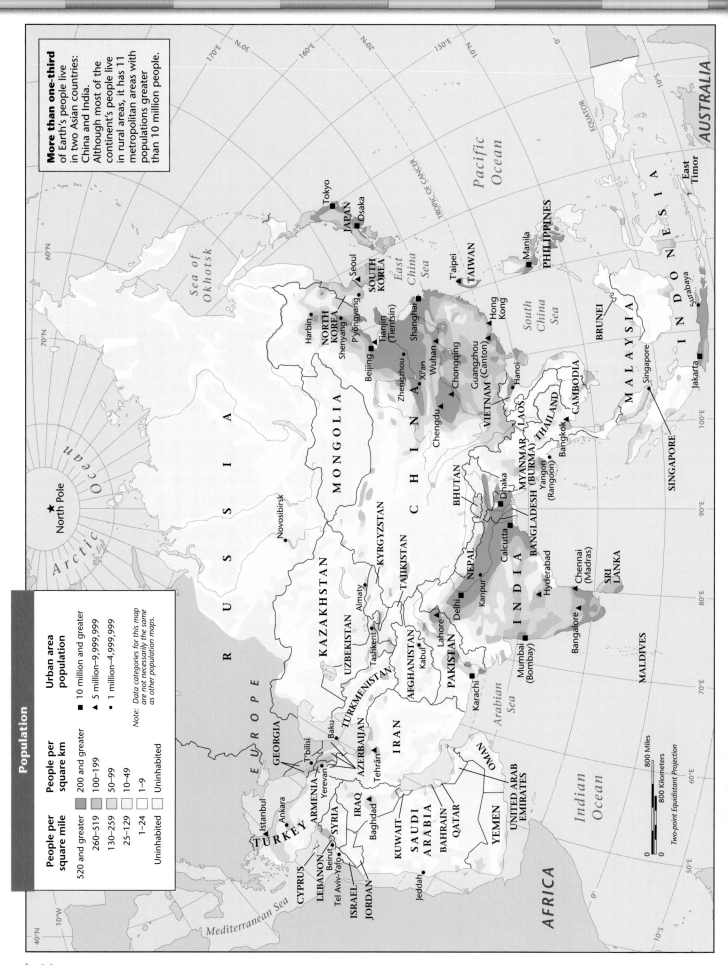

Population

People per square mile
- 520 and greater
- 260–519
- 130–259
- 25–129
- 1–24
- Uninhabited

People per square km
- 200 and greater
- 100–199
- 50–99
- 10–49
- 1–9
- Uninhabited

Urban area population
- ■ 10 million and greater
- ▲ 5 million–9,999,999
- • 1 million–4,999,999

Note: Data categories for this map are not necessarily the same as other population maps.

More than one-third of Earth's people live in two Asian countries: China and India. Although most of the continent's people live in rural areas, it has 11 metropolitan areas with populations greater than 10 million people.

Asia

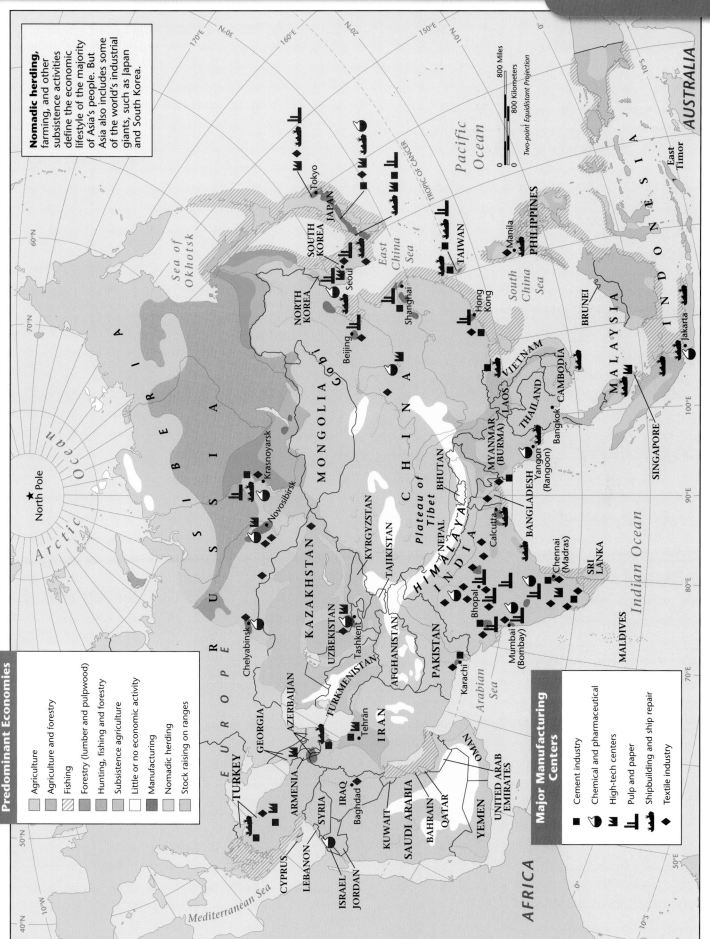

Nomadic herding, farming, and other subsistence activities define the economic lifestyle of the majority of Asia's people. But Asia also includes some of the world's industrial giants, such as Japan and South Korea.

Predominant Economies

- Agriculture
- Agriculture and forestry
- Fishing
- Forestry (lumber and pulpwood)
- Hunting, fishing and forestry
- Subsistence agriculture
- Little or no economic activity
- Manufacturing
- Nomadic herding
- Stock raising on ranges

Major Manufacturing Centers

- ■ Cement industry
- ◑ Chemical and pharmaceutical
- ⊥ High-tech centers
- ⊥ Pulp and paper
- ⛴ Shipbuilding and ship repair
- ◆ Textile industry

800 Miles
800 Kilometers
Two-point Equidistant Projection

North Pole ★

Arctic Ocean

Pacific Ocean

Sea of Okhotsk

East China Sea

South China Sea

Indian Ocean

Arabian Sea

Mediterranean Sea

S I B E R I A

R U S S I A

E U R O P E

AFRICA

AUSTRALIA

I N D O N E S I A

MONGOLIA
Gobi
C H I N A
Plateau of Tibet
KAZAKHSTAN
UZBEKISTAN
TURKMENISTAN
KYRGYZSTAN
TAJIKISTAN
AFGHANISTAN
PAKISTAN
I N D I A
HIMALAYA
NEPAL
BHUTAN
BANGLADESH
MYANMAR (BURMA)
LAOS
THAILAND
CAMBODIA
VIETNAM
MALAYSIA
BRUNEI
SINGAPORE
PHILIPPINES
TAIWAN
JAPAN
SOUTH KOREA
NORTH KOREA
SRI LANKA
MALDIVES
East Timor

TURKEY
GEORGIA
ARMENIA
AZERBAIJAN
SYRIA
IRAQ
IRAN
CYPRUS
LEBANON
ISRAEL
JORDAN
KUWAIT
SAUDI ARABIA
BAHRAIN
QATAR
UNITED ARAB EMIRATES
OMAN
YEMEN

Tokyo
Seoul
Beijing
Shanghai
Hong Kong
Manila
Jakarta
Bangkok
Yangon (Rangoon)
Calcutta
Chennai (Madras)
Bhopal
Mumbai (Bombay)
Karachi
Tehrān
Baghdad
Tashkent
Krasnoyarsk
Novosibirsk
Chelyabinsk

World Heritage Sites

In 1972, the United Nations Educational, Scientific and Cultural Organization (UNESCO) adopted a treaty, signed by more than 150 countries, dedicated to the preservation of cultural and natural sites of "outstanding universal value" that are "testimonies to an enduring past." These sites are designated as World Heritage Sites because they are part of the universal heritage of people everywhere.

Since much of human history is rooted in Asia, the continent is home to many of the best known World Heritage Sites, including the Taj Mahal, in India, and the temple complex at Angkor in Cambodia. Some of the world's endangered and vulnerable animals, such as the tiger and the komodo dragon, are native to Asia, and their habitats also are preserved as World Heritage Sites.

In December 1999, the World Heritage List included 630 sites in 118 countries. Among these, 148 sites are in Asian countries, including four in the part of Russia that lies east of the Ural Mountains.

▲ **Cappadocia,** a centuries-old complex of caves, dwellings, and Christian churches carved into ancient volcanic rock in central Turkey, is an example of a mixed World Heritage Site.

World Heritage Sites

These sites are chosen for their universal value. Cultural sites reflect unusual human ingenuity or represent the traditions or values of an established culture or civilization. Natural sites are often examples of important geological processes or the habitats of endangered species. A few sites are selected because they combine cultural and natural characteristics.

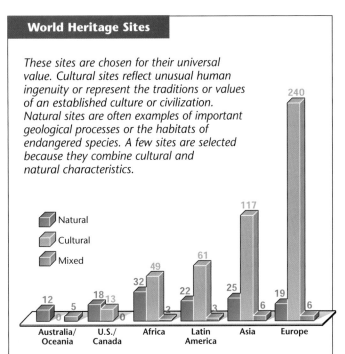

Legend:
- Natural
- Cultural
- Mixed

	Natural	Cultural	Mixed
Australia/Oceania	12	5	0
U.S./Canada	18	13	0
Africa	32	49	2
Latin America	22	61	3
Asia	25	117	6
Europe	19	240	6

▲ **Angkor Wat,** which is part of a cultural site in Cambodia, honors the Hindu god Vishnu. Nearby temples at Angkor Thom are Buddhist.

Web Link for information on World Heritage Sites: www.unesco.org/whc/

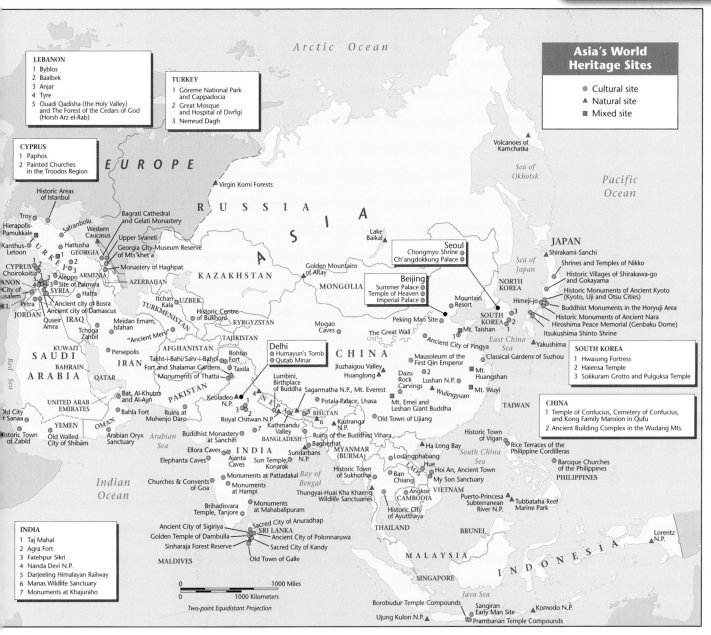

Arctic Ocean

Asia's World Heritage Sites

● Cultural site
▲ Natural site
■ Mixed site

LEBANON
1 Byblos
2 Baalbek
3 Anjar
4 Tyre
5 Ouadi Qadisha (the Holy Valley) and The Forest of the Cedars of God (Horsh Arz el-Rab)

TURKEY
1 Göreme National Park and Cappadocia
2 Great Mosque and Hospital of Divrĭgi
3 Nemrud Dagh

CYPRUS
1 Paphos
2 Painted Churches in the Troodos Region

EUROPE

Virgin Komi Forests

RUSSIA

ASIA

Lake Baikal

Volcanoes of Kamchatka

Sea of Okhotsk

Pacific Ocean

Sea of Japan

Golden Mountains of Altay

KAZAKHSTAN

MONGOLIA

JAPAN
Shirakami-Sanchi
Shrines and Temples of Nikko
Historic Villages of Shirakawa-go and Gokayama
Historic Monuments of Ancient Kyoto (Kyoto, Uji and Otsu Cities)
Buddhist Monuments in the Horyuji Area
Historic Monuments of Ancient Nara
Hiroshima Peace Memorial (Genbaku Dome)
Itsukushima Shinto Shrine

Historic Areas of Istanbul
Troy
Hierapolis-Pamukkale
Safranbolu
Western Caucasus
Bagrati Cathedral and Gelati Monastery
Upper Svaneti
Georgia City-Museum Reserve of Mts'khet'a
Monastery of Haghpat
Xanthus-Letoon
Hattusha
TURKEY
GEORGIA
ARMENIA
AZERBAIJAN
Itchan Kala
UZBEK.
Historic Centre of Bukhoro
KYRGYZSTAN
TAJIKISTAN

Seoul
Chongmyo Shrine
Ch'angdokkung Palace

Beijing
Summer Palace
Temple of Heaven
Imperial Palace

Mountain Resort

Peking Man Site

Himeji-jo

NORTH KOREA

SOUTH KOREA

Mogao Caves

The Great Wall

Mt. Taishan

Ancient City of Pingya

Yakushima

East China Sea

SOUTH KOREA
1 Hwasong Fortress
2 Haiensa Temple
3 Sokkuram Grotto and Pulguksa Temple

CYPRUS
Choirokoitia
Aleppo
Site of Palmyra
SYRIA
Ancient city of Bosra
Ancient city of Damascus
Quseir Amra
Petra
JORDAN
IRAQ
Tchoga Zanbil
Hatra
Meidan Emam, Isfahan
"Ancient Merv"
AFGHANISTAN
Persepolis
IRAN
KUWAIT
SAUDI ARABIA
BAHRAIN
QATAR
Takht-i-Bahi/Sahr-i-Bahol
Fort and Shalamar Gardens
Monuments of Thatta
PAKISTAN

Delhi
Humayun's Tomb
Qutab Minar

CHINA

Rohtas Fort
Taxila

Jiuzhaigou Valley
Huanglong

Mausoleum of the First Qin Emperor

Dazu Rock Carvings

Lushan N.P.

Mt. Huangshan

Mt. Wuyi

Classical Gardens of Suzhou

Wulingyuan

Mt. Emei and Leshan Giant Buddha

TAIWAN

CHINA
1 Temple of Confucius, Cemetery of Confucius, and Kong Family Mansion in Qufu
2 Ancient Building Complex in the Wudang Mts.

UNITED ARAB EMIRATES
Bat, Al-Khutm and Al-Ayn
Bahla Fort
OMAN
Arabian Oryx Sanctuary

Keoladeo N.P.

Lumbini, Birthplace of Buddha

Sagarmatha N.P., Mt. Everest

Potala Palace, Lhasa

Old Town of Lijiang

Historic Town of Vigan

Rice Terraces of the Philippine Cordilleras

Ruins at Mohenjo Daro
Buddhist Monastery at Sanchih
Royal Chitwan N.P.
Kathmandu Valley
BHUTAN
Kaziranga N.P.
Ruins of the Buddhist Vihara
Bagerhat

INDIA
1 Taj Mahal
2 Agra Fort
3 Fatehpur Sikri
4 Nanda Devi N.P.
5 Darjeeling Himalayan Railway
6 Manas Wildlife Sanctuary
7 Monuments at Khajuraho

Ellora Caves
Ajanta Caves
INDIA
Elephanta Caves
Churches & Convents of Goa
Monuments at Pattadakal
Monuments at Hampi
Brihadisvara Temple, Tanjore
Monuments at Mahabalipuram
Sun Temple, Konarak
BANGLADESH
Sundarbans N.P.
MYANMAR (BURMA)
Historic Town of Sukhothai
Thungyai-Huai Kha Khaeng Wildlife Sanctuaries
Ban Chiang
Louangphabang
Hue
Hoi An, Ancient Town
My Son Sanctuary
Ha Long Bay
VIETNAM
LAOS
Angkor
CAMBODIA
Historic City of Ayutthaya
THAILAND

Puerto-Princesa Subterranean River N.P.
Tubbataha Reef Marine Park
Baroque Churches of the Philippines
PHILIPPINES

BRUNEI

Lorentz N.P.

Ancient City of Sigiriya
Golden Temple of Dambulla
Sinharaja Forest Reserve
MALDIVES
Sacred City of Anuradhap
SRI LANKA
Ancient City of Polonnaruwa
Sacred City of Kandy
Old Town of Galle

MALAYSIA

INDONESIA

SINGAPORE

Java Sea

Borobudur Temple Compounds
Ujung Kulon N.P.
Sangiran Early Man Site
Prambanan Temple Compounds
Komodo N.P.

0 ___ 1000 Miles
0 ___ 1000 Kilometers
Two-point Equidistant Projection

South China Sea

Bay of Bengal

Arabian Sea

Indian Ocean

▲ **The Taj Mahal,** a cultural site in India, is an outstanding example of Muslim architecture in a country most often associated with Hinduism.

▲ **Tubbataha Reef Marine Park,** a natural site in the Philippines, is habitat for birds, sea turtles, and fish.

Australia & Oceania

Smallest of Earth's great landmasses, Australia is the only continent that is both a continent and a country. It is part of the greater region of Oceania, which includes New Zealand, the eastern part of New Guinea, and hundreds of smaller islands scattered across the Pacific Ocean. Although Hawaii is politically part of the United States, geographically and culturally it is part of Oceania.

Facts & Figures

▶ **Land area:** 3,284,000 sq mi (8,505,000 sq km)

▶ **Population:** 30,663,000

▶ **Highest point:** Mount Wilhelm, Papua New Guinea: 14,793 ft (4,509 m)

▶ **Lowest point:** Lake Eyre, Australia: 52 ft (16 m) below sea level

▶ **Longest river:** Murray-Darling, Australia: 2,911 mi (4,685 km)

▶ **Largest lake:** Lake Eyre, Australia: 3,430 sq mi (8,884 sq km)

▶ **Number of independent countries:** 14

▶ **Largest country:** Australia: 2,968,000 sq mi (7,687,000 sq km)

▶ **Smallest country:** Nauru: 8 sq mi (21 sq km)

▶ **Most populous country:** Australia: Pop. 19,195,000

▶ **Least populous country:** Nauru: Pop. 12,000

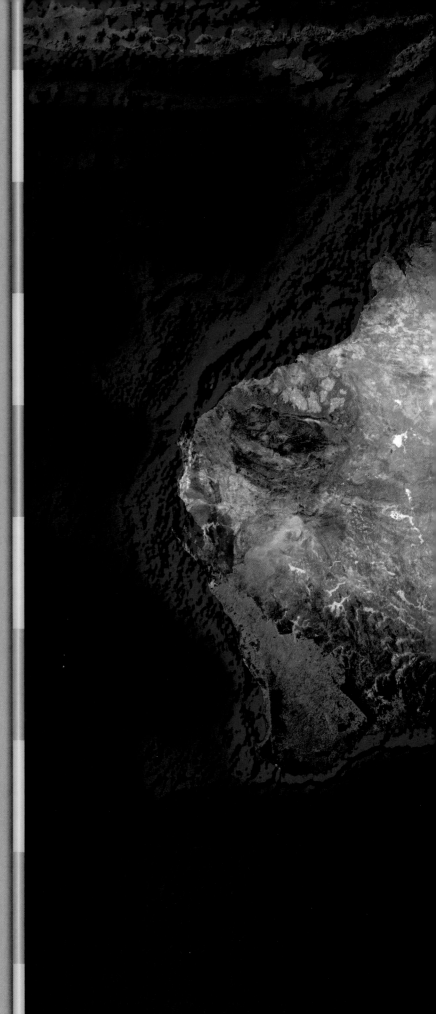

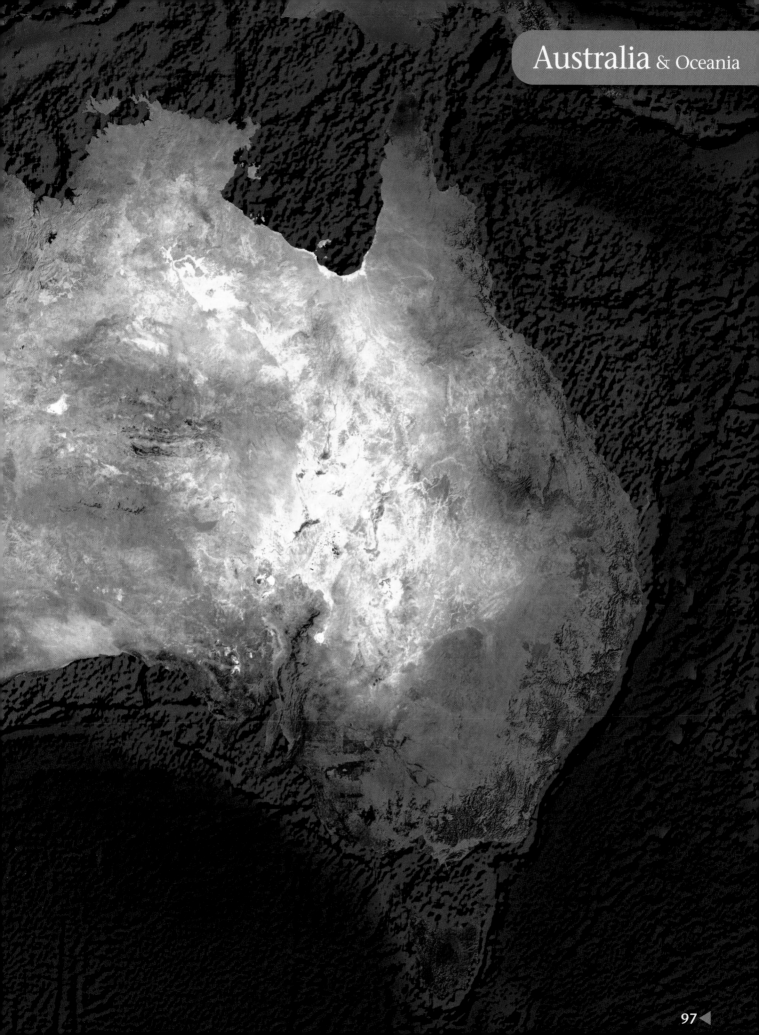

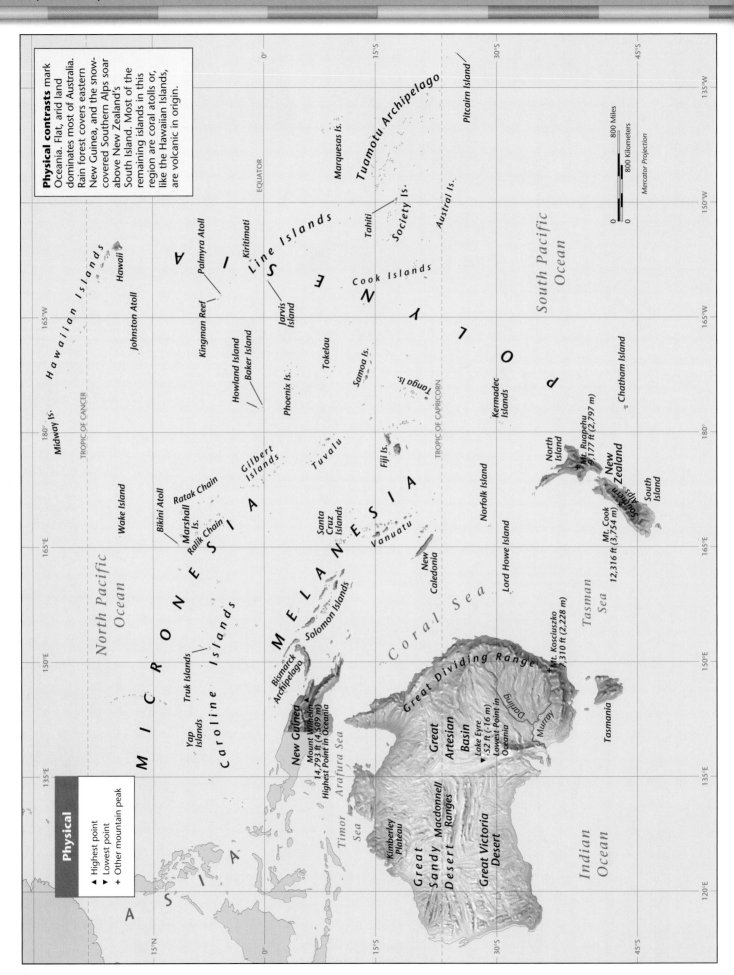

Physical contrasts mark Oceania. Flat, arid land dominates most of Australia. Rain forest covers eastern New Guinea, and the snow-covered Southern Alps soar above New Zealand's South Island. Most of the remaining islands in this region are coral atolls or, like the Hawaiian Islands, are volcanic in origin.

EQUATOR

Physical

▲ Highest point
▼ Lowest point
+ Other mountain peak

800 Miles
800 Kilometers

Mercator Projection

TROPIC OF CANCER

TROPIC OF CAPRICORN

North Pacific Ocean

South Pacific Ocean

Indian Ocean

Hawaiian Islands

Midway Is.

Johnston Atoll

Palmyra Atoll

Kingman Reef

Kiritimati

Line Islands

Howland Island

Baker Island

Jarvis Island

Phoenix Is.

Tokelau

Samoa Is.

Tonga Is.

Cook Islands

Tahiti

Society Is.

Austral Is.

Marquesas Is.

Tuamotu Archipelago

Pitcairn Island

MICRONESIA

POLYNESIA

MELANESIA

Wake Island

Bikini Atoll

Ratak Chain

Marshall Is.

Ralik Chain

Gilbert Islands

Tuvalu

Fiji Is.

Santa Cruz Islands

Vanuatu

New Caledonia

Norfolk Island

Lord Howe Island

Kermadec Islands

Chatham Island

Yap Islands

Truk Islands

Caroline Islands

Solomon Islands

Bismarck Archipelago

New Guinea

▲ Mount Wilhelm
14,793 ft (4,509 m)
Highest Point in Oceania

Timor Sea

Arafura Sea

Coral Sea

Tasman Sea

Great Dividing Range

+ Mt. Kosciuszko
7,310 ft (2,228 m)

Darling

Murray

▼ Lake Eyre
-52 ft (-16 m)
Lowest Point in Oceania

Great Artesian Basin

Macdonnell Ranges

Great Sandy Desert

Great Victoria Desert

Kimberley Plateau

Tasmania

North Island

New Zealand

▲ Mt. Ruapehu
9,177 ft (2,797 m)

Southern Alps

Mt. Cook
12,316 ft (3,754 m)

South Island

ASIA

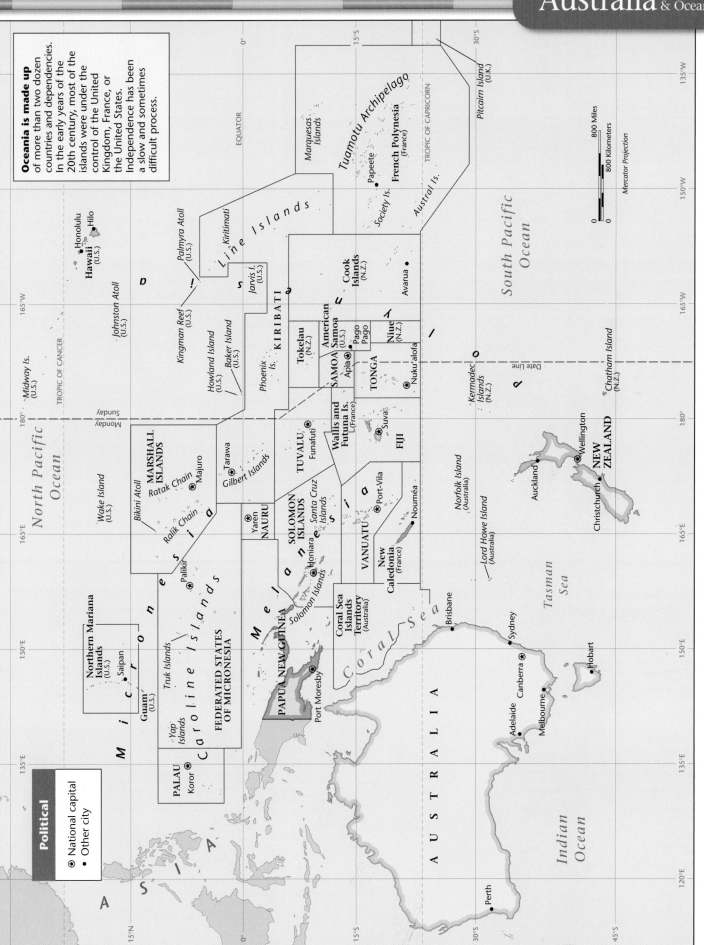

Oceania is made up of more than two dozen countries and dependencies. In the early years of the 20th century, most of the islands were under the control of the United Kingdom, France, or the United States. Independence has been a slow and sometimes difficult process.

Political

⊕ National capital
• Other city

EQUATOR

TROPIC OF CANCER

TROPIC OF CAPRICORN

Date Line

800 Miles

800 Kilometers

Mercator Projection

North Pacific Ocean

South Pacific Ocean

Indian Ocean

Tasman Sea

Coral Sea

Micronesia

Melanesia

Polynesia

Midway Is. (U.S.)

Honolulu
Hilo
Hawaii (U.S.)

Johnston Atoll (U.S.)

Wake Island (U.S.)

Palmyra Atoll (U.S.)

Kingman Reef (U.S.)

Line Islands

Kiritimati

Jarvis I. (U.S.)

Howland Island (U.S.)
Baker Island (U.S.)

Phoenix Is.

KIRIBATI

Marquesas Islands

Tuamotu Archipelago

Papeete
French Polynesia (France)

Society Is.
Austral Is.

Pitcairn Island (U.K.)

Cook Islands (N.Z.)
Avarua

Tokelau (N.Z.)

American Samoa (U.S.)
Pago Pago

SAMOA
Apia

Niue (N.Z.)

TONGA
Nuku'alofa

Kermadec Islands (N.Z.)

Chatham Island (N.Z.)

Wake Island (U.S.)

Bikini Atoll
Ratak Chain
Ralik Chain

MARSHALL ISLANDS

Majuro

Tarawa
Gilbert Islands

TUVALU
Funafuti

Wallis and Futuna Is. (France)

Suva
FIJI

NEW ZEALAND
Wellington
Auckland
Christchurch

Norfolk Island (Australia)

Lord Howe Island (Australia)

Northern Mariana Islands (U.S.)
Saipan

Guam (U.S.)

Yap Islands
Truk Islands

Caroline Islands

FEDERATED STATES OF MICRONESIA
Palikir

PALAU
Koror

Yaren
NAURU

SOLOMON ISLANDS
Honiara
Santa Cruz Islands

Solomon Islands

VANUATU
Port-Vila

New Caledonia (France)
Nouméa

Coral Sea Islands Territory (Australia)

PAPUA NEW GUINEA
Port Moresby

ASIA

AUSTRALIA

Brisbane
Sydney
Canberra
Melbourne
Adelaide
Hobart
Perth

Monday
Sunday

99

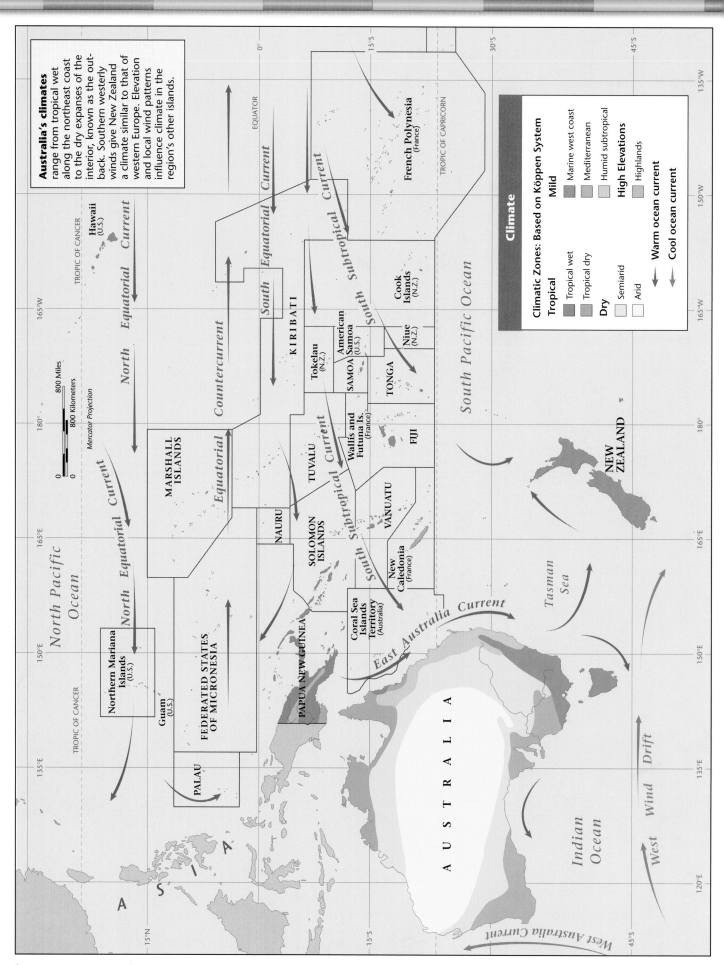

Australia's climates range from tropical wet along the northeast coast to the dry expanses of the interior, known as the outback. Southern westerly winds give New Zealand a climate similar to that of western Europe. Elevation and local wind patterns influence climate in the region's other islands.

Climate

Climatic Zones: Based on Köppen System

Tropical
- Tropical wet
- Tropical dry

Dry
- Semiarid
- Arid

Mild
- Marine west coast

Mediterranean
- Mediterranean
- Humid subtropical

High Elevations
- Highlands

→ Warm ocean current
→ Cool ocean current

North Pacific Ocean

North Equatorial Current

North Equatorial Current

North Equatorial Current

Equatorial Countercurrent

South Equatorial Current

South Equatorial Current

South Subtropical Current

South Subtropical Current

South Subtropical Current

South Pacific Ocean

East Australia Current

Tasman Sea

West Wind Drift

Indian Ocean

West Australia Current

Hawaii (U.S.)

TROPIC OF CANCER

EQUATOR

TROPIC OF CAPRICORN

Northern Mariana Islands (U.S.)

Guam (U.S.)

PALAU

FEDERATED STATES OF MICRONESIA

MARSHALL ISLANDS

NAURU

SOLOMON ISLANDS

PAPUA NEW GUINEA

KIRIBATI

TUVALU

Tokelau (N.Z.)

American Samoa (U.S.)

SAMOA

Wallis and Futuna Is. (France)

FIJI

VANUATU

New Caledonia (France)

Coral Sea Islands Territory (Australia)

TONGA

Niue (N.Z.)

Cook Islands (N.Z.)

French Polynesia (France)

NEW ZEALAND

A U S T R A L I A

A S I A

800 Miles
800 Kilometers
Mercator Projection

15°N

TROPIC OF CANCER

15°S

45°S

0°

15°S

30°S

45°S

120°E

135°E

150°E

165°E

180°

165°W

150°W

135°W

Australia & Oceania

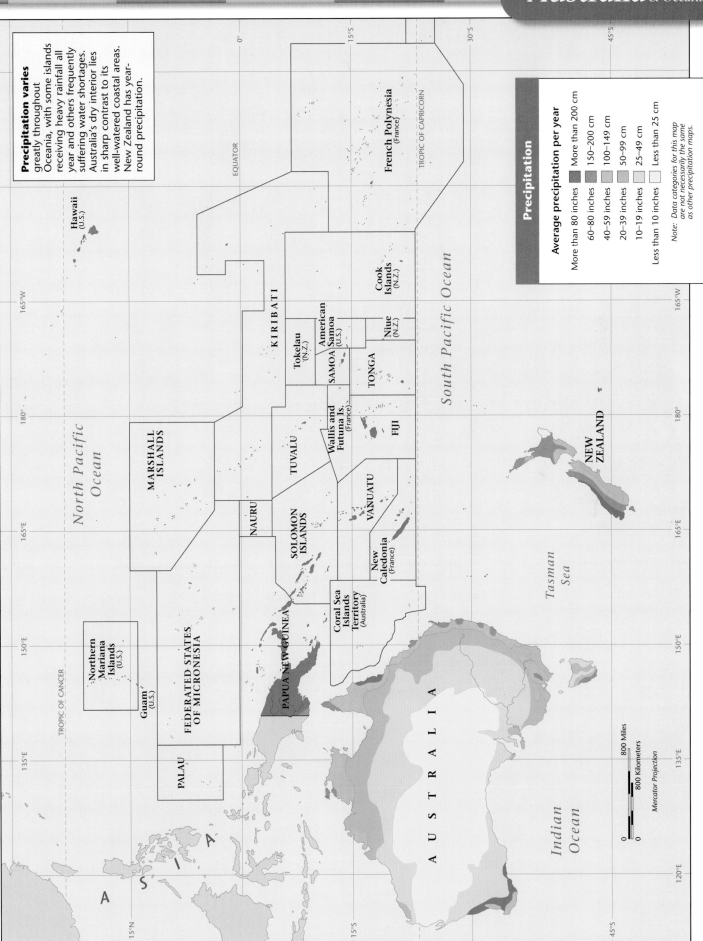

Precipitation varies greatly throughout Oceania, with some islands receiving heavy rainfall all year and others frequently suffering water shortages. Australia's dry interior lies in sharp contrast to its well-watered coastal areas. New Zealand has year-round precipitation.

Precipitation

Average precipitation per year

More than 80 inches	More than 200 cm
60–80 inches	150–200 cm
40–59 inches	100–149 cm
20–39 inches	50–99 cm
10–19 inches	25–49 cm
Less than 10 inches	Less than 25 cm

Note: Data categories for this map are not necessarily the same as other precipitation maps.

Hawaii (U.S.)

North Pacific Ocean

KIRIBATI

French Polynesia (France)

EQUATOR

TROPIC OF CAPRICORN

Cook Islands (N.Z.)

Tokelau (N.Z.)

American Samoa (U.S.)

SAMOA

Niue (N.Z.)

TONGA

Wallis and Futuna Is. (France)

FIJI

South Pacific Ocean

MARSHALL ISLANDS

TUVALU

NAURU

SOLOMON ISLANDS

VANUATU

New Caledonia (France)

NEW ZEALAND

Tasman Sea

Northern Mariana Islands (U.S.)

Guam (U.S.)

FEDERATED STATES OF MICRONESIA

PALAU

PAPUA NEW GUINEA

Coral Sea Islands Territory (Australia)

AUSTRALIA

Indian Ocean

TROPIC OF CANCER

A S I A

800 Miles

800 Kilometers

Mercator Projection

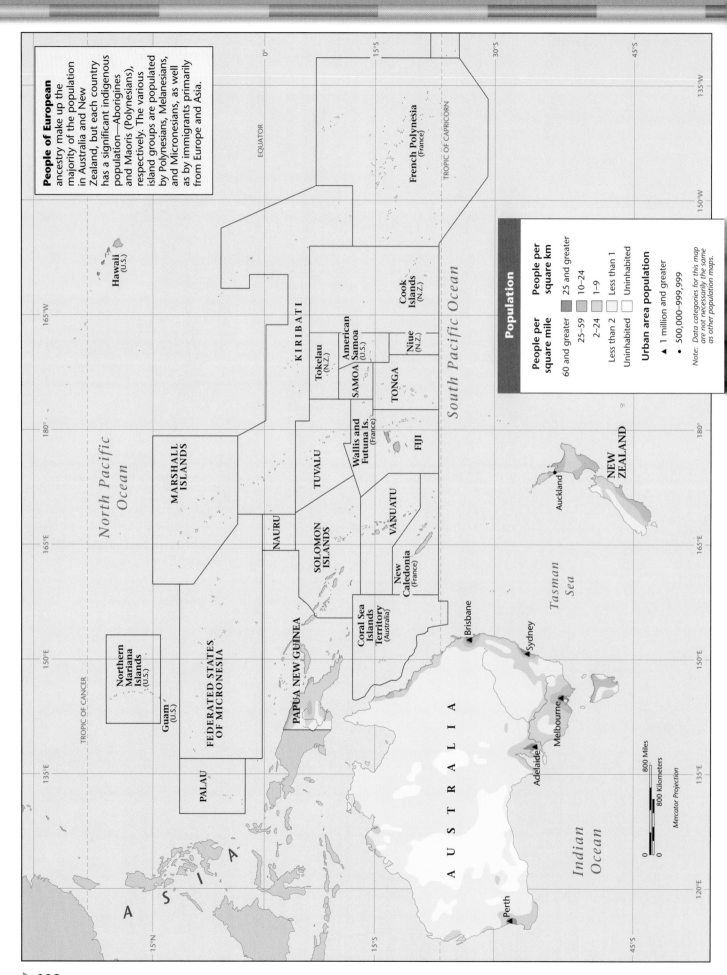

People of European ancestry make up the majority of the population in Australia and New Zealand, but each country has a significant indigenous population—Aborigines and Maoris (Polynesians), respectively. The various island groups are populated by Polynesians, Melanesians, and Micronesians, as well as by immigrants primarily from Europe and Asia.

Population

People per square mile	People per square km
60 and greater	25 and greater
25–59	10–24
2–24	1–9
Less than 2	Less than 1
Uninhabited	Uninhabited

Urban area population

▲ 1 million and greater

• 500,000–999,999

Note: Data categories for this map are not necessarily the same as other population maps.

North Pacific Ocean

South Pacific Ocean

Indian Ocean

Tasman Sea

A S I A

AUSTRALIA

NEW ZEALAND

Hawaii (U.S.)

KIRIBATI

MARSHALL ISLANDS

Tokelau (N.Z.)

American Samoa (U.S.)

SAMOA

Niue (N.Z.)

Cook Islands (N.Z.)

TONGA

French Polynesia (France)

TUVALU

Wallis and Futuna Is. (France)

FIJI

NAURU

VANUATU

New Caledonia (France)

SOLOMON ISLANDS

Coral Sea Islands Territory (Australia)

Northern Mariana Islands (U.S.)

Guam (U.S.)

FEDERATED STATES OF MICRONESIA

PALAU

PAPUA NEW GUINEA

Auckland

Brisbane

Sydney

Melbourne

Adelaide

Perth

EQUATOR

TROPIC OF CANCER

TROPIC OF CAPRICORN

800 Miles

800 Kilometers

Mercator Projection

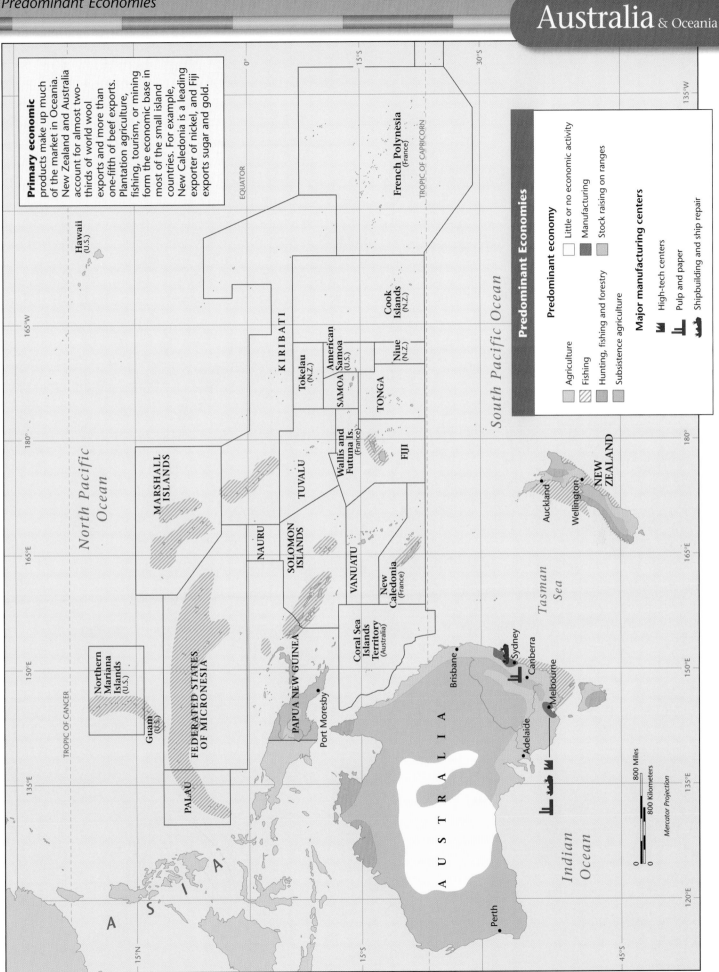

Primary economic products make up much of the market in Oceania. New Zealand and Australia account for almost two-thirds of world wool exports and more than one-fifth of beef exports. Plantation agriculture, fishing, tourism, or mining form the economic base in most of the small island countries. For example, New Caledonia is a leading exporter of nickel, and Fiji exports sugar and gold.

Predominant Economies

Predominant economy

- Agriculture
- Fishing
- Hunting, fishing and forestry
- Subsistence agriculture
- Little or no economic activity
- Manufacturing
- Stock raising on ranges

Major manufacturing centers

- High-tech centers
- Pulp and paper
- Shipbuilding and ship repair

North Pacific Ocean

South Pacific Ocean

Indian Ocean

Tasman Sea

Hawaii (U.S.)

French Polynesia (France)

Cook Islands (N.Z.)

Niue (N.Z.)

American Samoa (U.S.)

SAMOA

Tokelau (N.Z.)

KIRIBATI

TONGA

Wallis and Futuna Is. (France)

FIJI

TUVALU

MARSHALL ISLANDS

NAURU

SOLOMON ISLANDS

VANUATU

New Caledonia (France)

NEW ZEALAND

Auckland

Wellington

Northern Mariana Islands (U.S.)

Guam (U.S.)

FEDERATED STATES OF MICRONESIA

PALAU

PAPUA NEW GUINEA

Port Moresby

Coral Sea Islands Territory (Australia)

A U S T R A L I A

Brisbane

Sydney

Canberra

Melbourne

Adelaide

Perth

ASIA

EQUATOR

TROPIC OF CAPRICORN

TROPIC OF CANCER

0 800 Miles
0 800 Kilometers

Mercator Projection

103

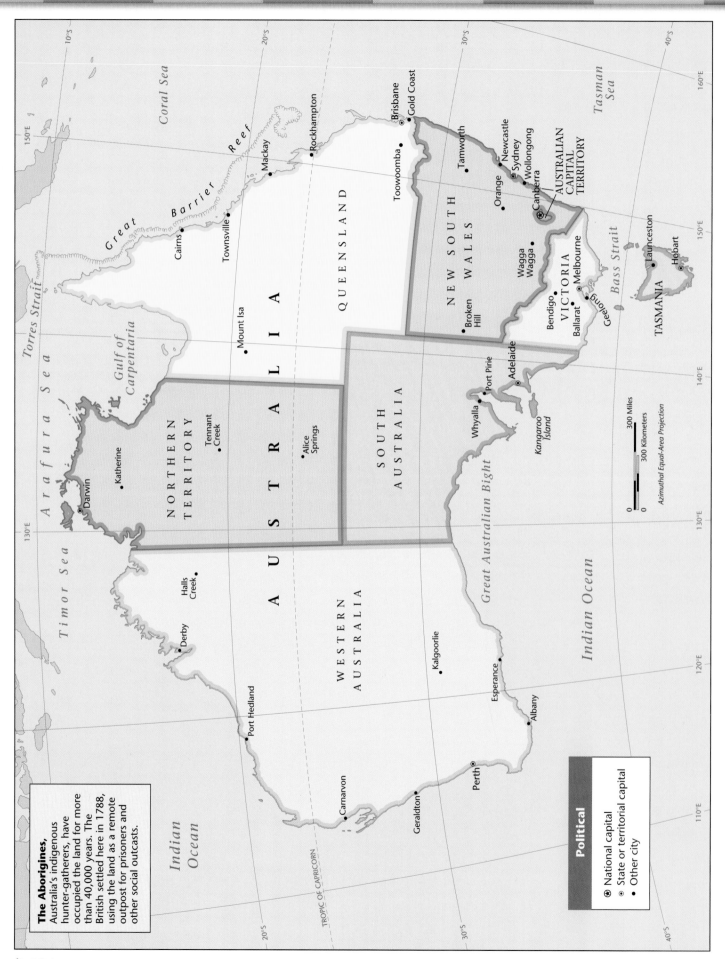

The Aborigines,
Australia's indigenous
hunter-gatherers, have
occupied the land for more
than 40,000 years. The
British settled here in 1788,
using the land as a remote
outpost for prisoners and
other social outcasts.

Political

⊛ National capital
⊙ State or territorial capital
• Other city

Coral Sea

Great Barrier Reef

Torres Strait

Arafura Sea

Gulf of Carpentaria

Timor Sea

Indian Ocean

Tasman Sea

Bass Strait

Great Australian Bight

Indian Ocean

TROPIC OF CAPRICORN

Rockhampton
Mackay
Cairns
Townsville
Brisbane
Gold Coast
Toowoomba
Tamworth
Newcastle
Orange
Sydney
Wollongong
Canberra
AUSTRALIAN
CAPITAL
TERRITORY
Mount Isa

QUEENSLAND

NEW SOUTH WALES

Wagga Wagga
Broken Hill
Bendigo
Ballarat
VICTORIA
Melbourne
Geelong

Launceston
Hobart
TASMANIA

Katherine
Tennant Creek
Alice Springs
NORTHERN TERRITORY

AUSTRALIA

Darwin

Port Pirie
Adelaide
Whyalla
Kangaroo Island

SOUTH AUSTRALIA

Halls Creek
Derby

WESTERN AUSTRALIA

Kalgoorlie

Esperance
Albany

Port Hedland

Carnarvon
Geraldton
Perth

300 Miles
300 Kilometers
Azimuthal Equal-Area Projection

Political

⊛ National capital
• Other city

35°S

170°E   175°E

Kaitaia   Kerikeri

Whangarei

Great Barrier
Island

Tasman
Sea

Takapuna
Waitemata   Manukau
Auckland

North
Island

Hamilton   Mount Maùnganui
Tauranga
Whakatane
Rotorua

Taupo   Gisborne

New Plymouth

Raetihi

Napier
Hastings

Wanganui

Feilding
Palmerston North
Porirua   Levin
Masterton
Nelson   Upper Hutt
Picton   Lower Hutt
Blenheim   Wellington

Cook Strait

Westport

Molesworth

Greymouth   Kaikoura
Hokitika   Parnassus
Arthur's
Pass

Pacific
Ocean

Fox Glacier   Christchurch   Lyttelton
Franz Josef
Glacier   Ashburton

Haast

Timaru   Canterbury
Bight

Milford
Sound   Wanaka

Oamaru

South
Island

Dunedin
Gore
Balclutha
Invercargill

Foveaux Strait

Stewart
Island

0   150 Miles
0   150 Kilometers
Azimuthal Equal-Area Projection

35°S

40°S   40°S

45°S

165°E   170°E   175°E

Two large islands
and several smaller ones
make up New Zealand.
The country averages 37
people per square mile
(14 people per sq km), but
most of the population
lives in urban areas. The
economy relies on primary
activities, such as raising
sheep, dairying, and
forestry. Wellington,
Christchurch, and other
place-names reflect a
strong British influence.

Time Zones & the Date Line

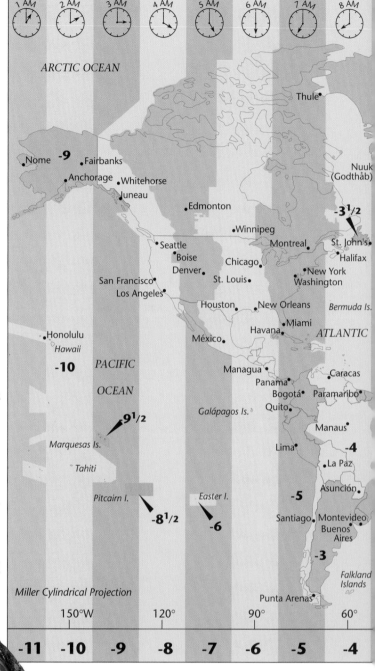

The *Fiji Times,* a newspaper published in Suva, capital of the Fiji Islands, carries the message "The First Newspaper Published in the World Today" on the front page of each edition. How can this newspaper from a small island country make such a claim? Fiji and most of the other islands that make up Oceania, including Australia and New Zealand, lie west of the date line, an invisible boundary designated to mark the beginning of each new day. The date line is just part of the system we have adopted to keep track of the passage of days.

For most of human history, people determined time by observing the position of the sun in the sky. Slight differences in time did not matter until, in the mid-19th century, the spread of railroads and telegraph lines changed forever the importance of time. High-speed transportation and communications required schedules, and schedules required that everyone agree on the time.

In 1884, an international conference, convened in Washington, D.C., established an international system of 24 time zones based on the fact that Earth turns from west to east 15 degrees of longitude every hour. Each time zone has a central meridian and is 15 degrees wide, 7$\frac{1}{2}$ degrees to either side of the named central meridian.

▶ **The prime meridian's** path is lit up by light bulbs strung across Greenwich Park just north of the Royal Observatory, in England. The photographer used a special lens called a fish-eye to make the park resemble a globe. Of course, on the real Earth, meridians and parallels (lines of longitude and latitude) are imaginary and cannot be seen.

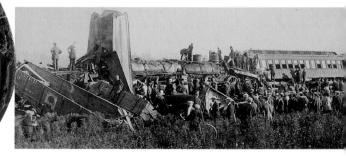

▲ **A system of standard time** put trains on schedules, which helped reduce the chance of collisions and the loss of lives and property caused by them.

Web Link for information on time zones: http://tycho.usno.navy.mil/tzones.html

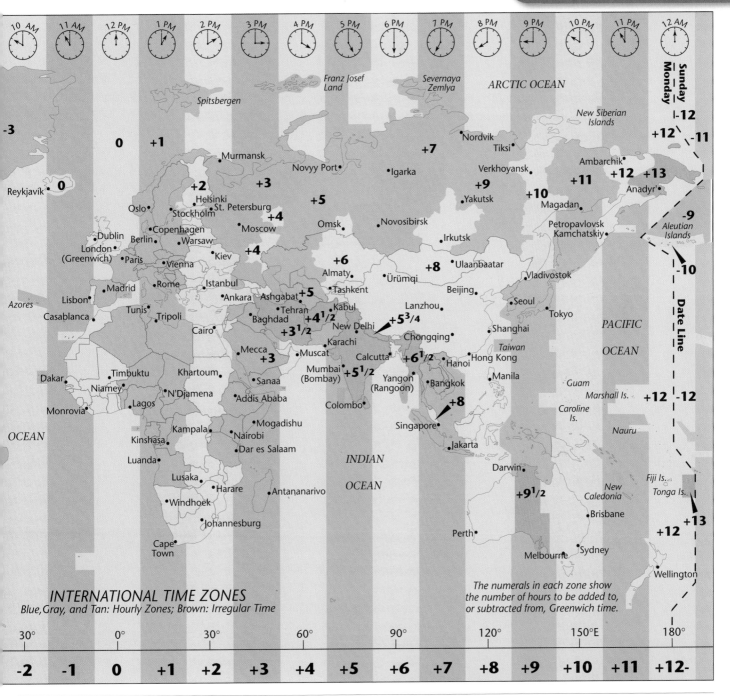

INTERNATIONAL TIME ZONES
Blue, Gray, and Tan: Hourly Zones; Brown: Irregular Time

The numerals in each zone show the number of hours to be added to, or subtracted from, Greenwich time.

30°		0°		30°		60°		90°		120°		150°E		180°	
-2	-1	0	+1	+2	+3	+4	+5	+6	+7	+8	+9	+10	+11	+12-	

Date Line

The date line (180°) is directly opposite the prime meridian (0°). As Earth rotates, each new day officially begins as the 180° line passes 12 midnight. If you travel west across the date line, you advance one day; if you travel east across the date line, you fall back one day.

Notice on the map how the line zigs to the east as it passes through the South Pacific so that the islands of Fiji will not be split between two different days. Also notice that India is 5½ hours ahead of Greenwich time, and China has only one time zone, even though the country spans more than 60 degrees of longitude. These differences are the result of decisions made at the country level.

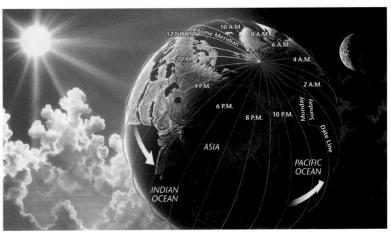

Antarctica

About 180 million years ago Antarctica broke away from the ancient supercontinent Gondwana. Slowly the continent drifted to its present location at the southernmost point on Earth. Approximately 98 percent of the continent lies under permanent ice sheets that are nearly 3 miles (5 km) thick in places. It is estimated that if all of Antarctica's ice were to melt, the global ocean level would rise more than 200 feet (60 m).

Facts & Figures

▶ **Land area:** 5,100,400 sq mi (13,209,000 sq km)

▶ **Population:** no permanent residents

▶ **Highest point:** Vinson Massif: 16,067 ft (4,897 m)

▶ **Lowest point:** Bentley Subglacial Trench: 8,366 ft (2,550 m) below sea level

▶ **Number of independent countries:** 0

▶ **Number of countries claiming land:** 7

▶ **Number of countries operating research stations:** 23

▶ **Number of research stations:** 44

▶ **Coldest temperature recorded:** minus 128.6°F (minus 89°C), July 21, 1983

▶ **Average precipitation on the polar plateau:** less than 2 in (5 cm) per year

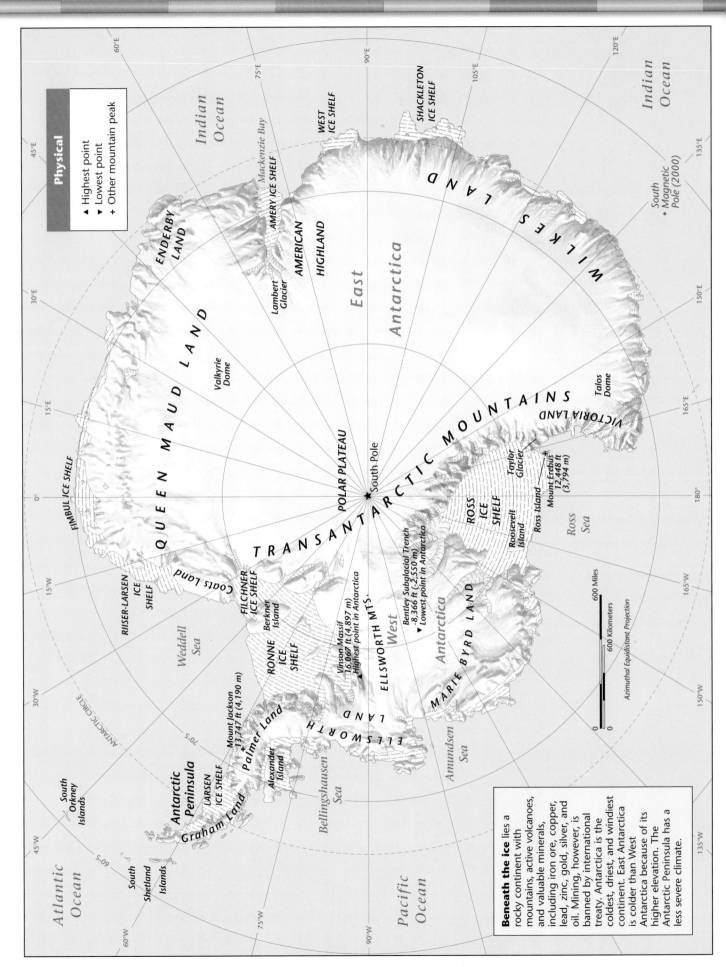

Physical
- ▲ Highest point
- ▼ Lowest point
- + Other mountain peak

Indian Ocean

SHACKLETON ICE SHELF

WEST ICE SHELF

South Magnetic Pole (2000)

Indian Ocean

Mackenzie Bay

AMERY ICE SHELF

ENDERBY LAND

AMERICAN HIGHLAND

W I L K E S   L A N D

Lambert Glacier

East Antarctica

Q U E E N   M A U D   L A N D

Valkyrie Dome

Talos Dome

VICTORIA LAND

FIMBUL ICE SHELF

T R A N S A N T A R C T I C   M O U N T A I N S

POLAR PLATEAU

★ South Pole

Taylor Glacier

+ Mount Erebus 12,448 ft (3,794 m)

RISER-LARSEN ICE SHELF

Coats Land

FILCHNER ICE SHELF

Berkner Island

ROSS ICE SHELF

Roosevelt Island

Ross Island

Ross Sea

Weddell Sea

Bentley Subglacial Trench -8,366 ft (-2,550 m) ▼ Lowest point in Antarctica

Vinson Massif 16,067 ft (4,897 m) ▲ Highest point in Antarctica

ELLSWORTH MTS.

West Antarctica

RONNE ICE SHELF

ELLSWORTH LAND

M A R I E   B Y R D   L A N D

Mount Jackson + 13,747 ft (4,190 m)

Palmer Land

Alexander Island

Amundsen Sea

Antarctic Peninsula

LARSEN ICE SHELF

Graham Land

Bellingshausen Sea

South Orkney Islands

South Shetland Islands

Atlantic Ocean

ANTARCTIC CIRCLE

Pacific Ocean

600 Miles
600 Kilometers
Azimuthal Equidistant Projection

Beneath the ice lies a rocky continent with mountains, active volcanoes, and valuable minerals, including iron ore, copper, lead, zinc, gold, silver, and oil. Mining, however, is banned by international treaty. Antarctica is the coldest, driest, and windiest continent. East Antarctica is colder than West Antarctica because of its higher elevation. The Antarctic Peninsula has a less severe climate.

Antarctica

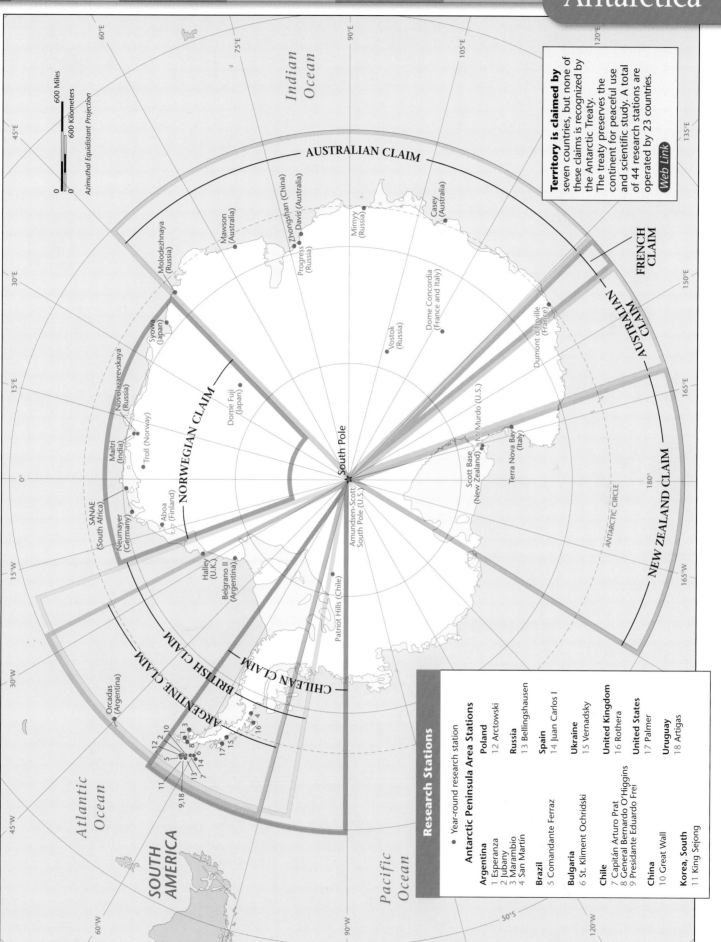

AUSTRALIAN CLAIM

Indian Ocean

600 Miles
600 Kilometers
Azimuthal Equidistant Projection

Casey (Australia)
Mirnyy (Russia)
Davis (Australia)
Zhongshan (China)
Progress (Russia)
Mawson (Australia)
Molodezhnaya (Russia)
Dome Concordia (France and Italy)
Vostok (Russia)
Dumont d'Urville (France)
FRENCH CLAIM
AUSTRALIAN CLAIM
Terra Nova Bay (Italy)
McMurdo (U.S.)
Scott Base (New Zealand)
NEW ZEALAND CLAIM
ANTARCTIC CIRCLE

Syowa (Japan)
Novolazarevskaya (Russia)
Dome Fuji (Japan)
Maitri (India)
Troll (Norway)
NORWEGIAN CLAIM
Neumayer (Germany)
SANAE (South Africa)
Aboa (Finland)
Halley (U.K.)
Belgrano II (Argentina)
Patriot Hills (Chile)
South Pole
Amundsen-Scott South Pole (U.S.)

CHILEAN CLAIM
BRITISH CLAIM
ARGENTINE CLAIM

Orcadas (Argentina)

12
11
2
10
5
8
3
1
13
7
14
6
4
16
15
17

Atlantic Ocean

SOUTH AMERICA

Pacific Ocean

Research Stations

• Year-round research station

Antarctic Peninsula Area Stations

Argentina
1 Esperanza
2 Jubany
3 Marambio
4 San Martín

Brazil
5 Comandante Ferraz

Bulgaria
6 St. Kliment Ochridski

Chile
7 Capitán Arturo Prat
8 General Bernardo O'Higgins
9 Presidante Eduardo Frei

China
10 Great Wall

Korea, South
11 King Sejong

Poland
12 Arctowski

Russia
13 Bellingshausen

Spain
14 Juan Carlos I

Ukraine
15 Vernadsky

United Kingdom
16 Rothera

United States
17 Palmer

Uruguay
18 Artigas

The flags and fact boxes below represent the world's 191 independent countries—those with national governments that are the highest legal authority over the land and people within their boundaries. The flags shown are national flags recognized by the United Nations. Area figures are for land only. They do not include surface areas for inland bodies of water. Population figures are for the year 2000 as provided by the Population Reference Bureau of the United States. The languages listed are either the ones most commonly spoken within a country or official languages of a country.

NORTH AMERICA

Antigua and Barbuda
Area: 170 sq mi (440 sq km)
Population: 68,000
Capital: St. John's
Languages: English, local dialects

Bahamas
Area: 5,382 sq mi (13,939 sq km)
Population: 310,000
Capital: Nassau
Languages: English, Creole

Barbados
Area: 166 sq mi (430 sq km)
Population: 259,000
Capital: Bridgetown
Language: English

Belize
Area: 8,867 sq mi (22,965 sq km)
Population: 254,000
Capital: Belmopan
Languages: English, Spanish, Mayan, Carib

Canada
Area: 3,849,670 sq mi (9,970,610 sq km)
Population: 30,764,000
Capital: Ottawa
Languages: English, French (both official)

Costa Rica
Area: 19,730 sq mi (51,100 sq km)
Population: 3,589,000
Capital: San José
Languages: Spanish, English

Cuba
Area: 42,804 sq mi (110,861 sq km)
Population: 11,139,000
Capital: Havana
Language: Spanish

Dominica
Area: 290 sq mi (751 sq km)
Population: 76,000
Capital: Roseau
Languages: English, French patois

Dominican Republic
Area: 18,816 sq mi (48,734 sq km)
Population: 8,443,000
Capital: Santo Domingo
Language: Spanish

El Salvador
Area: 8,124 sq mi (21,041 sq km)
Population: 6,280,000
Capital: San Salvador
Languages: Spanish, Nahuatl

Grenada
Area: 133 sq mi (344 sq km)
Population: 98,000
Capital: St. George's
Languages: English, French patois

Guatemala
Area: 42,042 sq mi (108,889 sq km)
Population: 12,670,000
Capital: Guatemala City
Languages: Spanish, Amerindian dialects

Haiti
Area: 10,714 sq mi (27,750 sq km)
Population: 6,423,000
Capital: Port-au-Prince
Languages: French, Creole

Honduras
Area: 43,277 sq mi (112,088 sq km)
Population: 6,130,000
Capital: Tegucigalpa
Languages: Spanish, Amerindian dialects

Jamaica
Area: 4,244 sq mi (10,991 sq km)
Population: 2,609,000
Capital: Kingston
Languages: English, Creole

Mexico
Area: 756,066 sq mi (1,958,201 sq km)
Population: 99,639,000
Capital: Mexico City
Languages: Spanish, regional indigenous languages

Nicaragua
Area: 50,193 sq mi (129,999 sq km)
Population: 5,074,000
Capital: Managua
Languages: Spanish, English, Amerindian dialects

Panama
Area: 29,762 sq mi (77,082 sq km)
Population: 2,857,000
Capital: Panama City
Languages: Spanish, English

St. Kitts and Nevis
Area: 101 sq mi (261 sq km)
Population: 43,000
Capital: Basseterre
Language: English

St. Lucia
Area: 238 sq mi (617 sq km)
Population: 157,000
Capital: Castries
Languages: English, French patois

St. Vincent and the Grenadines
Area: 150 sq mi (388 sq km)
Population: 112,000
Capital: Kingstown
Languages: English, French patois

Trinidad and Tobago
Area: 1,981 sq mi (5,131 sq km)
Population: 1,295,000
Capital: Port of Spain
Languages: English, Hindi, French, Spanish

United States
Area: 3,717,796 sq mi (9,629,091 sq km)
Population: 275,600,000
Capital: Washington, D.C.
Languages: English, Spanish

SOUTH AMERICA

Argentina
Area: 1,068,302 sq mi (2,766,889 sq km)
Population: 37,048,000
Capital: Buenos Aires
Languages: Spanish, English, Italian, German

Bolivia
Area: 424,164 sq mi (1,098,581 sq km)
Population: 8,281,000
Capitals: La Paz, Sucre
Languages: Spanish, Quechua, Aymara (all official)

Brazil
Area: 3,286,488 sq mi (8,511,965 sq km)
Population: 170,115,000
Capital: Brasília
Languages: Portuguese, Spanish, English

Chile
Area: 292,135 sq mi (756,626 sq km)
Population: 15,211,000
Capital: Santiago
Language: Spanish

Colombia
Area: 439,737 sq mi (1,138,914 sq km)
Population: 40,037,000
Capital: Bogotá
Language: Spanish

Ecuador
Area: 109,484 sq mi (283,561 sq km)
Population: 12,646,000
Capital: Quito
Languages: Spanish, Quechua

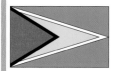

Guyana
Area: 83,000 sq mi (214,969 sq km)
Population: 698,000
Capital: Georgetown
Languages: English, Amerindian dialects

Paraguay
Area: 157,048 sq mi (406,752 sq km)
Population: 5,505,000
Capital: Asunción
Languages: Spanish, Guaraní

Peru
Area: 496,225 sq mi (1,285,217 sq km)
Population: 27,136,000
Capital: Lima
Languages: Spanish, Quechua (both official), Aymara

Suriname
Area: 63,037 sq mi (163,265 sq km)
Population: 434,000
Capital: Paramaribo
Languages: Dutch, English, Sranang Tongo (Taki-Taki), Hindustani, Javanese

Uruguay
Area: 68,037 sq mi (176,215 sq km)
Population: 3,313,000
Capital: Montevideo
Languages: Spanish, Portunol, Brazilero

Venezuela
Area: 352,144 sq mi (912,050 sq km)
Population: 24,170,000
Capital: Caracas
Language: Spanish

EUROPE

Albania
Area: 11,100 sq mi (28,748 sq km)
Population: 3,431,000
Capital: Tirana
Languages: Albanian, Greek

Andorra
Area: 175 sq mi (453 sq km)
Population: 67,000
Capital: Andorra la Vella
Languages: Catalan, French, Spanish

Austria
Area: 32,377 sq mi (83,856 sq km)
Population: 8,094,000
Capital: Vienna
Language: German

Belarus
Area: 80,154 sq mi (207,598 sq km)
Population: 10,004,000
Capital: Minsk
Languages: Belorussian, Russian

Belgium
Area: 11,783 sq mi (30,518 sq km)
Population: 10,246,000
Capital: Brussels
Languages: Flemish, French, German

Bosnia and Herzegovina
Area: 19,741 sq mi (51,129 sq km)
Population: 3,809,000
Capital: Sarajevo
Language: Serbo-Croat (Bosnian)

Bulgaria
Area: 42,823 sq mi (110,912 sq km)
Population: 8,152,000
Capital: Sofia
Language: Bulgarian

Croatia
Area: 21,829 sq mi (56,538 sq km)
Population: 4,600,000
Capital: Zagreb
Language: Serbo-Croat

Czech Republic
Area: 30,450 sq mi (78,864 sq km)
Population: 10,275,000
Capital: Prague
Languages: Czech, Slovak

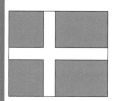

Denmark
Area: 16,638 sq mi (43,092 sq km)
Population: 5,330,000
Capital: Copenhagen
Languages: Danish, Faeroese, Greenlandic

Estonia
Area: 17,413 sq mi (45,099 sq km)
Population: 1,433,000
Capital: Tallinn
Languages: Estonian, Russian, Ukrainian

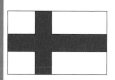

Finland
Area: 130,558 sq mi (338,145 sq km)
Population: 5,177,000
Capital: Helisinki
Languages: Finnish, Swedish (both official)

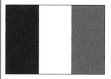

France
Area: 210,026 sq mi (543,965 sq km)
Population: 59,353,000
Capital: Paris
Language: French

Germany
Area: 137,857 sq mi
(357,046 sq km)
Population: 82,141,000
Capital: Berlin
Language: German

Greece
Area: 50,962 sq mi
(131,990 sq km)
Population: 10,596,000
Capital: Athens
Languages: Greek, English,
French

Hungary
Area: 35,919 sq mi
(93,030 sq km)
Population: 10,020,000
Capital: Budapest
Language: Hungarian

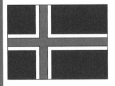

Iceland
Area: 39,769 sq mi
(103,001 sq km)
Population: 281,000
Capital: Reykjavík
Language: Icelandic

Ireland
Area: 27,137 sq mi
(70,284 sq km)
Population: 3,795,000
Capital: Dublin
Languages: English, Irish
(Gaelic)

Italy
Area: 116,324 sq mi
(301,277 sq km)
Population: 57,820,000
Capital: Rome
Languages: Italian,
German, French

Latvia
Area: 24,942 sq mi
(64,599 sq km)
Population: 2,416,000
Capital: Riga
Languages: Latvian,
Lithuanian, Russian

Liechtenstein
Area: 62 sq mi
(160 sq km)
Population: 33,000
Capital: Vaduz
Languages: German,
Alemannic dialect

Lithuania
Area: 25,174 sq mi
(65,200 sq km)
Population: 3,697,000
Capital: Vilnius
Languages: Lithuanian,
Polish, Russian

Luxembourg
Area: 998 sq mi
(2,586 sq km)
Population: 438,000
Capital: Luxembourg
Languages:
Luxembourgian, German,
French

Macedonia
Area: 9,928 sq mi
(25,713 sq km)
Population: 2,033,000
Capital: Skopje
Languages: Macedonian,
Albanian

Malta
Area: 122 sq mi
(316 sq km)
Population: 390,000
Capital: Valletta
Languages: Maltese,
English (both official)

Moldova
Area: 13,217 sq mi
(33,999 sq km)
Population: 4,276,000
Capital: Chişinău
Languages: Moldavian,
Russian

Monaco
Area: 0.6 sq mi
(1.9 sq km)
Population: 34,000
Capital: Monaco
Languages: French,
English, Italian

Netherlands
Area: 16,023 sq mi
(41,499 sq km)
Population: 15,921,000
Capital: Amsterdam
Language: Dutch

Norway
Area: 125,182 sq mi
(324,220 sq km)
Population: 4,487,000
Capital: Oslo
Language: Norwegian

Poland
Area: 120,725 sq mi
(312,677 sq km)
Population: 38,648,000
Capital: Warsaw
Language: Polish

Portugal
Area: 35,672 sq mi
(92,389 sq km)
Population: 10,013,000
Capital: Lisbon
Language: Portuguese

Romania
Area: 91,699 sq mi
(237,499 sq km)
Population: 22,432,000
Capital: Bucharest
Languages: Romanian,
Hungarian, German

Russia
Area: 6,592,692 sq mi
(17,074,993 sq km)
Population: 145,231,000
Capital: Moscow
Language: Russian

San Marino
Area: 24 sq mi
(61 sq km)
Population: 27,000
Capital: San Marino
Language: Italian

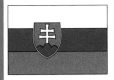

Slovakia
Area: 18,921 sq mi
(49,006 km)
Population: 5,401,000
Capital: Bratislava
Languages: Slovak,
Hungarian

Slovenia
Area: 7,819 sq mi
(20,251 sq km)
Population: 1,968,000
Capital: Ljubljana
Languages: Slovene,
Serbo-Croat

Spain
Area: 194,897 sq mi
(504,782 sq km)
Population: 39,466,000
Capital: Madrid
Languages: Spanish,
Catalan, Galician, Basque

Sweden
Area: 173,732 sq mi
(449,964 sq km)
Population: 8,866,000
Capital: Stockholm
Language: Swedish

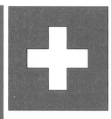

Switzerland
Area: 15,941 sq mi
(41,288 sq km)
Population: 7,142,000
Capital: Bern
Languages: German,
French, Italian, Romansch

Ukraine
Area: 233,206 sq mi
(604,001 sq km)
Population: 49,509,000
Capital: Kiev
Languages: Ukrainian,
Russian, Romanian

United Kingdom
Area: 94,248 sq mi
(24,101 sq km)
Population: 59,750,000
Capital: London
Languages: English, Welsh,
Gaelic

Vatican City
Area: 0.2 sq mi
(0.4 sq km)
Population: 1,000
Languages: Italian, Latin

Yugoslavia
Area: 39,450 sq mi
(102,173 sq km)
Population: 10,662,000
Capital: Belgrade
Languages: Serbo-Croat,
Albanian

AFRICA

Algeria
Area: 919,595 sq mi
(2,381,741 sq km)
Population: 31,471,000
Capital: Algiers
Languages: Arabic, French,
Berber dialects

Angola
Area: 481,354 sq mi
(1,246,700 sq km)
Population: 12,878,000
Capital: Luanda
Languages: Portuguese,
Bantu

Benin
Area: 43,484 sq mi
(112,622 sq km)
Population: 6,396,000
Capitals: Porto-Novo,
Cotonou
Languages: French, Fon,
Yoruba, indigenous languages

Botswana
Area: 231,805 sq mi
(600,372 sq km)
Population: 1,576,000
Capital: Gaborone
Languages: English, Setswana

Burkina Faso
Area: 105,869 sq mi
(274,200 sq km)
Population: 11,946,000
Capital: Ouagadougou
Languages: French,
indigenous languages

Burundi
Area: 10,747 sq mi
(27,834 sq km)
Population: 6,054,000
Capital: Bujumbura
Languages: Kirundi,
French (both official)

Cameroon
Area: 183,569 sq mi
(475,442 sq km)
Population: 15,422,000
Capital: Yaoundé
Languages: French, English
(both official), 24 major
African language groups

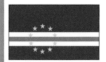

Cape Verde
Area: 1,557 sq mi
(4,033 sq km)
Population: 401,000
Capital: Praia
Languages: Portuguese,
Crioulo

Central African
Republic
Area: 240,535 sq mi
(622,984 sq km)
Population: 3,513,000
Capital: Bangui
Languages: French,
Sango, Arabic, Hunsa

Chad
Area: 495,755 sq mi
(1,284,000 sq km)
Population: 7,977,000
Capital: N'Djamena
Languages: French, Arabic
(both official), Sara, Sango,
more than 100 different
languages and dialects

Comoros
Area: 719 sq mi
(1,862 sq km)
Population: 578,000
Capital: Moroni
Languages: Arabic, French
(both official), Comoran

Congo
Area: 132,047 sq mi
(342,000 sq km)
Population: 2,831,000
Capital: Brazzaville
Languages: French,
Lingala, Monokutuba, many
local languages, dialects

Congo, Democratic
Republic of the
Area: 905,568 sq mi
(2,345,409 sq km)
Population: 51,965,000
Capital: Kinshasa
Languages: French,
Lingala, Kingwana

Côte d'Ivoire
Area: 124,504 sq mi
(322,463 sq km)
Population: 15,980,000
Capitals: Yamoussoukro,
Abidjan
Languages: French,
Dioula, 60 native dialects

Djibouti
Area: 8,958 sq mi
(23,200 sq km)
Population: 638,000
Capital: Djibouti
Languages: French, Arabic
(both official)

Egypt
Area: 386,662 sq mi
(1,001,449 sq km)
Population: 68,344,000
Capital: Cairo
Languages: Arabic,
English, French

Equatorial Guinea
Area: 10,831 sq mi
(28,051 sq km)
Population: 453,000
Capital: Malabo
Languages: Spanish,
French (both official), pid-
gin English, Fang, Bubi, Ibo

Eritrea
Area: 46,842 sq mi
(121,320 sq km)
Population: 4,142,000
Capital: Asmara
Languages: Afar, Amharic,
Arabic, Tigre

Ethiopia
Area: 424,934 sq mi
(1,100,574 sq km)
Population: 64,117,000
Capital: Addis Ababa
Languages: Amharic,
Tigrinya, Orominga,
Guaraginga, Somali, Arabic

Gabon
Area: 103,347 sq mi
(267,667 sq km)
Population: 1,226,000
Capital: Libreville
Languages: French, Fang,
Myene, Bateke, Bapounou/
Eschira,Bandjabi

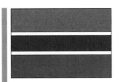

Gambia
Area: 4,361 sq mi
(11,295 sq km)
Population: 1,305,000
Capital: Banjul
Languages: English,
Mandinka, Wolof, Fula

Ghana
Area: 92,100 sq mi
(238,537 sq km)
Population: 19,534,000
Capital: Accra
Languages: English,
African languages (includ-
ing Akan, Moshi-Dagomba,
Ewe and Ga)

Guinea
Area: 94,926 sq mi
(245,857 sq km)
Population: 7,466,000
Capital: Conakry
Languages: French,
indigenous languages

Guinea-Bissau
Area: 13,948 sq mi
(36,125 sq km)
Population: 1,213,000
Capital: Bissau
Languages: Portuguese,
Crioulo, indigenous languages

Kenya
Area: 228,861 sq mi
(592,747 sq km)
Population: 30,340,000
Capital: Nairobi
Languages: English,
Swahili (both official),
indigenous languages

Lesotho
Area: 11,720 sq mi
(30,355 sq km)
Population: 2,143,000
Capital: Maseru
Languages: English,
Sesotho, Zulo, Xhosa

Liberia
Area: 43,000 sq mi
(111,369 sq km)
Population: 3,164,000
Capital: Monrovia
Languages: English,
indigenous languages

Libya
Area: 679,362 sq mi
(1,759,540 sq km)
Population: 5,114,000
Capital: Tripoli
Languages: Arabic, Italian,
English

Madagascar
Area: 226,658 sq mi
(587,041 sq km)
Population: 14,858,000
Capital: Antananarivo
Languages: French,
Malagasy (both official)

Malawi
Area: 45,747 sq mi
(118,484 sq km)
Population: 10,385,000
Capital: Lilongwe
Languages: Chewa,
English (both official)

Mali
Area: 478,841 sq mi
(1,240,192 sq km)
Population: 11,234,000
Capital: Bamako
Languages: French,
Bambara, numerous
African languages

Mauritania
Area: 397,955 sq mi
(1,030,700 sq km)
Population: 2,670,000
Capital: Nouakchott
Languages: Hasaniya
Arabic, Wolof (both offi-
cial), Pula, Soninke, French

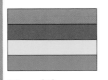

Mauritius
Area: 788 sq mi
(2,040 sq km)
Population: 1,189,000
Capital: Port Louis
Languages: English,
Creole, French, Hindi,
Urdu, Hakka, Bojpoori

Morocco
Area: 275,117 sq mi
(712,550 sq km)
Population: 28,778,000
Capital: Rabat
Languages: Arabic, Berber
dialects, French

Mozambique
Area: 308,642 sq mi
(799,380 sq km)
Population: 19,105,000
Capital: Maputo
Languages: Portuguese,
indigenous dialects

Namibia
Area: 318,261 sq mi
(824,292 sq km)
Population: 1,771,000
Capital: Windhoek
Languages: English,
Afrikaans, German, indige-
nous languages

Niger
Area: 489,191 sq mi
(1,267,000 sq km)
Population: 10,076,000
Capital: Niamey
Languages: French, Hausa,
Djerma

Nigeria
Area: 356,669 sq mi
(923,768 sq km)
Population: 123,338,000
Capital: Abuja
Languages: English,
Hausa, Yoruba, Igbo

Rwanda
Area: 10,169 sq mi
(26,338 sq km)
Population: 7,229,000
Capital: Kigali
Languages: Kinyarwanda,
French, English (all official),
Kiswahili (Swahili)

Sao Tome and
Principe
Area: 372 sq mi
(964 sq km)
Population: 160,000
Capital: São Tomé
Language: Portuguese

Senegal
Area: 75,955 sq mi
(196,722 sq km)
Population: 9,481,000
Capital: Dakar
Languages: French, Wolof,
Pulaar, Diola

Seychelles
Area: 175 sq mi
(453 sq km)
Population: 82,000
Capital: Victoria
Languages: English, French
(both official), Creole

Sierra Leone
Area: 27,699 sq mi
(71,740 sq km)
Population: 5,233,000
Capital: Freetown
Languages: English,
Mende, Temne, Krio

Somalia
Area: 246,201 sq mi
(637,657 sq km)
Population: 7,253,000
Capital: Mogadishu
Languages: Somali, Arabic,
Italian, English

South Africa
Area: 471,445 sq mi
(1,221,037 sq km)
Population: 43,421,000
Capitals: Pretoria (adminis-
trative), Cape Town (legisla-
tive), Bloemfontein (judicial)
Languages: Afrikaans, English,
Ndebele, Pedi, Sotho, Swazi,
Tsonga, Tswana, Venda,
Xhosa, Zulu (all official)

Sudan
Area: 963,600 sq mi
(2,495,712 sq km)
Population: 29,490,000
Capital: Khartoum
Languages: Arabic,
Nuban, Ta Bedawie

Swaziland
Area: 6,704 sq mi
(17,364 sq km)
Population: 1,004,000
Capital: Mbabane
Languages: English, Swazi
(both official)

Tanzania
Area: 364,900 sq mi
(945,087 sq km)
Population: 35,306,000
Capital: Dar es Salaam
Languages: Swahili, English
(both official), Arabic, many
local languages

Togo
Area: 21,925 sq mi
(56,785 sq km)
Population: 5,019,000
Capital: Lomé
Languages: French, Ewe,
Mina, Kabye, Dagomba

Tunisia
Area: 63,170 sq mi
(163,610 sq km)
Population: 9,619,000
Capital: Tunis
Languages: Arabic, French

Uganda
Area: 91,134 sq mi
(236,036 sq km)
Population: 23,318,000
Capital: Kampala
Languages: English, Ganda
or Luganda

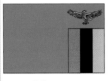

Zambia
Area: 290,586 sq mi
(752,614 sq km)
Population: 9,582,000
Capital: Lusaka
Languages: English,
indigenous languages

Zimbabwe
Area: 150,804 sq mi
(390,580 sq km)
Population: 11,343,000
Capital: Harare
Languages: English,
Shona, Sindebele

ASIA

Afghanistan
Area: 251,773 sq mi
(652,090 sq km)
Population: 26,668,000
Capital: Kabul
Languages: Pashto, Dari,
Turkic languages

Armenia
Area: 11,583 sq mi
(30,000 sq km)
Population: 3,809,000
Capital: Yerevan
Languages: Armenian,
Russian

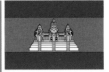

Azerbaijan
Area: 33,591 sq mi
(87,000 sq km)
Population: 7,734,000
Capital: Baku
Languages: Azeri, Russian,
Armenian

Bahrain
Area: 267 sq mi
(691 sq km)
Population: 691,000
Capital: Manama
Languages: Arabic,
English, Persian, Urdu

Bangladesh
Area: 55,598 sq mi
(143,998 sq km)
Population: 128,133,000
Capital: Dhaka
Languages: Bengali,
English

Bhutan
Area: 18,147 sq mi
(47,001 sq km)
Population: 877,000
Capital: Thimphu
Languages: Dzonkha,
Tibetan, and Nepali
dialects

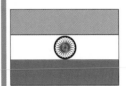

Brunei
Area: 2,226 sq mi
(5,765 sq km)
Population: 331,000
Capital: Bandar Seri
Begawan
Languages: Malay, English,
Chinese

Cambodia
Area: 69,898 sq mi
(181,035 sq km)
Population: 12,127,000
Capital: Phnom Penh
Languages: Khmer, French

China
Area: 3,705,820 sq mi
(9,598,032 sq km)
Population:
1,264,536,000
Capital: Beijing
Languages: Chinese,
Mandarin, dialects

Cyprus
Area: 2,277 sq mi
(5,897 sq km)
Population: 882,000
Capital: Nicosia
Languages: Greek, Turkish,
English

Georgia
Area: 27,027 sq mi
(70,000 sq km)
Population: 5,454,000
Capital: T'bilisi
Languages: Georgian,
Russian, Armenian

India
Area: 1,269,346 sq mi
(3,287,591 sq km)
Population: 1,002,142,000
Capital: New Delhi
Languages: Hindi, 14
other official languages,
English

Indonesia
Area: 741,101 sq mi
(1,919,443 sq km)
Population: 212,207,000
Capital: Jakarta
Languages: Bahasa
Indonesia, English, Dutch,
Javanese and other local
dialects

Iran
Area: 636,296 sq mi
(1,647,999 sq km)
Population: 67,411,000
Capital: Tehran
Languages: Persian, Turkic,
Kurdish, Luri

Iraq
Area: 169,235 sq mi
(438,317 sq km)
Population: 23,115,000
Capital: Baghdad
Languages: Arabic,
Kurdish (official in Kurdish
regions), Assyrian,
Armenian

Israel
Area: 8,019 sq mi
(20,770 sq km)
Population: 6,227,000
Capital: Jerusalem
Languages: Hebrew,
Arabic, English

Japan
Area: 145,875 sq mi
(377,815 sq km)
Population: 126,876,000
Capital: Tokyo
Language: Japanese

Jordan
Area: 35,467 sq mi
(91,860 sq km)
Population: 5,083,000
Capital: Amman
Languages: Arabic, English
understood

Kazakhstan
Area: 1,049,039 sq mi
(2,716,998 sq km)
Population: 14,865,000
Capital: Astana
Languages: Kazakh,
Russian

Korea, North
Area: 46,540 sq mi
(120,538 sq km)
Population: 21,688,000
Capital: Pyongyang
Language: Korean

Korea, South
Area: 38,230 sq mi
(99,016 sq km)
Population: 47,275,000
Capital: Seoul
Languages: Korean,
English widely taught

Kuwait
Area: 6,880 sq mi
(17,818 sq km)
Population: 2,190,000
Capital: Kuwait
Languages: Arabic, English

Kyrgyzstan
Area: 76,834 sq mi
(198,999 sq km)
Population: 4,929,000
Capital: Bishkek
Languages: Kirghiz,
Russian (both official)

Laos
Area: 91,429 sq mi
(236,800 sq km)
Population: 5,218,000
Capital: Vientiane
Languages: Lao, French,
English, ethnic

Lebanon
Area: 4,015 sq mi
(10,399 sq km)
Population: 4,202,000
Capital: Beirut
Languages: Arabic, French,
English

Malaysia
Area: 127,317 sq mi
(329,749 sq km)
Population: 23,253,000
Capital: Kuala Lumpur
Languages: Malay, English,
Chinese

Maldives
Area: 115 sq mi
(298 sq km)
Population: 286,000
Capital: Male
Languages: Maldivian
Divehi, English

Mongolia
Area: 604,250 sq mi
(1,565,000 sq km)
Population: 2,472,000
Capital: Ulaanbaatar
Languages: Khalkha
Mongol, Turkic, Russian,
Chinese

Myanmar
Area: 261,218 sq mi
(676,552 sq km)
Population: 48,852,000
Capital: Yangon (Rangoon)
Languages: Burmese,
minority ethnic

Nepal
Area: 54,362 sq mi
(140,797 sq km)
Population: 23,930,000
Capital: Kathmandu
Languages: Nepali, 20
other languages

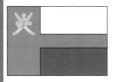

Oman
Area: 82,030 sq mi
(212,457 sq km)
Population: 2,353,000
Capital: Muscat
Languages: Arabic,
English, Baluchi, Urdu

Pakistan
Area: 307,374 sq mi
(796,095 sq km)
Population: 150,648,000
Capital: Islamabad
Languages: Urdu, English,
Punjabi, Sindhi

Philippines
Area: 115,831 sq mi
(300,001 sq km)
Population: 80,298,000
Capital: Manila
Languages: Tagalog,
English (both official)

Qatar
Area: 4,247 sq mi
(11,000 sq km)
Population: 591,000
Capital: Doha
Languages: Arabic, English

Saudi Arabia
Area: 830,000 sq mi
(2,149,690 sq km)
Population: 21,607,000
Capital: Riyadh
Language: Arabic

Singapore
Area: 239 sq mi
(618 sq km)
Population: 4,001,000
Capital: Singapore
Languages: Chinese,
Malay, Tamil, English

Sri Lanka
Area: 25,332 sq mi
(65,610 sq km)
Population: 19,169,000
Capitals: Colombo,
Sri Jayewardenepura Kotte
Languages: Sinhalese,
Tamil, English

Syria
Area: 71,044 sq mi
(184,004 sq km)
Population: 16,482,000
Capital: Damascus
Languages: Arabic,
Kurdish, Armenian

Tajikistan
Area: 55,213 sq mi
(143,001 sq km)
Population: 6,374,000
Capital: Dushanbe
Languages: Tajik, Russian

Thailand
Area: 198,457 sq mi
(514,001 sq km)
Population: 62,043,000
Capital: Bangkok
Languages: Thai, English,
regional dialects

Turkey
Area: 300,948 sq mi
(779,452 sq km)
Population: 65,311,000
Capital: Ankara
Languages: Turkish,
Kurdish, Arabic

Turkmenistan
Area: 188,418 sq mi
(488,000 sq km)
Population: 5,239,000
Capital: Ashgabat
Languages: Turkmenian,
Russian, Uzbek

United Arab Emirates
Area: 32,278 sq mi
(83,600 sq km)
Population: 2,835,000
Capital: Abu Dhabi
Languages: Arabic,
Persian, English, Hindi,
Urdu

Uzbekistan
Area: 172,588 sq mi
(447,001 sq km)
Population: 24,760,000
Capital: Tashkent
Languages: Uzbek,
Russian, Tajik

Vietnam
Area: 127,242 sq mi
(329,556 sq km)
Population: 78,697,000
Capital: Hanoi
Languages: Vietnamese,
Chinese, English, French,
Khmer, indigenous languages

Yemen
Area: 203,850 sq mi
(527,968 sq km)
Population: 17,030,000
Capital: Sanaa
Language: Arabic

AUSTRALIA & OCEANIA

Australia
Area: 2,968,000 sq mi
(7,687,000 sq km)
Population: 19,195,000
Capital: Canberra
Languages: English,
indigenous languages

Fiji Islands
Area: 7,056 sq mi
(18,274 sq km)
Population: 811,000
Capital: Suva
Languages: English, Fijian,
Hindi

Kiribati
Area: 277 sq mi
(717 sq km)
Population: 92,000
Capital: Tarawa
Languages: English,
Gilbertese

Marshall Islands
Area: 70 sq mi
(181 sq km)
Population: 68,000
Capital: Majuro
Languages: English, local
dialects, Japanese

Micronesia
Population: 271 sq mi
(702 sq km)
Population: 119,000
Capital: Palikir
Languages: English,
Trukese, Pohnpeian

Nauru
Area: 8 sq mi
(21 sq km)
Population: 12,000
Capital: Yaren
Languages: Nauruan,
English

New Zealand
Area: 103,883 sq mi
(269,057 sq km)
Population: 3,836,000
Capital: Wellington
Languages: English, Maori

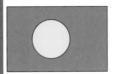

Palau
Area: 188 sq mi
(487 sq km)
Population: 19,000
Capital: Koror
Languages: English,
Palaun, 3 local official

Papua New Guinea
Area: 178,260 sq mi
(461,691 sq km)
Population: 4,810,000
Capital: Port Moresby
Languages: 715 indige-
nous languages

Samoa
Area: 1,093 sq mi
(2,831 sq km)
Population: 176,000
Capital: Apia
Languages: Samoan
(Polynesian), English

Solomon Islands
Area: 10,985 sq mi
(28,450 sq km)
Population: 434,000
Capital: Honiara
Languages: Melanesian
pidgin, 120 indigenous
languages, English

Tonga
Area: 270 sq mi
(699 sq km)
Population: 108,000
Capital: Nuku'alofa
Languages: Tongan,
English

Tuvalu
Area: 10 sq mi
(26 sq km)
Population: 10,000
Capital: Funafuti
Languages: Tuvalu, English

Vanuatu
Area: 5,700 sq mi
(14,760 sq km)
Population: 195,000
Capital: Port-Vila
Languages: English,
French, pidgin (Bislama)

Glossary

Note: Terms defined within the main body of the atlas text are not listed below.

Alkaline term describing soil or natural body of water that has a high salt content; most often found in dry areas where soluble salts have not been washed away or where evaporation rates are high (p. 84)

Arid climate type of dry climate in which annual precipitation is often less than 10 inches (25 cm); experiences great daily variations in day-night temperatures (pp. 18–19)

Boundary line established by people to separate one political or mapped area from another; physical features, such as mountains and rivers, or latitude and longitude lines sometimes act as boundaries (p. 10)

Breadbasket geographic region that is a principal source of grain (p. 34)

Brine solution containing a much higher concentration of salt than seawater (p. 84)

Canadian Shield region containing the oldest rock in North America; areas are exposed in much of eastern Canada and some bordering U.S. regions (p. 42)

Coastal plain any comparatively level land of low elevation that borders the ocean (p. 50)

Continental climate mid-latitude climate zone occurring on large landmasses in the Northern Hemisphere and characterized by great variations of temperature, both seasonally and between day and night; continental cool summer climates

are influenced by nearby colder subarctic climates; continental warm summer climates are influenced by nearby mild or dry climates (pp. 18–19)

Culture hearth center from which major cultural traditions spread and are adopted by people in a wide geographic area (p. 86)

Desert and dry shrub vegetation region with either hot or cold temperatures that annually receives 10 inches (25 cm) or less of precipitation (pp. 22–23)

Ecosystem term for classifying Earth's natural communities according to how all the things in an environment, such as a forest or a coral reef, interact with each other (p. 10)

Fault break in Earth's crust along which movement up, down, or sideways occurs (pp. 14–15)

Flooded grassland wetland dominated by grasses and covered by water (pp. 22–23)

Fossil fuel group of nonrenewable mineral resources—coal, oil, natural gas—formed over millions of years from plant and animal remains (pp. 38–39)

Geothermal energy heat energy generated within Earth (p. 39)

Glacier large, slow-moving mass of ice that forms over time from snow (p. 42)

Gondwana name given to the southern part of the supercontinent Pangaea; made up of what we now call Africa, South America, Australia, Antarctica, and India (pp. 14, 84)

Hemisphere one-half of the globe; the Equator divides Earth into Northern and Southern Hemispheres; the prime meridian and the 180 degree meridian divide it into Eastern and Western Hemispheres (p. 5)

Highland/upland climate region associated with mountains or plateaus that varies depending on elevation, latitude, continental location, and exposure to sun and wind; in general, temperature decreases and precipitation increases with elevation (pp. 18–19)

Humid subtropical climate region characterized by hot summers, mild to cool winters, and year-round precipitation that is heaviest in summer; generally located on the southeastern margins of continents (pp. 18–19)

Ice cap climate one of two kinds of polar climate; summer temperatures rarely rise above freezing, and what little precipitation occurs is mostly in the form of snow (pp. 18–19)

Indigenous native to or occurring naturally in a specific area or environment (p. 102)

Infiltration process that occurs in the water, or hydrologic, cycle when gravity causes surface water to seep down through the soil (p. 36)

Isthmus narrow strip of land that connects two larger landmasses and has water on two sides (p. 56–57)

Landform physical feature shaped by uplifting, weathering, and erosion; mountains, plateaus, hills, and plains are the four major types (p. 20)

Language family group of languages that come from a common ancestry (pp. 30–31)

Latin America cultural region generally considered to include Mexico, Central America, South America, and the West Indies; Portuguese and Spanish are the principal languages (pp. 28–29)

Llanos extensive, mostly treeless grasslands in the Orinoco River basin of northern South America (p. 58)

Lowlands fairly level land at a lower elevation than surrounding areas (p. 12)

Mangrove vegetation tropical trees and shrubs with dense root systems that grow in tidal mud flats and extend coastlines by trapping soil (pp. 22–23)

Marine west coast type of mild climate common on the west coasts of continents in midlatitude regions; characterized by small variations in annual temperature range and wet, foggy winters (pp. 18–19)

Median age midpoint of a population's age; half the population is older than this age; half is younger (p. 27)

Mediterranean climate type of mild climate common on the west coasts of continents, named for the dominant climate along the Mediterranean coast; characterized by mild rainy winters and hot dry summers (pp. 18–19)

Mediterranean shrub low-growing, mostly small-leaved evergreen vegetation, such as chaparral, that thrives in Mediterranean climate regions (p. 22–23)

Melanesia one of three major island groups that make up Oceania; includes the Fiji Islands, New Guinea, Vanuatu, the Solomon Islands, and New Caledonia (pp. 102–103)

Melanesian indigenous to Melanesia (p. 102)

Mestizo person of mixed Native American and European ancestry; most commonly used in Latin America (p. 53)

Microclimate climate of a very limited area that varies from the overall climate of the surrounding region (p. 20)

Micronesia one of three major island groups that make up Oceania; made up of some 2,000 mostly coral islands, including Guam, Kiribati, the Mariana Islands, Palau, and the Federated States of Micronesia (pp. 102–103)

Micronesian indigenous to Micronesia (p. 102)

Monsoon seasonal change in the direction of the prevailing winds, which causes wet and dry seasons in some tropical areas (p. 90)

Mountain grassland vegetation region characterized by clumps of long grass that grow beyond the limit of forests at high elevations (pp. 22–23)

Nonrenewable resource elements of the natural environment, such as metals, minerals, and fossil fuels, that form within Earth by geological processes over millions of years and thus cannot be readily replaced (pp. 38–39)

Northern coniferous forest vegetation region composed primarily of cone-bearing, needle-leafed or scale-leafed evergreen trees that grow in regions with long winters and moderate to high annual precipitation; also called boreal forest or taiga (pp. 22–23)

Oceania name for the widely scattered islands of Polynesia, Micronesia, and Melanesia; often includes Australia and New Zealand (pp. 96–107)

Pampas temperate grassland primarily in Argentina between the Andes and the Atlantic Ocean; one of the richest agricultural regions in the world (pp. 56, 58)

Patagonia cool, windy, arid plateau region primarily in southern Argentina between the Andes and the Atlantic Ocean (p. 58)

Plain large area of relatively flat land; one of the four major kinds of landforms (p. 16)

Plate tectonics study of the interaction of slabs of Earth's crust as molten rock within Earth causes them to slowly move across the surface (pp. 14–15)

Plateau large, relatively flat area that rises above the surrounding landscape; one of the four major kinds of landforms (pp. 16–17)

Polar climates climates that occur at very high latitudes; generally too cold to support tree growth; include tundra and ice cap (pp. 22–23)

Polynesia one of three major regions in Oceania made up mostly of volcanic and coral islands, including the Hawaiian Islands, the Society Islands, Samoa, and French Polynesia (pp. 102–103)

Polynesian indigenous to Polynesia (p. 102)

Predominant economy main type of work that most people do to meet their wants and needs in a particular country (pp. 32–33, 47, 63, 73, 83, 93, 103)

Province land governed as a political or administrative unit of a country or empire; Canadian

provinces, like U.S. states, have substantial powers of self-government (p. 49)

River basin area drained by a single river and its tributaries (p. 58)

Sahel in Africa the semiarid region of short tropical grassland that lies between the dry Sahara and the humid savanna and that is prone to frequent droughts (p. 78)

Savanna tropical tall grassland with scattered low trees (p. 23)

Selva Portuguese word referring to tropical rain forests, especially in the Amazon Basin (p. 64)

Semiarid dry climate region that experiences great daily variation in day-night temperatures; receives enough rainfall to support grasslands (pp. 18–19)

Silt mineral particles that are larger than grains of clay but smaller than grains of sand (p. 65)

Sisal tropical plant with leaves made up of strong fibers that are used to make rope (p. 84)

Steppe Slavic word referring to relatively flat, mostly treeless temperate grasslands that stretch across much of central Europe and central Asia (p. 88)

Subarctic climate region characterized by short, cool, sometimes freezing summers and long, bitter cold winters; most precipitation falls in summer (pp. 18–19)

Subcontinent large landmass such as India that, although part of a continent, is considered a separate feature either geographically or politically (p. 84)

Subtropical climate region between tropical

and continental climates characterized by distinct seasons but with milder temperatures than continental climates (pp. 18–19)

Temperate broadleaf forest vegetation region with distinct seasons and dependable rainfall; predominant species include oak, maple, and beech, all of which lose their leaves in the cold season (pp. 22–23)

Temperate coniferous forest vegetation region that has mild winters with heavy precipitation; made up of mostly evergreen, needleleaf trees that bear seeds in cones (pp. 22–23)

Temperate grassland vegetation region where grasses are dominant and the climate is characterized by hot summers, cold winters, and moderate rainfall (pp. 22–23)

Territory land under the jurisdiction of a country but that is not a state or a province (p. 43)

Tropical coniferous forest vegetation region that occurs in a cooler climate than tropical rain

forests; has distinct wet and dry seasons; made up of mostly evergreen trees with seed-bearing cones (pp. 22–23)

Tropical dry climate region characterized by year-round high temperatures and sufficient precipitation to support savannas (pp. 18–19)

Tropical dry forest vegetation region that has distinct wet and dry seasons and a cooler climate than tropical moist forests; has shorter trees than rain forests and many shed their leaves in the dry season (pp. 22–23)

Tropical grassland and savanna vegetation region characterized by scattered individual trees; occurs in warm or hot climates with annual rainfall of 20 to 50 inches (50–130 cm) (pp. 22–23)

Tropical moist broadleaf forest vegetation region occurring mostly in a belt between the Tropic of Cancer and the Tropic of Capricorn in areas that have at least 80 inches (200 cm) of rain annually and an average annual temperature of 80°F (20°C) (pp. 22–23)

Tropical wet climate region characterized by year-round warm temperatures and rainfall ranging from 60 to150 inches (150–400 cm) annually (pp. 18–19)

Troposphere region of Earth's atmosphere that is closest to the surface; where weather occurs (p. 5)

Tundra vegetation region at high latitudes and high elevations characterized by cold temperatures, low vegetation, and a short growing season (pp. 22–23)

Tundra climate region with one or more months of temperatures slightly above freezing when the ground is free of snow (pp. 18–19)

Upland climate see Highland/upland climate

Web Sites (Web Link)

Thematic Index

Place-name Index

Due to limited space, only countries, their capitals, cities with populations of one million or more, and selected physical features are listed here.

National Geographic Society

John M. Fahey, Jr.
President and Chief Executive Officer

Gilbert M. Grosvenor
Chairman of the Board

Nina D. Hoffman
President, Books and School Publishing Group

William R. Gray
Vice President and Director of the Book Division

Ericka Markman
Vice President and Director, School Publishing

Staff for this book

Children's Books

Nancy Laties Feresten
Publishing Director, Children's Books

Suzanne Patrick Fonda
Project Editor

Carl Mehler
Director of Maps

Marianne R. Koszorus
Design Director

Dorrit Green
Art Director and Designer

Martha B. Sharma
Writer and Chief Consultant

Marilyn Mofford Gibbons
Illustrations Editor

Jerome N. Cookson
Map Production Manager

Matt Chwastyk
Thomas L. Gray
Nicholas P. Rosenbach
Gregory Ugiansky
Martin S. Walz
National Geographic Maps
XNR Productions
Map Research and Production

Marcia Pires-Harwood
Text Research

Marilyn "Minh" Le
Jessica Ann Peterson
Anjali M. Shenai
Research Assistance

Stuart Armstrong
Graphs

Sharon K. Berry
Illustrations Assistant

Connie B. Binder
Indexer

Ellen Teguis
Director
Trade Sales and Marketing

Lawrence M. Porges
Marketing Specialist

R. Gary Colbert
Production Director

Lewis R. Bassford
Production Manager

Vincent R. Ryan
Manufacturing Manager

School Publishing Division

Steve Mico
Editorial Director

Richard Easby
Editorial Manager

Carolyn Hatt
Lydia Lewis
Editors

Jean Stringer
Anika Trahan
Associate Editors

Education Foundation

Lanny Proffer
Executive Director

Joe Ferguson
Director of Programs
Geography Education Outreach

Christopher Shearer
Program Officer

Consultants

Deborah Batchelor
Specialist
Baltimore City Public
School System
Baltimore, Maryland

Sari J. Bennett
Department of Geography
& Environmental Systems
University of Maryland
Baltimore County

Acknowledgments: We are grateful for the assistance of Richard W. Bullington, Jan D. Morris, Karla H. Tucker, and Alfred L. Zebarth of NG Maps; the National Geographic Image Collection; and Jo H. Tunstall, Robert W. Witt, and Lyle Rosbotham, NG Book Division

Illustrations Credits: Abbreviations for terms appearing below: (t) top; (b) bottom; (l) left; (r) right; (c) center; NGS: National Geographic Staff

Locator globes on pages 2–3 and in chapter openers created by Theophilus Britt Griswold

Graphs created by Stuart Armstrong

Continent chapter openers: NASA/JPL/California Institute of Technology/Advanced Very High Resolution Radiometer Project/Cartographic Applications Group

Cover: NOAA satellite mosaic prepared for National Geographic Television by NASA/ JPL, color enhanced by Alfred L. Zebarth; background art digitally created by Slim Films

Back cover: photograph, Steve Raymer; satellite image map, NOAA/NESDIS/NGDC

About The Earth
4 (art) © NGS; 4–5 (t) Shusei Nagaska; (b) Earth Satellite Corporation; 5 (bl) Robert Hynes; 6–7 (art) Shusei Nagaska; 10 (l) Vlad Kharitonov NGS; 11 (t–b) NASA/GISS, NOAA/NESDIS/NGDC, NASA/GSFC, University of Miami; 14–15 (t) NASA/JPL/CalTech/CAG, (b) Christopher R. Scotese/PALEOMAP Project, U. of TX, Arlington; 16–17 (t) NOAA/ NESDIS/NGDC; 22–3 (l–r) Jen & Des Bartlett; Raymond Gehman; Cosmo Condina/stone; Walter M. Edwards; Tom Bean/stone; Steve Jackson; Timothy G. Lamar; Medford Taylor; 26 Stuart Franklin; 32 (graph) Theopholis Britt Griswold, revised by Stuart Armstrong; 32–3 (l–r) Martin Rogers; James P. Blair; Phil Schermeister; James L. Stanfield; Mark Thiessen NGS; © NGS; 34 (l) Steve Raymer; (c) Sisse Brimberg; (r) Stephen G. St. John; 36–7 (l–r) Steve Winter; Annie Griffiths Belt; Loren McIntyre; Jim Brandenburg; 39 (tl) James A. Sugar/Black Star; (tr) Marc Moritsch; (bl) Bob Krist; (r) stone

North America
54 (tl) Roger Werth/Woodfin Camp Inc; (tr) Ravi Miro Fry; (b) Chris Stewart/Black Star

South America
65 (bl, br) Michael Nichols NGS; (tr) Bill Curtsinger; (c) Mattias Klum

Europe
74 Bert Blokhuis/stone; 75 (br) Index Stock

Africa
84 (l) Paul Zahl; (tr, br) Chris Johns NGS

Asia
94 (t) James L. Stanfield; (b) Steve McCurry; 95 (l) James P. Blair; (r) Lynn Funkhouser

Australia
106 (l) Bob Sacha; (r) The Granger Collection; 107 Shusei Nagaska

Library of Congress Cataloging-in-Publication Data

National Geographic Society (U.S.)
National Geographic student atlas of the world.
p. cm.
Includes index and glossary.
ISBN 0-7922-7221-8 (pbk.)
ISBN 0-7922-7235-8 (hc.)
1. Children's atlases. 2. Earth—remote-sensing images. 3. Physical geography—Maps for children.
[1.Atlases.] I. Title: Student atlas of the world. II. Title.
G1021 .N42 2001
912–dc21   00-030006

Published by the National Geographic Society
1145 17th St. N.W.
Washington, D.C. 20036-4688
Copyright © 2001 National Geographic Society

Metric Tables

CONVERSION TO METRIC MEASURES

SYMBOL	WHEN YOU KNOW	MULTIPLY BY	TO FIND	SYMBOL
LENGTH				
in	inches	2.54	centimeters	cm
ft	feet	0.30	meters	m
yd	yards	0.91	meters	m
mi	miles	1.61	kilometers	km
AREA				
in^2	square inches	6.45	square centimeters	cm^2
ft^2	square feet	0.09	square meters	m^2
yd^2	square yards	0.84	square meters	m^2
mi^2	square miles	2.59	square kilometers	km^2
—	acres	0.40	hectares	ha
MASS				
oz	ounces	28.35	grams	g
lb	pounds	0.45	kilograms	kg
—	short tons	0.91	metric tons	t
VOLUME				
in^3	c...		...illiliters	mL
liq oz	li...		...illiliters	mL
pt	p...		...ers	L
qt	q...		...ers	L
gal	g...		...ers	L
ft^3	c...		...bic meters	m^3
yd^3	c...		...bic meters	m^3
TEMPERATURE				
°F	...F		...grees Celsius (centigrade)	°C

CONVERSION FROM METRIC MEASURES

SYMBOL	WHEN...		...TO FIND	SYMBOL
LENGTH				
cm	cen...		...hes	in
m	met...		...t	ft
m	met...		...rds	yd
km	kilo...		...les	mi
AREA				
cm^2	squ...		square inches	in^2
m^2	squ...		square feet	ft^2
m^2	sq...		...are yards	yd^2
km^2	sq...		...are miles	mi^2
ha	he...		...s	—
MASS				
g	gr...		...ces	oz
kg	kil...		...nds	lb
t	m...		...t tons	—
VOLUME				
mL	m...		...c inches	in^3
mL	m...		...d ounces	liq oz
L	lit...		...pt	pt
L	lit...		...rts	qt
L	lit...		...ons	gal
m^3	cu...		...c feet	ft^3
m^3	cu...		...c yards	yd^3
TEMPERATURE				
°C	degrees Celsius (centigrade)	9/5 then add 32	degrees Fahrenheit	°F